P9-CMO-754

IT'S NOT ABOUT THE TRUTH

The Untold Story

of the

Duke Lacrosse Case

and the

Lives It Shattered

Don Yaeger
with Mike Pressler

THRESHOLD EDITIONS
New York London Toronto Sydney

Threshold Editions
A Division of Simon & Schuster, Inc.
1230 Avenue of the Americas
New York, NY 10020

First Threshold Editions hardcover edition June 2007

THRESHOLD EDITIONS and colophon are trademarks of Simon & Schuster, Inc.

For information about special discounts for bulk purchases,
please contact Simon & Schuster
Special Sales at 1-800-456-6798 or
business@simonandschuster.com.

Manufactured in the United States of America

10 9 8 7 6 5 4 3 2 1

Library of Congress Cataloging-in-Publication Data

ISBN-13: 978-1-4165-5146-1
ISBN-10: 1-4165-5146-8

To Jeanette:

By the time this is published,
we'll be back from the honeymoon.
Thanks for sharing—and shaping—my life dream.

—DY

To my girls:

Your strength and support through the worst of times
inspired me no end.
True toughness comes in all different shapes and sizes.
To the 2006 Duke lacrosse team:
Thank you for "staying the course."
As I promised, "We will have our day."

—MP

Contents

Author's Note

If it takes a village to raise a child, it took a city to write this book, especially on compressed time frames. That is where good help, lots of clip research, great editing, and a strong publisher come into play. Without those elements, this project never ends up on the shelf.

The work of many journalists can be found in these pages. Their efforts at reporting this story helped me track its path and allowed me to ask better questions of the more than one hundred people interviewed for the book.

Among those whose work I turned to are: Scott Price, Farrell Evans, and Lester Munson, my longtime colleagues at *Sports Illustrated,* Kurt Anderson at *New York* magazine, and *ESPN the Magazine*'s Greg Garber and Jon Pess. At *Rolling Stone,* Janet Reitman; ABC11 Eyewitness News; ABC News, Aaron Beard, Chris Cuomo, Chris Francescani, Eamon McNiff, David Scot; *New York Times,* David Brooks, Jack Shafer; *Duke Chronicle,* Adam Eaglin, Saidi Chen, Jared Mueller, Emily Rotberg, Gregory Beaton, Rob Copeland, William Chafe, Steven Baldwin, Steve Veres, Matt Sullivan, Victoria Ward, David Graham, Bolin Niu, Sheya Rao, Stefanie Williams; *TIME,* Greg Fulton; WRAL, Kelcey Carlson, Julia Lewis, Melissa Buscher, Erin Coleman, Ken Smith; ESPN, Darren Rovel; *New York Daily News,* Tamer El-Ghobashy, Dave Goldiner; *USA Today,* Eddie Timanus, Steve Wieberg, Erik Brady, Mary Beth Markein; *The O'Reilly Factor,* FOX News, Megyn Kendall, Liza Porteus; MSNBC, Dan Abrams, Susannah Meadows, Rita Cosby, Evan Thomas; Slate, Stuart Taylor, Jr.; CBS *Early Show;* CBS News *60 Minutes,* Ed Bradley, Lesley Stahl; *Chicago Defender,* Reverend Jesse L. Jackson, Sr.; *Herald-Sun,* John Stevenson, William F. West; *News &*

Observer, Benjamin Niolet, Joseph Neff, Anne Blythe, Jane Stancill, Samiha Khanna, Ruth Sheehan, Michael Biesecker, Eric Ferreri, Jim Nesbitt, Lorenzo Perez, Matt Dees, Jenifer Brevorka, Ted Vaden, Nikole Hannah-Jones, Allen G. Breed, J. Andrew Curliss, Steve Ford, Jonathan B. Cox; *Wall Street Journal,* Stuart Taylor, K. C. Johnson; *Washington Post; Wilmington Journal,* Cash Michaels; NBC 17; *New York Sun,* Eliana Johnson; *Weekly Standard,* Charlotte Allen; *Duke* magazine; Durham-In-Wonderland.com, K. C. Johnson; Renew America, Michael Gaynor; LieStoppers.com; FreeRepublic.com; Johnsville.blogspot.com; *Essence,* Kristal Brent Zook, Bridget A. Lacy; CNN; JohnInCarolina.blogspot.com; *Charlotte Observer,* Gary L. Wright; *New York Post,* Frank Ryan; *Newsweek,* Susannah Meadows; *Newsday,* Steven Marcus; and WPTF Radio's Kevin Miller.

On the writing and research end, Jim Henry was the glue that held this book together. An enormously talented sportswriter, Jim came to work with me a year ago and, when the deadline on this book was pushed up by four months, put everything aside to make sure this book was thorough and a pleasure to read. Four young and talented college students, Jenny Fernandez, Erica Foti, Leah Porter, and Sarah Kwak, worked night and day on this as well. I hope their professors prove to be as understanding as Jim's wife. The talented Tiffany Brooks also brought her special blend of skills, and once again delivered like a champion.

Literary agent Ian Kleinert, editor Margaret Clark, and publishers Louise Burke, Mary Matalin, and Anthony Ziccardi were there to offer whatever support was needed. Lee Southren and Keith Askenas, agents for Mike Pressler, couldn't have been more helpful.

The greatest challenge, though, proved to be writing this book without input from some of the story's most central players. Not long after signing a contract to author this book, I Federal Expressed letters to Duke President Richard Brodhead, Athletic Director Joe Alleva, and District Attorney Mike Nifong. As they were central figures in the story, I wanted to hear explanations for decisions. None of them responded to requests for interviews.

As the reporting on this project continued, I met and interviewed

Mike Pressler, Duke's longtime lacrosse coach, who was the one university employee who was fired during this debacle. Pressler came to the interview with a bombshell: He had kept a diary from day one, filled with details of conversations and his reactions and emotions. It was a writer's dream.

Pressler also told me he was going to write his own book. "Why not," I suggested, "combine the two projects?" That is how this book fell together. Add a hundred interviews to the insight of the story's ultimate insider and you get a tale that has both graphic detail and personal passion. More important, as Mike Pressler stressed, you get to the two words that have been at the root of his support for the players: The Truth.

Weeks after my letter to Brodhead—and after Coach Pressler had decided to fold his project into mine—I received a call from John Burness, Duke's senior vice president and chief spokesman. Burness told me he was to consider my request to interview the president, but that doing so could only occur after he had spent time briefing me—even telling me another reporter had spent fourteen hours with Burness before getting to Brodhead. I had to pass the Burness test. We met for more than four hours one night in his Duke office. In emails Burness sent later it was apparent I failed the test. Burness believed that I held such strong opinions about the case after having done so many interviews with "opponents" of Brodhead that he did not allow an interview with the president.

That is my one regret. Despite the hours I spent with Burness, Duke's leader didn't want to answer these questions. Later, Burness would imply that my interview request was rejected because I now had Pressler's involvement in my book. As a result, you will find Burness speaking for Duke and Brodhead throughout this book. Reporters always want to get their information from the horse's mouth. That didn't happen here.

—*Don Yaeger*

CHAPTER ONE

The Perfect Storm

It was a postcard-perfect Monday afternoon in North Carolina on March 13, 2006. A brilliant sun was accompanied by temperatures in the midseventies. The campus of Duke University was peaceful and relatively empty with the arrival of spring break. Dukies, with the exception of athletic teams in season such as men's lacrosse, welcomed the reprieve. The city of Durham, meanwhile, embraced a new work week. Durhamites savored the crisp, clean air as they scurried around town and tackled their to-do lists. Little did they know the perfect storm had started to churn on the horizon.

The Perfect Storm?

Yes, that's exactly what would occur. Not a drop of rain would fall in Durham over the next twelve hours, but an extraordinary combination of events would devastate a prestigious university and a proud city, changing many lives forever. Not rain, not snow, not wind would cause this massive destruction.

The elements that produced this perfect storm were in a powder keg, just waiting to be ignited. That powder keg, located in the living room at 610 North Buchanan Boulevard, was packed with the politics of privilege, race, sex, and money. As the alcohol flowed, and music filled the air, the fuse was lit.

There was an explosion around midnight.

Duke University, ranked as the thirteenth "Best University in the World" in 2006 by the *New York Times Higher Education Supplement,* is extraordinarily picturesque. Grand Gothic buildings covered in warm, gold-toned brick stand high above the magnolia and dogwood trees that fill the campus. An aura of privilege and excellence surround the thousands of eager, bright students who pay an annual tuition in excess of forty-four thousand dollars and rush to keep pace with their demanding academic and social schedules. However, the university's beautiful exterior couldn't conceal the turmoil beneath.

People love to hate Duke. Though no one can pinpoint exactly why, everyone has a theory. John Burness, Duke's senior vice president for public affairs and government relations, believes it stems from the school's reputation. Once the darling underdog, Duke is now viewed as a powerful elitist. Its attitude, intellect, and wealth set an exclusive standard, similar to the success exhibited by professional baseball's New York Yankees. Most of the Ivy League despise the thought that Duke is trying to be something it's not: one of them. In the Ivies' minds, Duke is a poser, striving to emulate an image Harvard, Yale, Cornell, Stanford, Brown, Columbia, Dartmouth, and the University of Pennsylvania spent centuries developing.

"I really believe that if this had occurred almost anywhere else in the country, it wouldn't have been this big," Burness said. "It would have been big, but nowhere as big as Duke. We are on a pedestal. I think the factor that put this one over the top, with all the other elements—and God, it had all the other elements—was that this was Duke."

Those "other elements":

- Outside the "Duke Bubble," as many students call it, you enter Durham, a vibrant and growing city that can also be especially dangerous in places. It was the murder capital of North Carolina in 2005, boasting thirty-seven murders, the highest murder rate per capita. Though not all of Durham adheres to the poor, blue-collar family image the media portrays, nevertheless, its crime rate and poverty levels are alarming. The contrast between the surrounding community and the young, elite, predominately white Dukie is startling and cause for friction. The national media have described Durham as "a small Southern town where conflict over race and class dominates daily life." Even the *Princeton Review* noted in

2006 that "Duke and Durham have one of the most strained town-gown relationships in the nation."

- Duke's president, Richard Brodhead, entered uncharted waters when he walked onto Duke's campus four years earlier. He was a shy, scholarly man from Yale, and big-time sports at the Division I level were foreign to him. Brodhead was unsure how to balance athletics and academics, a combination that Duke views with beaming pride. In fact, 10 percent of Duke's undergraduate students are athletes. Brodhead speaks in long, elegant passages and often quotes Shakespeare. His timid, calm demeanor is surprising for a man of such power. In the midst of this struggle to establish himself, he was forced to manage a faculty becoming more vocally radical in its political views. Brodhead had watched just a month earlier as his contemporary Harvard President Lawrence Summers fell victim to that university's more extreme professors and wanted to ensure he didn't suffer a similar fate. It was a balancing act that could easily tip with the slightest disturbance.
- Mike Nifong was nearing the end of his term as Durham's interim district attorney. Despite the promise he had made to Governor Mike Easley, Nifong went back on his word and decided to run for the office. However, he trailed badly in the polls to a former colleague in the district attorney's office, Freda Black, who helped successfully handle the explosive and televised Michael Peterson murder case in 2003. As the gap between the two candidates grew, so did Nifong's desperation: He used thirty thousand dollars of his own money to continue campaigning. What he needed was a moment that would guarantee him free publicity.
- Some police officers seemed to specifically target Duke students. Sergeant Mark Gottlieb had arrested ten times as many Duke students as the district's other three squad commanders combined. Students whom he had arrested alleged that Gottlieb occasionally used violent tactics and misrepresented the truth in court. Gottlieb arrested or incarcerated Duke students at a higher rate than nonstudents, even when they were accused of less serious crimes than the nonstudents, according to a news report.
- Duke's lacrosse team had, in the minds of some, developed a reputa-

tion for living loud and large. Players were athletic, smart, and handsome, a trifecta that generated adulation and envy. "In the order of the social universe of Duke undergraduates, the lacrosse players ranked at the top of the dominance hierarchy," wrote Peter J. Boyer of *The New Yorker.* "They tended to be the children of white, prosperous families, products of Northeastern preparatory schools, where the game is a fixture; after graduation most of them go on to lucrative careers in fields like finance . . . they were also known as enthusiastically social creatures, partiers of the very highest order." The team exemplified the Duke student body motto of "work hard, play hard," causing resentment on and off campus. The team traveled in packs and "got all the best women," joked former Duke lacrosse captain Matt Zash. Though many involved with the team would dispute the image, *Baltimore Sun* columnist David Steel wrote, "It's a sport of privilege played by children of privilege and supported by families of privilege."

• Add to this volatile mixture two African-American strippers—with criminal records and wild imaginations. Kim Roberts, who went by the stage name "Nikki," dropped out of college after two years when she got pregnant. She married the father of her child but was divorced soon after. After she took a job as a payroll specialist, her employers caught her stealing twenty-five thousand dollars. Embezzlement charges stood in the way of any future employment, so she began stripping. Crystal Gail Mangum, also known as "Precious," was a North Carolina Central University student and divorced mother of two. It was known within the community that she had a history of mental instability and abused drugs and alcohol. In 2002, Mangum pled guilty to misdemeanor charges of larceny, speeding to elude arrest, assault on a government official, and driving while impaired.

The perfect storm.

On the afternoon of March 13, Duke's nationally ranked lacrosse team searched for ways to escape the spring-break boredom. Golf was a popular option. Many other guys spent the afternoon at 610 North Buchanan Boulevard, drinking beer, talking about women, and playing an outdoor game called washers. In this version, players tossed small washers underhand through holes cut into wooden panes the size of doors on the ground five feet away. When conversation turned to the night's entertainment, faces lit up. A few years ago the team unveiled a tradition of meeting at Teasers Men's Club one night during spring break. However, players had run into a problem that threatened the fun at this local strip club: Some of their underage teammates were carded and denied entry in 2005. In what they thought was a stroke of genius, the players decided to bring the strip club to them. "The reality is that every guy that we know in every fraternity and on every sports team had had strippers to their house," one player said. "We thought, 'What's the downside?' We could control what we got. The thinking was we needed to control the atmosphere."

The elements began to spin.

In this age of instant access, there's no need to flip through Durham's 151-page telephone book to find live entertainment. The Internet was easier. Only a few keystrokes were needed to find escort services and dancers on yellowpages.com. Among the first to pop up: Allure Escort Services. No one knew, when one of the team's four lacrosse captains, Dan Flannery, made the call, using the name Dan Flannigan, that his afternoon call would ring in the ghetto of East Durham. "The address is actually an out-of-service gas station on some random street," senior lacrosse captain Matt Zash recalls. "It's just a front. It doesn't even exist. It's just someone with a cell phone that has a network of girls that he can call up."

After first dialing a number that was out of order, Flannery punched in the telephone number for Allure Escort Services in his cellular phone at 2:00 P.M. He had a connection. A ring followed. Flannery explained he was looking for entertainment for a party.

"What do you want?" the woman from Allure Escort Services asked.

"What do you mean?" Flannery replied, unsure of striptease etiquette in his first call for such a request.

"How many girls do you need?" she responded, impatiently.

"I need two for this party, possibly twenty or thirty guys," Flannery answered.

The woman said it wasn't a problem and she would call Flannery back in ten minutes to tell him what she had available for the party that night. As scheduled, Flannery's cell phone rang. It was the woman from Allure Escort Services.

"I've got two girls that would be perfect for a group like yours," said the woman, who recited their measurements and added they were comfortable dancing at parties of this size.

"One is Hispanic and one has brown hair with blond highlights."

That's fine, Flannery thought.

Visions of two beautiful, curvy, tanned girls dancing sensually with vertical poles, moving their bodies to the beat of the music, filled the players' minds. The seniors were so convinced that attractive women were due to arrive that they assigned freshmen the chore of cleaning up the living room—running the vacuum, taking out trash, straightening up the furniture—so as not to offend their guests. Some of the older players had been to off-campus parties with strippers, saying the scene had been fun and appropriate. Many others had never seen strippers at all, much less up close and personal. Though some in the group were apprehensive about the late-night show, the wheels were in motion. The party was set. The strippers were to come to a house just off the edge of Duke's East Campus, a house that served as the de facto gathering place for the fraternity that was Duke lacrosse: 610 North Buchanan Boulevard.

Underage drinking had once been an extracurricular activity the Duke administration treated with a wink and smile. But several years ago, then Duke President Nannerl Keohane issued an edict that no alcohol could be consumed on East Campus by students. Keg parties were allowed on West Campus, where older students lived, but revelers had to buy the keg from university catering (Keohane jacked up keg prices to make it less appealing), and the beer had to be served by campus bartenders (even more expensive) who checked everyone's IDs, effectively making drinking on-campus so unappealing to most students that all parties were moved to neighborhoods on the edge of campus. It was a decision Keohane felt was necessary to prove that Duke was not deserving of its growing "party school" reputation. (So well known was Duke's "work hard, play hard" student motto that novelist Tom Wolfe's *I Am Charlotte Simmons* is set in an oversexed, alcohol-crazed parody of Duke named Dupont University.) The unintended consequence was that the off-campus parties further strained the relationship between Duke students and residents of the surrounding community.

Trinity Park is a neighborhood "where people walk their dogs and children play outside," Samiha Khanna, a writer for the Raleigh, North Carolina, newspaper *News & Observer*, told North Carolina Public Radio. "It's a great friendly neighborhood and everybody knows each other." Blue houses, yellow houses, white houses, and brick houses with sprawling front porches line streets that are separated from Duke's East Campus by a three-foot-high stone wall. When Keohane's policy of non-campus drinking went into effect, however, this wall suddenly divided neighborhood from university. Seniors from the school's fraternities and athletic teams, as well as other senior students, began renting homes in Trinity Park. Those homes would become the unofficial gathering spots for members of their groups.

The lacrosse team was just one of several groups that had moved its rowdiness and late-night parties off-campus. The white clapboard house at 610 North Buchanan, rented by senior captains Zash, Flannery, and David Evans, became popular with teammates and friends. Though they never threw parties with baby oil wrestling pits and dozens of kegs like some of their student neighbors, their home became the site of many "late nights," Zash admitted with a grin. Players from New York and New Jersey, such as Zash and many of his teammates, were accustomed to clubs and bars that kept music thumping and alcohol flowing well into the wee morning hours. When curfew struck at 2:00 A.M. in Durham, laxers (slang for lacrosse players) and friends knew where to head: 610.

An increasing number of neighbors grew tired of loud music in the middle of the night and the sight of empty beer cans strewn in their yards after the get-togethers. Jason Bissey was one of those Trinity Park residents. His complaints about the players, largely ignored before that night, would become significant.

After a quick visit to his home in Long Island, New York, freshman Devon Sherwood landed in Durham and caught a ride from a friend back to his dormitory on East Campus. Although a walk-on and the team's only African-American player, Sherwood was part of the tight-knit lacrosse team.

"It's like, once you earn the respect, you are part of the family," Sherwood said.

After ten that night, Sherwood's telephone rang and a teammate let him know there was a party at 610. Though the party had already started, he was in for a surprise.

The two strippers were scheduled to arrive at 11:00 P.M. The clock read 11:15 and only one woman, Kim, had shown, parking her black Honda Accord on the street in front of the house. Kim was in her early thirties, with chocolate skin and wavy hair. She wore tight blue jeans and a long-sleeved dress shirt. Kim had a pretty face, but an alternative lifestyle and pregnancy had aged her beyond her years. Though Kim was fully clothed, her stomach sagged under the weight of cellulite and her breasts fell deflated on her chest. A captain and another player met Kim on the back stoop. They talked about school and Kim smoked a cigarette while they waited for the other dancer to arrive. The player offered Kim a drink, and Kim responded "please." The player excused himself to fix the drink and, more important, alert the crowd inside the house of an important detail.

The player told his teammates that Kim, an African-American, was not what was promised by the agency. Most of the guys just shrugged, saying that was okay, and continued drinking beer from red plastic cups. The marathon party was prepared for its featured act. The carpeted living room had been turned into a makeshift dance floor. The furniture was pushed against the walls. Music played from an iPod hooked to portable speakers. Players had chipped in twenty to forty dollars each to cover the eight-hundred-dollar fee for the two dancers. "It was fine and great," recalled Tony McDevitt, who had arrived around 9:00 P.M. "Everybody was having a good time and it was under control. It wasn't loud or anything. People weren't like crazy drunk, people weren't breaking things."

Still, everyone started to get anxious when the second stripper hadn't arrived by eleven-thirty. She was thirty minutes late, so Kim telephoned her contact, Melissa, from the escort agency. Melissa informed Kim that the second dancer was on her way and should arrive soon.

Fifteen minutes later at eleven forty-five, Crystal Gail Mangum was dropped off by her friend Brian Taylor, who quickly left in his dark sedan. Unlike Kim, Crystal was dressed in uniform, ready to perform: a short, red, lace and glitter negligee and shiny white, patent-leather platform shoes. Crystal's brown and blond extensions were pinned behind her ears to keep them from hanging in her face. Her noticeably large breasts had been enhanced through surgery. Bruises and scars covered her body. She was only twenty-seven but time and neglect had already conspired against her. A player who watched Crystal emerge from the passenger side of the car remembers, "Yeah, she didn't get out of the car the way I get out of a car normally when I'm not impaired," he said. "She didn't spring out of the car. It was kind of like a slow-moving process."

Kim said she met Crystal at the back door of 610. The women had never met before that night and worked for two different escort agencies—Kim was with Allure Escort Services and Crystal was with Bunny Hole Entertainment. They introduced themselves to each other and began planning their performance. They entered the house and were each paid their four hundred dollars in cash in advance as agreed. At midnight, the exotic dancers emerged from the back bathroom, where Kim had changed into her outfit. They strolled down a short hallway and into the living room, where nearly thirty guys, some of whom were friends of Duke lacrosse players, waited for the show.

Kim began, shaking her hips like a pendulum to the beat of the music provided by the players. She later told police that the guys "hooted and hollered" as each of the dancers peeled off her bra. But the smiling and cheering didn't last long. Things began to get awkward when Crystal, intoxicated and on a powerful muscle relaxant, repeatedly tripped and stumbled over Kim. Kim later recalled giving her a look during the performance like, "C'mon, girl, what's going on?," but got no response.

At one point, Crystal—barely able to stand, much less put on a show—tumbled to the floor. While that was not a rare sight, according to Yolanda Haynes, the former manager of the Platinum Club, where Crystal frequently worked, this badly choreographed dance only aroused suspicion and disappointment among the players. With Crystal on the floor, Kim hovered over her partner and "they for some reason started mimicking oral sex," one player said. "We didn't ask them to. One girl got on top of the other one, and everyone was like . . . ugh."

The uninspiring performance led some, among them Devon Sherwood, to begin leaving. "They had no poles or flashing lights," he said. "They were just dancing around a group of guys on beat-up couches and carpets that probably hadn't been cleaned in ten years." Someone decided to help the dancers, asking if they had brought any sex toys.

"I'd use your dick, but it's too small," an annoyed Kim retorted.

That prompted a tragic decision. One player grabbed a brown broom handle and said, "Well, how about this?" That suggestion set the strippers on edge. A photograph snapped by a player showed an agitated Kim reacting and reaching out toward the players during the show. Kim later said the commotion had Crystal "riled up and irate," so Kim said she pulled Crystal into the nearby bathroom of the three-bedroom house and locked the door.

The five-minute striptease had ended. The show had not.

After a few minutes, one of the nervous captains became suspicious of what the women were doing in the locked bathroom, adjacent to the bedroom of one of the captains. One player said, "I didn't know what they were doing. I thought they were shooting up, doing something stupid." Desperate to regain control of the situation and get the strippers out of the bathroom, a player began to slip bills underneath the locked door.

At 12:14 A.M., Reade Seligmann, a sophomore Duke lacrosse player at the party, telephoned On Time Taxi and asked for a taxi to pick him up at the nearby corner of Watts Street and Urban Avenue. Moez Mostafa, owner of On Time Taxi, said in a sworn statement that he picked up Seligmann and another person on that street corner at twelve-nineteen, driving them directly to Wachovia Bank. The bank's security camera showed Seligmann withdrawing money from the ATM at 12:24 A.M.

Back at the house, the strippers finally emerged from the bathroom at 12:20 A.M. An incoherent Crystal followed Kim out of the back door. As they were leaving, Kim saw the player who had grabbed the broomstick and "loses her shit again," according to another player. "Kim ran to the car and I followed her," one player said. "I was apologizing to Kim and she was saying, 'It's not your fault, it's not your fault.' "

Players, who had paid the dancers for a two-hour performance, were angry about the abbreviated performance. Bissey, a next-door neighbor, reported hearing players in the alley between the two houses, saying, "I want my money back." One of the players said, "I got guys that are pissed off because they got ripped off. I know we got ripped off and I was trying to do damage control here and get these girls out of the house. But I don't want the cops to show up in the middle of this whole thing and see all of us drunk and have this girl lie and say she was threatened or felt unsafe or uncomfortable."

One player approached the driver's side of Kim's car and apologized to the women, asking them to come back into the house to collect their belongings. Crystal had left her purse in the bathroom and a shoe in the living room. "I wasn't trying to get them back in the house to dance," the player said. "I just wanted to calm them down so the cops wouldn't come. We were worried about getting cited for having guys drinking underage."

Crystal got out of the car, made her way down the alley next to the house, and stumbled up the back doorstep. She stepped in and grabbed her purse from the bathroom, which was three feet from the back door. She also grabbed Dave Evans's shaving kit. As she stepped back outside, players locked the doors and wouldn't allow her back in.

Crystal began pounding on the back door and reached into her purse to grab her phone. And, at 12:26 A.M., she made a call to Centerfold Escorts, another service with which she worked. Drunk and confused, Crystal stood at the top of the steps for a moment, trying to decide what to do. She smiled at a player who was standing in the driveway and snapping photographs. Then she lost her balance. Crystal's hands slowly reached for the iron railing, to no avail. She tumbled down, adding even more scratches and bruises to her tattered body. The fall didn't really hurt her, but embarrassment and muscle relaxants made it difficult for her to get up. She lay at the bottom of the stairs, pretending to be passed out, until one of the players left to get help from her dancing partner. "I go back and she's not moving and I am like, 'Holy shit, this girl's going to OD [overdose] on my back porch and die, and now we're really fucked,' " a player said.

Kim later said to police she told Flannery, ". . . If they could get her [Crystal] to my car, I would get her out of their hair." Flannery agreed, helping Crystal up and leaning her against his shoulder as he made his way to Kim's car. The player-turned-photographer, once again documenting the bizarre events, snapped a shot of a disoriented Crystal being placed into Kim's vehicle at 12:41 A.M.

As the women were preparing to drive away, one player, still upset by his monetary losses, made a comment about Kim's appearance. Kim, enraged and defensive, called him a 'little-dick white boy, who probably couldn't get it on his own and had to pay for it."

The player countered with, "Tell your grandfather I said thanks for my cotton shirt."

That was it. The elements had collided.

At 12:53 A.M., the perfect storm, involving sex, race, class, politics, and lies, was set in motion when Kim Roberts grabbed her cell phone and dialed the fateful numbers: 911.

CHAPTER TWO

Don't Worry, This Will Blow Over

Duke lacrosse coach Mike Pressler understood the challenge of spring break for his troops. Though NCAA regulations allowed the team to practice every day during the week, the lack of classroom requirements often left the players with most of their days open. Because Duke prides itself on being a national university, nearly all of their classmates were long gone to homes many miles away. As a result, the laxers and a handful of other spring sport athletes were alone on campus. For years, Pressler had searched for creative ways to keep his team entertained during the break. The coach's efforts had led to an annual bowling showdown for his players at Durham Lanes.

Durham Lanes was the perfect location, close to the Duke campus on Chapel Hill Boulevard. It featured thirty-two lanes and fair prices: $4.00 per game and $4.54 to rent bowling shoes. On March 15, 2006, Pressler paid for the lanes, shoes, food, and soft drinks for his forty-seven players, as he had every previous year. Many players were dressed in bright, collared bowling shirts, nylon daisy dukes, argyle socks, and scuffed bowling shoes.

The competition among the four-man teams didn't offer prizes, just plenty of spirited razzing and a good time. Most of the players were admittedly lousy bowlers, barely able to break the century mark in scoring. Others, such as junior Nick O'Hara, who slicked back his hair and wore bushy, fake sideburns, and junior John Walsh, were exceptional bowlers. Walsh, who had his own bowling ball and could spin shots from any angle, bowled a 240 one game—300 is the perfect score. For Pressler, this was one of his favorite days of the season, a day when he could have his family—including daughters Janet and Maggie—together under one roof. But that roof would quickly cave in.

"It was supposed to be a day of fun," freshman Devon Sherwood remembered. "Instead it marked the beginning of a tumultuous time."

The team party two nights earlier at 610 wasn't on the players' minds when Pressler, checking his phone messages midway through the bowling tournament, received an urgent message on his cell phone at two-thirty in the afternoon from Sue Wasiolek, Duke's assistant dean of students. Pressler immediately stepped outside and returned the call from Wasiolek, who informed him of the disturbing news she had received from Bob Dean, the chief of the Duke Police Department.

"She told me there was a claim that a sexual assault had happened at 610 North Buchanan involving members of the lacrosse team," Pressler said. "And she said that Bob Dean, the chief of the Duke Police Department, had told her the accuser was not credible—that is a phrase we heard a thousand times over the next few days—and that 'this could go away.' "

Pressler went immediately back into the bowling alley to gather his four senior captains—Matt Zash, Dan Flannery, David Evans, and Bret Thompson.

Unbeknownst to Pressler and the team, Kim's 911 emergency telephone call as she pulled away from the party had been to file a false police report. Roberts claimed she and her "black girlfriend" were passing by the "big frat house" at 610 North Buchanan and had been taunted and called "niggers" by the white men hanging out at that address. In the call, during which she claimed to be both driving and walking by the house, she even faked tears.

"I was angry and I had to tell somebody," Kim said later, "but I didn't want everyone to know I'm a dancer."

Twenty-nine minutes after she pulled away from 610 and dialed 911, Kim was in need of real help. The inebriated Crystal Mangum had gone silent as Kim was driving, trying to decide what to do with her unanticipated passenger. Kim drove her black Honda away from Duke, passed a police station, and headed down Hillsborough Road, where she ended up in a parking lot of a Kroger Supermarket. There, Kim enlisted the help of Angel Altmon, a security guard, who telephoned police.

"There's a lady in someone else's car," Altmon explained to the 911 dispatcher, "and she will not get out of the car, period." Three minutes later, Sergeant John Shelton arrived in his squad car. Kim explained to Shelton that she had offered the woman a ride home because a group of boys were screaming racial slurs at her and she seemed incapable of making it out of the situation on her own. But now the woman wouldn't get out of her car.

Shelton walked over to Crystal, slumped over in the passenger seat of Kim's car, grabbed her lightly, and jostled her in hope of a response. His efforts went unacknowledged, so the officer returned to his cruiser for something that would surely wake her. "My experience is that unconscious people wake up rather quickly when exposed to ammonia capsules," he wrote in his report of the night. "When I used it she began mouth-breathing, which is a sign that she was not really unconscious." Whether she was actually passed out or not, she refused to get out of Kim's car. Shelton pulled at her waist in an attempt to remove her, but Crystal reached for the parking brake with her left hand and held on tight. When he finally pried her out she went limp once again, collapsing to the ground.

As she had no identification, the officer wasn't sure what to do with her. Shelton conferred with Officer Willie Barfield, who had arrived on the scene a few minutes behind him. "She wouldn't speak with us," Shelton wrote. "We didn't know her name or where she lived. Taking her home was not an option." Shelton considered Crystal too intoxicated for a twenty-four-hour hold in jail. An involuntary commitment to Durham Center Access, a mental health and substance abuse facility, was the only option. Barfield called dispatchers at 1:27 A.M. and told them that Crystal was "breathing, appears to be fine. She's not in distress. She's just passed out drunk."

Just before 2:00 A.M., Barfield arrived at the center with a conscious but dazed Crystal in his backseat. He stood by as a staff nurse went through the standard screening process, asking a series of questions to assess if she was at risk for suicide, violence, substance abuse, or victimization. The nurse said Crystal, who introduced herself as Honey, "was not capable of maintaining her lucid thinking," so she "began to zero in with questions."

"Have you been victimized in any way?" a staff member asked.

"Yes," Crystal replied.

Taking a second look at Crystal in her see-through negligee and lace panties, the nurse prompted, "Have you been raped?"

"Yes," Crystal replied this time.

Officer Barfield immediately contacted Sergeant Shelton to tell him that the woman said she had been raped inside the house at 610 North Buchanan Boulevard. Shelton recognized the address. The reason he was so quick to respond to Kim's cry for help in the Kroger parking lot was that he had just finished investigating the scene she complained about in her first 911 call; the same house.

Crystal was no longer eligible for involuntary commitment following her disclosure of rape. "I told him to take her to Duke Hospital and that I would meet them there," Shelton wrote in his report. He arrived at Duke University Medical Hospital at 2:30 A.M. and began questioning Crystal, who was finally conscious and cooperative, about the rape. She told him that she was a stripper and that she and one other girl were hired to "put on a show" for a group of men at 610. When they left the party she got into an argument with the other stripper, who wanted to go back inside. At that point, Crystal said several men pulled her out of the car and groped her.

No one forced her to have sex—there was no rape, she now said in the first of many changes to her story—but someone did steal her money. She told the nurse that "Nikki," the stage name Kim used, had taken her cash.

While Crystal was checking into the hospital at 2:45 A.M., Shelton walked to the parking lot and called the police station to say the woman had recanted her rape allegation. Before he could make it back inside, he got word that she had changed her story again, giving the nurse-in-training who was handling her case a new version. She told the Sexual Assault Nurse Examiner (SANE) she had, in fact, been raped. "I called the watch commander back and said she had changed her story back to being raped," Shelton wrote.

The sergeant confronted Crystal, asking which story was true. "She told me she did not want to talk to me anymore," Shelton wrote in his report. "And then she started crying and saying something about them dragging her into the bathroom."

A rape kit examination ensued. According to hospital reports, samples from the entire pelvic area, which includes the vulva, vagina, cervix, fundus, and rectal area, were taken and smeared onto slides to be examined at the state crime lab. Crystal complained of tenderness all over her body, but the ESI Pain Documentation portion of the medical record, which tracks vital stats and body movement, indicated she showed no signs of being uncomfortable or in pain. She was noted to be in "no obvious discomfort."

The only physical trauma the SANE nurse—still in training—could find was "diffuse edema of the vaginal walls" and a few scratches on her legs. "Physicians and nurses can determine whether there has been trauma to the body but they cannot usually determine the cause of the trauma," Dr. Thomas Sporn, assistant professor in Duke's Department of Pathology, told Duke's student newspaper, the *Chronicle.* "It's very difficult to tell if there's been consensual sex or rape."

Police documents indicate that the accuser had, in fact, been sexually active in the days leading up to the incident. Crystal admitted she'd performed using a vibrator in front of a couple earlier on the evening of the party at 610, and that she had slept with her boyfriend, Matthew Murchison, a week before the party. (Investigators later learned she had been paid for sex with a man at a little after 6:00 P.M. that same evening at the Millennium Hotel on Campus Walk Avenue in Durham.) But samples from her rape kit also contained DNA from several other men. Jarriel Johnson, who drives Crystal to most appointments but was unavailable to drive her to the party at 610, filed a police report stating that he and Crystal had sex less than a week before the party. He also told police that the weekend before the party he had driven her to several "appointments" at hotels in the area.

Accusations like Crystal's usually would have alarmed most law enforcement officers, but the Duke and Durham police present that night did not make an effort to examine the crime scene for almost three days. Why didn't police follow their usual protocol when allegations this severe were made? The only explanation is that the policemen who dealt with the woman that night agreed with what Duke officer Christopher Day wrote in his report of the incident: "The victim changed her story several times and eventually Durham Police stated that charges would not exceed misdemeanor simple assault against the occupants of 610 N. Buchanan."

While the players practiced the next day, on Thursday, none of them were aware their accuser was being further interviewed by police. Now she was sure of it: She had been raped. She wasn't sure how many men had violated her. The number changed from five to twenty to three in her statements.

But she was sure she had been raped.

When word spread through the bowling alley that Wasiolek, aka Dean Sue, was on the phone with Pressler, the players became concerned. One player remembers the team members whispering to each other, "Coach had to have found out about the party. Do you think he knows we had strippers?" They anticipated the consequences that would surely ensue. "We're going to have to do a lot of gassers; a lot of sprints," said another player. "He's going to run our asses off. Oh, man." Little did they know the situation beyond the double doors was worse than they could ever imagine.

Pressler had marched back inside and yanked his four captains—Flannery, Zash, Evans, and Bret Thompson—away from their bowling games and out to the front lawn. Flannery, Zash, and Evans rented the house at 610. The group was in clear view through the glass doors as players inside peered out.

"It was kind of weird," Tony McDevitt said. "We are all in the bowling alley and we see the four captains talking to coach and we could tell it was serious. All of a sudden, word starts getting around the whole team, 'What's going on? What's going on?' And then we see them on the phone. And we are like, 'This can't be good. What's happening?' I was thinking that somebody got in trouble. It was just an eerie feeling. We could tell it was something serious. You could look at Coach Pressler, you looked through the doors when they were outside and you could see Coach Pressler's face. He was pretty serious."

Pressler turned to his captains. "Did you guys have a stripper party Monday night?" he asked, almost screaming. "Yes," they admitted without hesitation. Pressler repeated what Dean Sue had just informed him, "That a woman is claiming she was gang-raped at 610 North Buchanan, involving members of the lacrosse team." Zash said his "jaw dropped" as Pressler spoke. "Is this true? Did this happen?" Pressler asked in an intimidating voice. Each player looked him straight in the eyes and vehemently denied the allegations, telling Pressler, "They never touched her."

Pressler was furious they had a party, especially one with strippers and underage drinking, but he believed they hadn't hurt anyone. "The astonishment on their faces, I knew right then and there the accusations were false," Pressler said. "They said we did have the party, it was a situation that escalated, but I swear to you, nobody touched that person. Guys look at me, in the eyes. I said to them, 'Nobody touched that person?' I went around to all of them and heard what I needed to hear. I believed them. I could see it in their eyes. I said, 'Okay, stand right here.' "

Pressler picked up his phone and dialed Dean Sue. Flannery, who witnessed the entire night's events, was the first on the phone. He acknowledged they threw a party and that he had ordered two strippers. That was the extent of their guilt. When the strippers arrived, one was already plastered and couldn't even dance, he told Wasiolek. They paid the women and the women ended up leaving early.

Zash was next. He reiterated what Flannery had said and added that the intoxicated stripper passed out on their back porch and had to be carried to the other stripper's car. Dean Sue, who was doubtful of the allegations from the beginning, assured the players she believed them. When Police Chief Dean had informed her of the situation earlier that day, he added that neither his officers nor the Durham police believed the accuser was credible. "Right now you don't need an attorney," Flannery said of Wasiolek's advice. "Just don't tell anyone, including your teammates or parents, and cooperate with police if they contact you. If you tell them the truth, it will work out."

Though the looming accusations weighed heavy on the minds of the four captains and their coach, Wasiolek's words helped calm them. Dean Sue was a lawyer, so they trusted her advice to have faith in the justice system. Pressler's mind was still spinning, however. "I really didn't want to hear about the details, all I wanted to hear is that they didn't touch her, that's all that resonated with me," he said. "I didn't want to get into the party, underage drinking; I was going to deal with all that . . . I was going to punish them all at the appropriate time and there were going to be suspensions—I never got the chance to do that. But, anyway, I just wanted to get to the bottom of the serious charge."

Most players were ending their games and heading home when Pressler and the captains walked back inside the bowling alley. "They were probably outside fifteen or twenty minutes," McDevitt said. "Obviously, when you're bowling, people are finishing up earlier than others. You are free to leave, get going. People were sort of scattering out—it was done. So nobody really had a chance to talk to coach or to the other guys."

The moment Pressler left the bowling alley and climbed into his Duke-blue Dodge Dakota, he called Chris Kennedy, Duke's senior associate athletic director, Pressler's superior and a huge supporter of the lacrosse team. The coach informed him of the allegations and repeated everything Dean Sue and the players discussed. "All right, Mike, just keep me posted," Kennedy said.

At 10:00 P.M. on Thursday, March 16, one day after the bowling tournament and three days after the lacrosse party, Pressler's phone rang. It was

Dean Sue calling to alert him of a search warrant that had been issued for 610. Pressler telephoned the captains at the house, but the call came too late.

Two hours earlier, Evans and Zash were taking a nap after a grueling practice when they awoke to fists pounding on their front door. Before either of them could get out of bed, eight police officers invaded the living room. When the players emerged from their bedrooms, they were frisked and ordered to sit on the sofa for the duration of the search. Benjamin Himan, a rookie investigator with the Durham police department, read them the search warrant that detailed their search.

In a scene straight out of a bad cop movie, several of the officers gathered around Zash and Evans in the living room so they could watch Duke's basketball team playing that night in the NCAA tournament. "It was surreal," Zash said, "would have made a great picture."

Just as Evans and Zash had promised to Dean Sue, they cooperated with police. As Zash read the search warrant and reviewed the items detailed, he voluntarily told police where to find them in the house. Zash said Crystal's makeup bag and cell phone were on the kegerator (a converted refrigerator used for a beer keg) in the living room. The players also gave investigators their cell phones, identification cards, computers, email accounts, and passwords, without hesitation. Nevertheless, Sergeant Mark Gottlieb, a veteran who led the investigation, and his team tore through 610 looking for any evidence that a brutal rape had occurred. Police found $120 still on the table from the party.

"We didn't know what to do with the money," Zash said. "We were going to put it into, whatever, buying beer for the rest of the team for the next outing we had or putting it toward the formal we had coming up. And he [Gottlieb] was like, 'Oh, it was $120, oh $120 in twenties, exactly what the stripper said she left here.' "

Zash couldn't believe what he was seeing or hearing. "They were being very cold with us," Zash said. "We were like, 'How can you guys believe this, this is a joke?' "

When investigators asked if they would like to come to the station and explain themselves, Zash and Evans jumped at the chance. "Absolutely, I don't want this investigation to go on a day longer," Zash said.

Evans was still sitting on the tattered sofa when Flannery, who had just finished his birthday dinner with a professor and his family, walked in. Flannery had passed five squad cars with their lights flashing outside the house and cops were inside searching the house. Flannery peered into the kitchen, where he noticed one of the investigators digging into a cake his girlfriend had mailed to him for his birthday. "What's going on here?" Flannery asked. "Dave, what's going on?"

Evans told Flannery to sit down and wait, they'd be leaving soon for the Durham police station to straighten everything out. Flannery had every intention of cooperating the way his roommates had, until a few of the investigators started giving him a hard time. When Richard Clayton, another investigator who assisted with the case, entered the room, his eyes locked in on the tall, athletic player with a shaved head. "You look like that kid," Clayton said, eyeing Flannery up and down. "You know, earlier in the school year you beat up one of our officers on the corner of Clarendon and West Markham. You are definitely the kid."

"I don't know what you're talking about," Flannery said nervously. All the police officers in the room were staring at him now. "I'm shitting my pants," Flannery remembers. "I'm like 'Oh, my God, I can just imagine what they're going to do to me.' " Clayton called to tell the officer who was assaulted to stop by 610 and identify the man who had beaten him. When he arrived and saw Flannery, he said they had the wrong guy. Flannery breathed a huge sigh of relief. Though he was not eager to help the police after the stunt Clayton pulled, Flannery followed Evans and Zash out the door and to the precinct.

The captains were separated into individual rooms at the police station and each gave a written statement of what happened the night of their party, which would remain consistent throughout the entire investigation. Then Gottlieb printed off the pictures of every Duke lacrosse team member and had each captain identify who was definitely at the party, who definitely was not, and who might have been there.

While Evans was looking through the pictures, Clayton called and claimed to have found cocaine in Evans's drawer at 610. Evans denied having it, and Clayton laughed and said he was just kidding. "They kept trying to scare us to gauge our reactions," Zash said. Zash was tired of their questions and constant intimidation techniques, so he offered to take a lie detector test to prove he was telling the truth. Gottlieb told him it would take too long to set up and it was not even admissible in court. "It's only used for investigative purposes," Gottlieb said. But Zash was confused. Wasn't this an investigation? He couldn't understand why they wouldn't let him take a test to prove he was telling them the truth. Little did he know that Gottlieb was denying him for a reason: He was more interested in DNA samples.

"I told Gottlieb that they were wasting their time and that they needed to bring the second dancer down to the station and she would corroborate our entire story," Flannery recalls.

Gottlieb visited each of the players' interview rooms with the same story. "Both of your roommates have agreed to a suspect kit. Will you take one?" he asked. The cocaptains had no idea they'd been deceived and happily agreed to the series of tests, which would obtain samples of their DNA. They agreed to go to the hospital, and while waiting there with Officer Clayton, they noticed that he had only two rape kits in his hand. The players asked where the other kit was. "Oh, one of you has been eliminated as a suspect," said Clayton. Their faces lit up. "Who?" they asked. "Just kidding," he replied, making his third cruel joke of the night; he was on a roll.

It was time to take DNA from the players. "Two female investigators, with industrial-sized tweezers, pulled fifty individual hairs from our head and pubic region," Flannery remembers. The worst part came when the industrial-sized tweezers went south, below their belts. "They couldn't just cut the hair because they had to get the root and all," Zash said, grimacing. After each guy had endured that and provided cheek swabs, the kit was complete. Their honesty and openness was viewed positively by police, who had gotten everything they needed from the guys and encountered almost no resistance. By the end of the search, police had seized their DNA, four laptop computers, three digital cameras, a bath mat, a bath rug, five artificial nails, a bottle of K-Y Jelly, a makeup bag, and a stack of twenty-dollar bills, among other items. As they were leaving the hospital and getting into Clayton's car for a ride home, the officer gave them all a reassuring look and repeated the words they would hear over and over for the next week.

"You know, guys," he said. "Don't worry about this. It's all going to blow over."

CHAPTER THREE

Duke and Durham

To some, Duke was referred to as an "Oasis in Durham." Others, mostly African-Americans, referred to it as "the plantation." Durham remains a segregated city, with East Durham often referred to as a "ghetto" where corner convenience stores have nicknames such as "Murder Mart" and "Shop and Rob" because of their connection to violent crimes. Just a few miles away—close enough for the echo of gunshots to be heard from East Durham—the Duke Forest neighborhood and its million-dollar homes sit nestled on the edge of Duke University.

Durham might not be North Carolina's largest city, but its crime rate and poverty levels are an alarming, if not embarrassing, combination for local officials. The contrast between the two sides of Durham's tracks can be startling.

Durham might also be *the* city in North Carolina that most suffers from low self-esteem. As Carl W. Kenney II wrote in the May 7, 2006, edition of the *Raleigh News & Observer,* "The national media have done a fine job of ruining the already fragile reputation of Durham. Before the Duke case arose, city leaders were stewing over a commentary by Michael Skube in the *Greensboro News and Record.* Skube claimed that Durham is the one city in the state that the rest wished would go away. It was hard reading those words, but there was a bit of truth. After the burning of three crosses, a few bouts with the Board of Education and a load of scandals in city and county government, those of us who love Durham find it difficult proving the City of Medicine is one of the best places to live in America."

• • •

Today, more than nineteen thousand Durham residents work at the university—15 percent of Durham's workforce—making it the city's largest employer. "Duke is the economic engine in Durham, most people would know that," said John Burness, Duke's senior vice president for public affairs and government relations. "The textiles and the tobacco have been demised, they are no longer here. They used to be major economic engines, and they no longer are. We are about all that's left in terms of a big powerful corporate nongovernmental entity. That's just the reality."

To make sure the city understood its impact, Duke began in 1997 to release a series of reports detailing just how much and in how many ways it contributed to the Durham community. The 2006 edition of the report yielded this conclusion: "Duke University's total economic impact on the city and county of Durham is estimated at $3.2 billion per year."

That wasn't always the case. Durham's rich soil had all the right ingredients to make money. Much of Durham's growth can be attributed to the establishment of a thriving tobacco industry. In fact, the city's nickname of the "Bull City" originated from a Blackwell Tobacco Company product, "Bull" Durham Tobacco. While the tobacco industry dominated the city's economy initially, it was soon rivaled by the establishment of multiple textile mills.

In 1854, Dr. Bartlett Durham sold four acres of land to the North Carolina Railroad Company to build a new railroad station. Located between Raleigh and Hillsborough, what began as a small settlement would soon become a central hub for the growing economy in North Carolina: the city of Durham.

In April, exactly twenty years later, Washington Duke purchased two acres of land near that railroad station. This would become the location of his new tobacco factory and the beginning of his tobacco empire. Given Duke's prior farming experience with Brightleaf tobacco, it did not take long for Duke and his sons to become major players in the tobacco industry. In 1878, through successful business ventures and partnerships, the business was renamed W. Duke, Sons and Company. Twelve years later, the Dukes would merge with their four largest competitors to create the American Tobacco Company.

Although the Supreme Court would later order the dissolution of this conglomerate, in 1911, the Dukes had established themselves as a prominent family in the Carolina community. Their growing wealth and influence in Durham allowed Washington Duke to dedicate time and money to new endeavors, one of which was Trinity College.

After the Civil War, Durham quickly developed a vibrant African-American community. The African-American economy prospered in this city through a combination of vocational training, land ownership, community leadership, and a powerful workforce. The center of the African-American community was an area known as "Hayti," just south of the center of town. Members of the African-American community established some of the most prominent and successful African-American–owned businesses in the country during the early twentieth century. These businesses, the best known of which are North Carolina Mutual Insurance Company and Mechanics & Farmers' Bank, were centered on Parrish Street, which would come to be known as the "Black Wall Street."

Trinity College, a Methodist school originally located in rural Randolph County, North Carolina, moved to Durham thanks to the financial assistance of Washington Duke and a sixty-two-acre land donation from Julian Carr, another North Carolina industrialist and philanthropist. In 1892, Trinity College opened the doors of its new location in the bustling New South city of Durham.

According to the Duke University Archives, "Washington Duke offered three gifts of $100,000 each for endowment, one of which was contingent upon the college admitting women 'on equal footing with men.' " By World War I, Trinity College had acquired a "relatively young, ambitious, and largely native faculty, recruited from the new graduate schools at Johns Hopkins, Columbia, and other Northern universities" to quickly become "one of the leading liberal arts colleges in the South."

In 1924, The Duke Endowment was formalized by James B. Duke, Washington Duke's son. This $40 million trust fund was intended to distribute its annual income to hospitals, orphanages, the Methodist Church, three colleges, and a university built around Trinity College. Accomplishing this goal would require $19 million in renovations to Trinity College to repair the old and to build the new. It seemed calling this institution by the same name would be an injustice to the man and the family who had donated so much to its improvements. James B. Duke agreed that renaming Trinity College "Duke University" would be a proper "memorial to his father and family."

Duke has developed into one of America's premier academic institutions. Its growth and academic focus have contributed to the university's reputation as an academic and research institution. Duke was ranked fifth in *U.S. News & World Report*'s annual college rankings. The school draws some of the best students from around the world, placing Duke in a quasi–Ivy League category.

Unfortunately, the university's "outrageous ambition" left many local students on the outside looking in, unable to gain entry. Stroll through a school parking lot and you are more likely to see out-of-state license plates than plates from the Tar Heel State. Many students hail from the Mid-Atlantic and Northeast, a fact not lost on locals who call Duke the "University of New Jersey in Durham."

In addition to the stiff academic competition, the tuition bill rules Duke out as an option for many locals. A 2006 article in *USA Today* made that clear: "Its [Duke's] tuition bill ($44,005, including room, board, expenses, and books) exceeds the median household income in Durham, N.C. ($43,337)."

Duke was not always ranked within the top five universities in the country. An attractive liberal arts school, Duke could only be transformed into an academic heavyweight with the recruitment of intellectual powerhouses prominent within the world of academia.

Previously the English department chair at Johns Hopkins University,

Stanley Fish was recruited to hold that same role for the Duke English Department from 1986 to 1992. Through his aggressive recruitment efforts, Fish was able to persuade other pioneering postmodern scholars to join Duke's liberal arts faculty, qualifying him as Duke's pied piper of academics.

With well-known and soon-to-be-well-known academics now teaching at Duke University, it did not take long for the school—especially its Arts & Sciences Department—to become recognized as one of the universities in the higher echelons of academic excellence.

Duke's ascent and Durham's decline happened almost simultaneously. It seemed that each freshman class at Duke brought a higher average SAT score, while the number rising in Durham was the crime rate.

The crime rate is such a troubling issue in present-day Durham that the mayor, William Bell, focused much of his 2006 State of the City Address on it. "I want to spend the majority of my report on what I feel is the one area the prevents us from being an excellent city, and that is crime," Bell said. He explained that there had been a 16 percent increase in the murder rate from 2004 to 2005—thirty-seven homicides in comparison to thirty-two.

Mayor Bell continued to break down the homicide statistics in order to make one specific point. "Let me say that as an African-American male and as your mayor, what is most disturbing to me personally about those numbers is that the vast majority of the victims and suspects are African-American males," said Bell. "As African-Americans, we are approximately 43 percent of the city's population, yet in the year 2005, we allegedly were responsible for committing over 80 percent of the homicides."

The high homicide rate is an obvious concern for Durham and its citizens. Earning the "dubious distinction of being North Carolina's murder capital," as proclaimed by the *News & Observer*, is not something that inspires civic pride. The only city in North Carolina with more murders than Durham is Charlotte—and that city is three times as big. When the number of murders is calculated against the city's population, which is the method used by the State Bureau of Investigation, Durham swamps Charlotte, at 18.9 to 12.7 per 100,000 residents.

You can almost hear them chanting, "We're number one," at the Durham County Jail.

When Duke's prospective students come to visit, Durham's reputation as the crime capital of the state is never mentioned. Rita Flannery, mother of former lacrosse captain Dan Flannery, admitted the high crime rates were never mentioned before she agreed to send her son to Duke. "That's never discussed with incoming parents," she said. "As a mother, I was not aware that they had such issues as gang violence."

Although some may call Duke "the plantation," complete segregation is impossible. The Duke students cannot avoid the fact that they will be Durham residents for the length of their academic career. The problems facing Durhamites will face Dukies as well.

The relationship between the university and the community surrounding it has been scrutinized from all angles. However, James Coleman, law professor at Duke, denies that racial tension is as serious as it has been portrayed as being. "People try to make it into a black-white thing," said Coleman. "The implication always was that this is the privileged white kids of Duke and poor black people in Durham and that's where the tension was. That wasn't it at all."

Coleman, like many who have studied the Duke-Durham relationship, say the challenge was less about race than it was about class. Indeed, Durham offers a stark contrast—one side young and privileged; the other side poor and working class. They are encouraged to avoid each other. When mixed, the combination can be lethal.

Duke and Durham are like two ships passing in the night; a relationship most people ignored, until Crystal made a false claim.

CHAPTER FOUR

Lacrosse at Duke

As Duke grew as an institution, it increasingly saw itself as the Harvard of the South. It pressed and pressed, trying to figure out ways to make itself an Ivy League equivalent. One way to build that reputation was by playing the very sports that the Ivies excelled in. Duke didn't just want to compete with Ivy League schools, the Blue Devils wanted to beat them. Duke refused to waver in its ambition: It was determined to contend at a championship level in sports across the board and do so without compromising academic standards.

Invented by Native North Americans as a way to prepare for war, lacrosse wasn't a sport for cowards. Early players concentrated on first injuring their opponents with their sticks, then moving to the goal. Games could be played on an open field over a mile wide and sometimes lasted for days. Often players were gravely injured or even killed. Early balls were made out of the heads of the enemy, deerskin, clay, stone, and sometimes wood.

Lacrosse became part of North Carolina history on April 7, 1938, when neighbors Duke and North Carolina met in the first game played in the state. With more than five hundred curious fans lining the muddy field, the Blue Devils beat the Tar Heels 2–1 behind player-coach Dick Lewis. Little did anyone realize at the time that game would serve as the foundation of a Duke program that would rise and fall over the next seven decades.

Duke Athletic Director Tom Butters had a struggling lacrosse program on his hands, one that had attempted to compete with the quickly growing powers on the East Coast. The Blue Devils had won their share of games, posting consecutive eleven-win seasons in 1986 and 1987 for the first time in school history. The coach, Tony Cullen, was considered one of the program's finest lacrosse players ever. The Blue Devils also had three lacrosse players inducted into the school's Hall of Fame—Jack Persons (1986), Gene Corrigan (1991), who would serve as commissioner of the Atlantic Coast Conference (ACC) and president of the National Collegiate Athletic Association (NCAA), and Charles Gilfillan (1994).

Despite a number of victories over the years, Duke was a miserable 2-45 in Atlantic Coast Conference play from 1977 to 1990. It is in conference play that teams advance to the NCAA Tournament and are measured for greatness. Much to the chagrin of Butters and others, the Blue Devils had little or no success against conference brethren North Carolina, Virginia, and Maryland. There was even talk that it might be time to put away Duke's lacrosse sticks for good.

In 1991, a resume from a young coach named Mike Pressler landed on Butters's desk. It was the right time for Pressler to jump to a major conference and it was the right time for Duke to jump back into the national lacrosse picture. Talent aside, Pressler was certain of one thing when he arrived in Durham: Nobody was going to outwork him or his team.

"It was a difficult hire for me," said Butters, who arrived at Duke in 1968 as the school's baseball coach before moving into administration, where he spent twenty-one years as the Blue Devils' legendary director of athletics before retiring in 1998. "I know I didn't want to hire a coach from a Division III program to a D I program and that person also be from my alma mater."

Pressler was both. He came to Duke as one of the most successful NCAA Division III coaches in the country. In five seasons at Ohio Wesleyan—Butters's alma mater—Pressler led the Battling Bishops to the NCAA Finals three straight times and to the semifinals twice. Pressler also served as an assistant at Army and guided Virginia Military Institute to a 7-4 record in the program's inaugural season and his only year as head coach in 1983.

Butters, who believed that defense won national championships, liked what he saw in Pressler—even if Pressler wasn't his first choice. But after Butters's top selection turned him down, Butters said he went with his gut, much as he did when he hired a little-known men's basketball coach named Mike Krzyzewski away from West Point to Duke in 1980. "I know people didn't know how to pronounce his name, and I know sure as hell they couldn't spell it," Butters said, laughing. "But we've done okay by him. I would try to hire good people and then get the hell out of the way."

And that's exactly what Butters did with Pressler, too. Confident and cocksure, Pressler quickly built a program that started to draw comparisons to tradition-rich lacrosse teams in the powerful Ivy League. The Blue Devils continued to improve during Pressler's tenure, winning the program's first ACC championship in forty-one years in 1995 and leading Duke to the national championship game in 2005. The Blue Devils lost to perennial power Johns Hopkins in that national title game, but the Blue Devils—and Pressler—had arrived.

Those who know Pressler weren't surprised by his success. A 1982 graduate of Washington and Lee University in Lexington, Virginia, Pressler was a four-year starter for both the football and lacrosse teams. Pressler, a lacrosse captain who went from a three-year starter on offense to defense his senior season, knew the importance of accountability and setting a high standard even as a young man.

"When he was a senior captain, we probably had more meetings than at any time I was a coach," said Jack Emmer, Pressler's lacrosse coach at Washington and Lee and a coach at Army for twenty-two years. "The meetings were about setting higher standards, about working harder. The key here was *he* called the meetings. The others had to respect him because he never asked anything of others he wasn't doing himself. He set such a high standard that if his teammates didn't give it all, he'd let them have it. A lot of captains don't do that because they want to be popular with their peers. That wasn't Mike. He was passionate about everyone getting the most of their ability. He certainly did."

During his tenure at Duke, which became fully funded in lacrosse with 12.6 scholarships in 2001, Pressler turned down the job at Maryland for the opportunity to continue his work with the Blue Devils. Duke Athletic Director Joe Alleva rewarded his coach with an unprecedented three-year contract extension in 2005, and Pressler joined Krzyzewski as one of the only two Duke coaches with multiyear deals. Alleva, in fact, told Pressler in a face-to-face meeting that Pressler would be his head coach as long as Alleva was the athletic director.

"Without question, Coach Pressler has done a magnificent job of taking our lacrosse program to the highest level," Alleva said in the Blue Devils' 2006 media guide. "Not only do his teams compete for ACC and national championships, but, more importantly his players graduate from Duke University."

"Every once in a while [Pressler] would get a job offer from somebody else or somebody would call on him, but we talked about it. Where else could you have what you have here?" said Chris Kennedy, Duke's senior associate athletic director and Pressler's close friend.

"The kind of kids you get to work with. You live three minutes from work. Quality of life. In terms of places to live, this place is pretty good. With all the cultural stuff, the weather, the beach, the mountains, all those kind of things. Where your family is happy. And you have achieved . . . you built a program that is one of the best five programs probably in the country. Where else can you do better? What's the top job in college lacrosse? Probably Johns Hopkins because it's Hopkins. But where do you live? I don't want to denigrate Baltimore but it's just . . . it's a different kind of experience."

Lacrosse, a lily-white sport, has helped student-athletes earn entry into some of the best academic institutions in the country. For many, it's a way out. Most popular in North America, especially in the Northeast, lacrosse is Canada's official national summer sport and the fastest-growing sport in the United States. In men's lacrosse at the collegiate level, there are 57 NCAA Division I, 35 Division II, and 130 Division III universities that field varsity teams. Additionally, almost 200 collegiate men's club teams compete at the Men's Collegiate Lacrosse Association level. NFL Hall of Fame running back Jim Brown is regarded as the best lacrosse player in the sport's history.

Each lacrosse team is composed of ten players on the field at a time: three attackmen, three midfielders, three defenders, and one goaltender. In men's lacrosse, players wear protective equipment on their heads, shoulders, arms, and hands, as body-checking is an integral part of the game, and stick checks to the arms and hands are considered legal.

"It's an up-speed game," said senior Tony McDevitt, who signed with the Blue Devils out of Penn Charter High School in Philadelphia and was also an all-state selection in football. "It combines a lot of sports. I played baseball and football growing up and I loved both. It [lacrosse] is basically like hockey on a field, without ice. You can hit, there's passing, there's scoring, a lot of goals, a lot of action. I think that's what makes it popular."

Lacrosse's impact can be felt in many areas, specifically on Wall Street. Actually, if you are looking to join the ranks of Wall Street stockbrokers, playing a varsity sport such as lacrosse may be just as powerful as a finance certificate. For some men's sports, a combination of on-the-field experience and strong alumni support, as is seen at Duke, draws a disproportionate number of athletes to the business world. It's believed that lacrosse teaches things that the classroom can't: teamwork, a positive reaction to adversity, and the ability to think on one's feet.

Former Duke captain Keat Crown, working in the Twin Towers when terrorists crashed airliners into the heart of New York City and the nation, relied on his lacrosse instincts to escape with his life on 9/11. Crown and his colleagues from Aon Chicago, an insurance brokerage firm, had a clear view of the damage inflicted by the first plane that crashed into Tower One that early morning of September 11, 2001. Crown, on the one hundredth floor of Tower Two, made his way down to the seventy-eighth floor as he tried to decide whether to evacuate or heed the advice of the tower-wide intercom message that alerted workers that the building was safe and they should return to their offices.

Just moments after he had telephoned his mother to tell her he was fine, the second plane barreled into Tower Two between the seventy-eighth and eighty-third floors. The seventy-eighth floor, where Crown was walking across the concourse, exploded in fire and fury. An elevator door that was blown off its hinges slammed Crown face-first to the floor, shattering his left ankle and left femur. Disoriented, confused, and bleeding profusely from a head wound (an elevator shaft spring had lodged in the back of his head), Crown was ready to die. Instead, he told family and friends that he heard Pressler's voice. Pressler teaches his players to rely on their training when faced with adversity, that they can always handle more than they believe that they can. What did Crown do? He fought for his life, crawling to safety, and was one of 12 persons out of 176 on his floor to survive.

"I don't know that I consciously thought about lacrosse at the time," said Crown, telling his story for the first time. "But there is no question in my mind that what I did, and my work ethic on the lacrosse fields and the lacrosse program on and off the field, kicked in immediately when I got in the crisis situation, where I'm on the seventy-eighth floor after we were hit. I can't say that I said, 'I learned this from lacrosse, and this from my training, so this is what I do.' But you absolutely just kick in to survival mode and crisis mode, I think both mentally and physically. Nothing's going to stop you, and you can endure more pain than you think because sometimes it is just inevitable.

"I wrote a letter to Coach Pressler in the weeks following and I sent him a big picture of the Trade Center, which he had on his wall the day he left Duke. I had him to thank him in part for surviving, and for instilling values. The things that he taught us that kept me from giving up. I don't remember the letter word for word, but I thanked him for turning boys into men. It was a constant theme in my mind of what he does year in and year out. He turns boys into men, and it's true."

When Pressler arrived at Duke in 1991, he brought a fiery, aggressive coaching style with him. Pressler stressed physical and mental toughness, and his approach wasn't for the faint of heart. He was a stern disciplinarian who challenged his players to become better players on the field and better students in the classroom. Pressler was nicknamed "Coach Tomato" by his players because his face would turn bright red when his emotions began to bubble to the surface, which was often.

"I wouldn't say he's laid back," said Joe Kennedy, who played for the Blue Devils from 2002 to 2005. "He's very fiery. He's a hard-ass. He demands a lot from you, but you respect him a lot. He's fair. If he yells at you, you deserve it. The thing I loved about him was it was never really about what you could do on the field. It didn't matter if you played every game, every minute, or if you didn't play at all, he showed each player respect. He would do anything for you."

The Blue Devils reached new heights under Pressler. They won their first game at Virginia in forty-two years (1992), earned their first bid to the NCAA Tournament (1992), won their first NCAA Tournament game (1994), won their first ACC Tournament title (1995), and advanced to the NCAA Final Four for the first time in history (1997). The 1997 team featured a school-record seven All-Americans, including two first-team selections in Jim Gonnella and David Stilley.

"When he built the program, he didn't get a lot of talent," Kennedy said. "It was more like take what he could get—coming up from nothing. It was guys who weren't great lacrosse players but who were great athletes. He would ride them and turn them into great lacrosse players. He used to call his team the Goon Squad. He would recruit those big, huge meatheads who can run. And then he stopped getting meatheads, and started getting real lacrosse players. He got guys who would go out on Saturday and work on their game. Pros."

It was the 2005 team that enjoyed the finest season in Duke history, winning an NCAA single-season record seventeen games and advancing to the national title game against Johns Hopkins. Pressler was named the USILA National Coach of the Year while players Matt Danowksi and Aaron Fenton earned top national honors at their respective positions of attackman and goalkeeper. Despite a heart-wrenching 9–8 setback to

Hopkins before more than forty-seven thousand fans at Lincoln Financial Field in Philadelphia, Pressler had taken Duke's lacrosse program from the edge of oblivion and turned it into a national contender.

The Blue Devils were just as successful in the classroom—in his sixteen years at Duke, Pressler's teams had a 100 percent graduation rate.

"He's definitely detail oriented," McDevitt said. "He's into the small things, the little things—when it's the fourth quarter and you are down a goal, and you have to lay back on your fundamentals. He definitely goes about things in a very meticulous manner. Coach Pressler was all about getting the edge any way possible. We watched film every day—sometimes on our practice, sometimes on our opponents. Anything he could do within the rules, he would do. He worked tirelessly. He was in the office at 6:00 A.M. Sometimes our scouting reports were fifteen to twenty pages long. He never wanted to leave any stone unturned. But overall coaching style, there's no doubt about it, he was a motivator. He knew how to push those buttons to get you going. And he still does to this day. When I get off the phone with him—I talk to him a bunch and we talk leisurely—I feel like I can go play in the national championship after I am done with him. He knows what to say to get you going."

There were a few players, however, who also knew how to turn the tables on Pressler. Kyle Dowd was one of those players. Dowd recalled an overtime game against Johns Hopkins during his sophomore season in 2004, when the Blue Devils tumbled 6–5 in overtime. "In the first overtime, we had the ball," Dowd said. "[Coach] calls a timeout and we bring it in and he goes over a play. I am in the game. I guess he thought I didn't understand what he was saying. Meanwhile, I did the whole time because I was paying attention. He started saying to me, 'You got that, you got that.' You know, he was yelling at me. I said, 'Coach, don't worry about it. I got it.' And I slapped him on the ass. I ran out on the field. I just remember the look on his face, and he had no idea what to do."

Pressler also went out of his way to make sure his support staff was comfortable and felt it was central to his lacrosse family. Lori Winters was hired as an assistant sports information director by Duke in 1992. Winters was raised in a football family—her father Bill Regnier was a head football and wrestling coach for thirty-one years in Lambertville, Michigan, and is in the National High School Coaches Hall of Fame—and knew nothing about lacrosse when she joined the Blue Devils' sports information staff. But Winters said Pressler's friendly, easy manner helped when it was time for her to cover men's lacrosse for the university.

"One thing I always remember and looked forward to was the first warm, spring day during lacrosse season," said Winters, thirty-seven, who left Duke in 1998. "Basketball season would be almost over—I traveled with the women's basketball team and helped with men's basketball when needed—and Coach Pressler would call the office and say, 'Lori, it's spring. The guys got the guns out today.' That meant they were practicing in tank tops and shorts instead of the usual sweats they wore in January and February. He would say, 'It's time for you to come out to practice.' It was the first sign of spring to me. I looked forward to that call every year."

Duke's administration reached out to Pressler and his lacrosse players to set a positive example on campus. The university had grown tired of "Tailgate," a quasisanctioned school function held in a parking lot before football games, and they asked Pressler for help in reining it in. At Tailgate, the lacrosse boys stood out among the revelers in their themed costumes—superheroes, cartoon charters, and so on.

For Duke officials, the problem was that the pregame revelry of Tailgate continued through the football games, meaning students stayed in the parking lot rather than heading into the stadium to support the woeful football team. So they asked Pressler for help, requesting that he get his players to leave the party and go into the game, in the hope that other students would follow suit.

The coach readily obliged, requiring that his players meet him fifteen minutes before kickoff to march to the near-vacant stadium. Unfortunately, they were the only Tailgaters to leave the party.

In this regard the lacrosse players, whose camaraderie off the field attracted criticism at times, exemplified the "work hard, play hard" Duke ideal. It wasn't lost on administrators either. As it happened, Sue Wasiolek, or Dean Sue, was reasonably attuned to the team's place in the school's culture, having been among those who attended the Tailgate. Even Duke President Richard Brodhead emerged from his private stadium box to talk with lacrosse players, in costume, as they entered one game. "He [Brodhead] was laughing, having a few yuks with the guys, and then he went back to his box," Pressler said.

As the lacrosse scandal unfolded, one would be led to believe the team was at the root of the most of the significant problems of our time—including world hunger. More specifically—and seriously—administrators connected lacrosse players with Tailgate trouble. John Burness, Duke's senior vice president for public affairs and government relations, called the event, started by basketball and lacrosse teams in the late 1990s, a "drunken brawl."

"There was lots of concern about Tailgate among people who cared about the health of the kids and had to deal with them—that's between the police and Student Affairs and whoever else," Burness said. "You regularly heard the lacrosse team was a big part of the problem under any circumstances. You didn't hear other teams were part of the problem."

Burness admits he has long been "concerned with the reputation" of the lacrosse team. It didn't matter to him that the facts didn't necessarily fit his image of the team. Several reporters who covered the lacrosse case said Burness was a "master of off-the-record trashing" of the players. Much of that trash found its way into the media.

As the media frenzy grew, Brodhead ordered an investigation of the lacrosse program, ostensibly to justify his actions. The results of the investigation were startling—and not what Burness had been implying to reporters.

The review was done by a faculty committee chaired by law professor James Coleman, who had been hand-picked by Brodhead. The committee said members of the team are "academically and athletically responsible students" who were not out of control while at Duke. The committee also made it clear many players have been irresponsible in their use of alcohol and engaged in "repetitive misconduct," and it acknowledged that the large number of players' citations was likely due to the "clannish nature" of the team—when one was out drinking, a dozen other teammates were likely right there with him.

The committee cited fifty-two incidents over a six-year span (2000–2006, during which the team's roster had a combined 250 players). The most common conduct for which disciplinary citations were issued involved drinking games in which several players living in the same residential hall participated, the report read. To put the number in perspective, though, the committee noted that the men's golf team had a higher percentage of its members with disciplinary records.

Coleman described the lacrosse team's repetitive conduct as "deplorable but pretty typical of what you see with other Duke students who abuse alcohol."

In the committee's review of the sixteen incidents that involved lacrosse players that resulted in citations from the Durham police and the Alcohol Enforcement Agency, all but two of the incidents involved typical alcohol-related misconduct. None of the misconduct involved fighting, sexual assault, harassment, or racial slurs, according to the report.

The committee found that "administrators responsible for the discipline of students were generally aware of the irresponsible conduct of lacrosse players associated with drinking. With the exception of the Office of Judicial Affairs, none of these administrators was especially alarmed by the conduct. Although some administrators claim that they communicated their concerns to Coach [Mike] Pressler, there is no evidence that they adequately did so."

The most important statistic the committee found: In the sixteen years Pressler had been head coach, he had graduated 100 percent of his players.

Pressler bristled at the charge his team was "a collection of thugs, as some in the administration tried to suggest." He also could not believe that Burness had suggested the team instigated all the boorish behavior related to Tailgate. "There are a thousand kids over there tailgating and they blame the rowdy behavior on forty lacrosse players," he said. While Pressler didn't feel comfortable intruding on his players' free time and certainly didn't condone their drinking, he was glad to see them together off the field—even when they were dressing up in SpongeBob SquarePants costumes for home football games.

"I knew they were always popular among the student body," Pressler said of his players. "And the one thing is the coach is a double-edged sword. You want your team to be together off the field—that's what we all want. You see one, you see thirty of them. You see one sophomore, you see nine of them. So as a coach I'm saying, why is that bad? The camaraderie, the bonds, the relationships that are built outside of practice are paramount to what we do. But on the other hand, the dean of students says this is a problem, the pack. I never really addressed that because I kind of liked it actually. I liked that kind of interaction off the field."

As did Kennedy, Duke's senior associate athletic director. "I think a little of it is one of the things we always say is we want our student athletes to be as much like other students as possible," Kennedy said. "But I think that in some ways, a lot of Duke students wanted to be as much like lacrosse players as possible."

As the rape allegations quickly went from local headline to national controversy, Butters watched the situation unravel from afar. His emotions ranged from disbelief to disappointment, from anger to rage. Butters couldn't fathom what was happening at an institution he loved and to a coach he admired. Butters wanted to be back at Duke, in his athletic director's chair, making decisions that benefited his university and, more important, Pressler. Butters, without hesitation, questioned the decisions made by Duke's administration in its handling of the situation.

"I know I am probably stepping on toes when I say this, but it was absurd," Butters, sixty-nine, said in late February from his home at Black Diamond, a golf community located in Central Florida between Orlando and Tampa, where he and wife, Lynn, spend the winter months before returning to their home in Durham.

"I spent thirty-some years at Duke, and I can assure you this would have been handled differently. Understand what I am saying here—not in my days, in Duke's days. Duke would have done something differently. When I was the AD at Duke I couldn't fail because I had people behind me that would not allow me to fail. That still may be the case, but I doubt it. It's a shame. We are not talking about a good man in [Pressler], we are talking about a great man."

Butters should know. He was known as a no-nonsense administrator whose trademark may have been his insistence on absolute integrity in every facet of the athletics operation. Also known as a champion fundraiser, Butters led the way in updating several facilities that hadn't been touched since they were first erected in the 1930s and 1940s. Butters knew coaches, too. He was a former pitcher with the Pittsburgh Pirates who came to Duke in 1968 as the school's baseball coach before moving into administration.

Butters was enshrined in Duke's Hall of Fame in 1999, and the Schwartz-Butters Athletic Center, part of a $75 million athletic facilities renovation project at Duke, was dedicated on April 15, 2000. Located adjacent to Cameron Indoor Stadium, the building is named after Butters and Alan D. Schwartz, a former Duke baseball player and the current executive vice president of Bear Stearns and Companies, Inc. Butters retired from Duke in 1998 after thirty years at the university, the last twenty-one as the Blue Devils' director of athletics.

Butters said he intentionally did not talk to Pressler during the lacrosse controversy. However, Butters knew on what side of the fence he would stand if forced to choose between Pressler and Duke. "If you are asking me to choose sides between Mike Pressler and a university that I love with all of my heart, I would choose Mike Pressler. You have no idea how hard that is for me to say. I am not against Duke, I am for Mike."

Butters, who stressed that a collegiate administrator couldn't have a better job than being the director of athletics at Duke, said the controversy surrounding Pressler has taken a toll on him. "I have the patience to see it unfold," he said. "I don't have the tolerance to see it unfold. To see what has happened to one of Duke's best [Pressler] is very difficult for an old man.

"I wanted somebody to step up for Mike and those kids and, by God, I would have done it if it cost me my job," Butters said. "Believe me when I say this, I would trust him [Pressler] with my life."

CHAPTER FIVE

The Strippers

When Durham's thriving tobacco industry and successful African-American–owned businesses began deteriorating in the 1960s, they left space for other businesses that weren't as reputable. Strip clubs and prostitution were just a couple of those industries. Though the presence of this adult entertainment bothered some who lived close to the downtown area, others enjoyed it.

H. P. Thomas, aka Fats, knows the dark side of Durham better than almost anyone. He used to be the security manager at a strip joint called Platinum Club and was, according to him, "A guy who was known for managing exotic dancers." According to Fats, this type of entertainment is quite the rage. "In Durham, exotic favors are popular amongst a lot of those well-to-do guys. I mean judges, lawyers, cops, you name it," he said.

In these clubs the drinks are cheap and the women, even cheaper.

Cigarette smoke billows around the red, blue, and yellow strobe lights. Men lean back in their chairs to take in the view. Narrow stages, which allow for the perfect peep show, are scattered throughout the club with metal poles reaching toward the ceiling. The ladies rotate every ten minutes as the DJ spins his thumping tunes. In these clubs it's not about the Benjamins. Here, men slip Washingtons into the ladies' G-strings. Others anxiously wait with a dollar bill, expecting one of the women to come snatch it.

The rule "look, but don't touch" does not always apply here. Most every girl has her price. There are plenty of dark corners and VIP rooms for men to have all their needs satisfied. "Most of these strippers are on drugs, have twenty kids, and will do just about anything for money," Fats said.

"There are two types of strippers. Some are classy. But most of the girls here are ghetto strippers," Fats explains. "The girls here are the bottom of the bottom. The best way to think of it is you have the pros, the semipros, and the guys who are just playing pick-up games. These girls are the pick-up players."

Many first-timers are disappointed when they realize the majority of girls who dance in Durham don't quite fit the Playboy Bunny stereotype they'd envisioned. The Duke lacrosse team and their friends were no exception. When the guys at 610 North Buchanan decided to take advantage of the thriving adult entertainment business in Durham, they expected the "classy" strippers Fats alluded to, but were disappointed to see two of the "other type of strippers" walk through the door. Perhaps, if the players had known the details of Kim Roberts's and Crystal Gail Mangum's troubling past, they wouldn't have let them past the front porch.

Kim Roberts, aka Kim Pittman, told the *Raleigh News & Observer* that when she attended college, she had visions of herself "one day wearing a power suit and carrying a briefcase." Instead, she has become infamous for wearing close to nothing and humping her fellow stripper's face at a Duke lacrosse party.

Kim, who was thirty-one years old the night of the lacrosse party, should have been on the path to reaching her goals. She graduated high school with a 4.0 GPA and studied psychology at UNC–Chapel Hill. Everything was progressing as planned until she got pregnant her junior year and dropped out of college. She married the father of her child, but their marriage quickly crumbled.

She still had dreams of becoming a businesswoman, but those plans came to a screeching halt when she was caught embezzling twenty-five thousand dollars from a photo-processing company called Qualex in 2001. She told Joseph Neff of the *News & Observer* that she doesn't know why she did it. Her job as a payroll specialist paid well and she wasn't under any financial stress. She just saw an opportunity and took advantage of it.

After her conviction, she began waitressing, but couldn't make enough money to offset her mounting legal bills. She needed to find a new job and, according to Fats, she was "pretty good-looking," so she decided to make the most of her appearance. She began working at an escort service where, she told the *News & Observer* her job was to "go in and look as pretty as possible and do a nice little dance for the person who calls."

She never wanted anyone to find out she was a stripper. But when her closet full of skeletons flew open in the weeks following the rape allegations, she called Butch Williams, a trusted attorney in Durham, for advice. He told her he represented lacrosse player Dan Flannery and couldn't help her, but asked if she remembered any details from the night. She said, "Well, [Dan] couldn't have done nothing because he was with me 99 percent of the night. He never really left my sight." Williams then asked her if she thought anyone had raped Crystal that night, to which she replied, "No." She told him she would think about giving a sworn statement, but when Williams mentioned pictures he had of her performing at the party, she got defensive and refused to cooperate. Little did he know Kim was a true opportunist. She knew how valuable her story was and would only share it in return for fame or money.

Williams tried to use Kim's story to his advantage, but when a PR firm released a note from Kim saying that she "didn't want this opportunity to pass [her] by," and asking them to help her "spin this to [her] advantage," her credibility went out the door. Kim never received the recognition she craved.

The woman who stole the media spotlight was the one who didn't even want it. In fact, she was so drunk the night of the party she couldn't even tell the officers her name. When the Duke lacrosse case surfaced in the media, a wholly sympathetic portrayal of Crystal Gail Mangum, the alleged victim, fell into place.

She was twenty-seven years old—the youngest of three children in a working-class family. Her father, Travis Mangum, was a truck driver, and her mother, Mary Mangum, worked in a paper mill. Crystal didn't have a lavish upbringing, but was raised in a religious household. The family attended church weekly.

"She usually kept to herself," Frederica Thomas, a former classmate, told the *News & Observer.* "She was quiet. . . . When I saw her, she was usually with her sister." Others who knew her told the *News & Observer* that she was a petite, soft-spoken woman, "a caring mother and a hard worker." She only stripped to feed her two children and afford her full-time tuition at North Carolina Central University.

The media made her look like "Sweet Polly Purebred, who met some hooligans that took advantage of her," said Williams. But as Crystal's gruesome rape allegations began unraveling, the sugar-coating melted and the truth finally appeared. "C'mon, kids. She wasn't this little poor North Carolina Central student working the fields. She was a whore," said Williams.

Joe Cheshire, also a defense lawyer, reviewed details of her life provided by investigators. "She rarely ever sees her children," he said. "Her parents basically take care of them. She was a stripper and somebody that engaged in sex for money. We can't even prove she was a full-time student."

Much of Crystal's income came from stripping at Platinum Club, which Fats called one of the dirtiest strip clubs in Durham. "You gotta understand," he said, "this [Platinum Strip Club] was just a hole in the wall where people go to get laid. The manager even sells condoms in the club." He further explained that the girls who danced at Platinum were different from the "Dollhouse" stereotype that comes to most people's minds. "Most of these girls are 'ghetto dancers,' a step removed from the streetcorner, the type of girls with bullet wounds, tattoos, and cuts," he said. "That's the type of girl Crystal is."

Fats said he worked with Crystal every day for four to five months and got to know her well. "This girl is a professional streetwalker from Raleigh," he said. "She would do things for twenty, thirty, forty dollars."

According to Fats, stripping was not Crystal's main source of income.

"She was more of a hooker than a stripper," he said. "She was stripping as advertising for hooking." When he read the *New York Times* article in which Crystal allegedly told police she had only slept with one client and it was not for money, Fats laughed so hard he almost fell out of his seat. "My best friend was her pimp," he said.

Though she claimed to be a college student, her behavior at the club showed she was not the brightest crayon in the box. "Crystal was so slow that she would give guys head for free," Fats said. Anyone who wanted to rent a VIP room at Platinum had to pay the owner a set fee. After the customer was in the room, he could pay a stripper a separate amount for her to dance privately inside the VIP room he rented. But Crystal didn't understand that she was supposed to be paid separate from the club when she danced privately. "Crystal would go into the VIP room with a guy who had already paid the club and just give him head for free," remembers Fats. "She thought that by paying the club for the room, they had paid enough. That's the level she was on."

For a woman who used her sexuality and physical appearance to make money, Crystal was not considered an attractive woman. "She was a hooker, but not a looker," Williams said. "I don't like to call people ugly," Fats said, but out of the estimated thirty dancers that worked at Platinum, "Crystal was in the bottom two when it came to looks and ability to make money."

She was also not as petite as many of the other strippers at the club. In fact, Williams said the first time he saw Crystal, he knew the lacrosse players were innocent. "She would have whooped any one of their asses," he said. "She would have fought them tooth and nail if they would've tried to do anything. Even a combination of them would be no match for her."

Unlike her more attractive dancing partner, Kim, it took Crystal a few auditions before she finally landed a position at a strip club. One of her first attempts—at Diamond Girl strip club in 2002—was especially awful. She not only failed to impress the manager, but wound up in jail later that night.

After her unsuccessful audition she proceeded to give a lap dance for a taxi driver who had come into the club. According to a report from the *Durham Herald-Sun,* "As she was feeling him up and putting her hands in his pockets, she removed the keys to his taxi cab without him knowing. He [the cabbie] told her he would drive her home but needed to go to the restroom first. While in the restroom he was advised that she was driving off in his taxi cab."

The cab driver immediately called 911. Deputy J. P. Carroll responded when he saw the blue 1992 Chevrolet Caprice fly by him. "The headlights were off and the woman was driving on the wrong side of the road," an article in the *News & Observer* reported. A high speed chase ensued from Angier Avenue, where Diamond Girl was located, to U.S. 70.

The car finally stopped when Crystal tried to drive the taxi through a fence. But, according to the *News & Observer* article, when the deputy got out and told the woman to turn off the car's engine, she laughed and backed up then nearly ran over him. She struck the corner of the deputy's car, but that didn't stop her from racing into oncoming traffic.

A flat tire finally put an end to Crystal's booze-fueled extravaganza. The officers cornered the stolen car and arrested her. According to the article in the *News & Observer,* her blood alcohol level was 0.19, more than twice the legal limit to drive in North Carolina.

Under a deal with prosecutors, she pleaded guilty to four misdemeanors in the car chase: larceny, speeding to elude arrest, assault on a government official, and DWI. She was required to serve three consecutive weekends in jail and was placed on two years' probation.

Crystal's actions led some who knew her to call her "crazy." But until lawyers in the lacrosse case started digging deeper into her past, no one was aware she had a deep history of mental instability. Her medical records have been sealed by a judge, but Chesire says they tell an "amazing and pathetic story."

Many close to Crystal attribute her deteriorating mental health to a traumatizing incident in her past. She filed a report in 1996 saying she had been raped three years earlier, when she was fourteen. Her boyfriend at the time, Kenneth McNeil, urged her to file the report after she told him that her boyfriend when she was fourteen—who was much older than her—took her to a house in Creedmoor and offered her body to his friends. "He let his boys take turns," McNeil told the *News & Observer.* According to the police report, the officer instructed her "to write a chronological ordered statement of the incidents [. . .] and return the statement for investigative purposes." Crystal never returned, but began seeing a psychiatrist and taking prescription medication shortly after, her parents told *Essence* magazine.

An overview of the Creedmoor incident proves eerily similar to her 2006 allegations: She was brutally raped. By three men.

The discovery of her previous rape claims raised even more suspicion of Crystal's accusations against the lacrosse players, especially after her father—who still believes Crystal was raped at the lacrosse party—told the *News & Observer* nothing happened that night when she was fourteen years old. "They didn't do anything to her," he said.

She was a ticking time bomb. Ready to explode at any time.

"That could've been any one of us," Fats said in an interview for this book. "Those boys just ended up with the wrong stripper. Forget white or black for a minute. That could've been any one of us."

Both of these women have lived lives full of betrayal, greed, and abuse. Each excused her behavior by saying they were "doing what they had to do to support their families." In their world of fake names, fake nails, and fake hair, no one knew them, or cared who they were. But soon, Kim and Crystal would emerge as two of the most infamous small-town strippers in America.

CHAPTER SIX

The Cops

For all the national media attention that would soon follow, it was a series of innocuous news briefs in the *Raleigh News & Observer* and the student paper, the *Duke Chronicle*, that started it all.

"Woman Reports Sexual Assault," was the headline over the three-sentence mention in the Triangle Briefs section of the *News & Observer.*

"Alleged rape was at party, police said," said the *News & Observer* headline the following day. A 123-word story followed.

"Off-East house site of reported rape" read the headline on page three of the March 20, *Chronicle,* preceding a 187-word brief.

The stories were light on details—nothing more, basically, than an electronic bulletin posting from police—but one fact jumped off the page when attorney Bob Ekstrand read them. The papers reported Sergeant M. D. Gottlieb was in charge of the investigation, that the officer said the alleged crime "was an act where alcohol was involved," and encouraged potential witnesses to contact Gottlieb if they "saw or heard anything unusual."

The quotations were insignificant. The speaker was not.

Ekstrand runs a small but successful law firm not far from the Duke campus where he earned his juris doctorate. A number of his clients are Duke students battling the various misdemeanor charges that are part of normal college life: open-container violations, defiance of the local noise ordinance, public urination citations, and the like.

In increasing numbers, two names were showing up on these police reports, those of Sergeant Mark Gottlieb and his protégé, Officer

R. D. Clayton. One might find that unexceptional until the students' stories started to add up.

Now the *Chronicle* was reporting that a rape had been alleged at 610 North Buchanan, and Ekstrand's antennae went up. The firm's paralegal, Stefanie Sparks, had finished a four-year career on Duke's women's lacrosse team the year before and Ekstrand's wife, Samantha, had once served as a lacrosse assistant coach to the women's program so they were, as a group, close enough to the men's program to know immediately that 610 North Buchanan wasn't simply any student residence. It was the home shared by three of Duke's best men's lacrosse players—all captains—and Sparks knew it.

"When I saw that Gottlieb was on the case and that he was talking to the media, my gut told me this was about to get ugly," Ekstrand said. "For months, we had been hearing stories about this guy, and they were often from students who would gain nothing from making something up. The stories were so outrageous that Stef had begun collecting them, and this was long before he became the lead investigator on this case."

It just happened that later on Monday, March 20, one of the home's residents, Dan Flannery was set to meet with Ekstrand, who was defending him on a noise violation that had drawn Durham police to the Buchanan street home on January 10, 2006. (Flannery would be found not guilty of the charge.)

When Flannery arrived, Ekstrand subtly asked about the article.

"He told me not to worry," Ekstrand recalled. "He said the university had hired a lawyer for them and it was all going to go away. I was suspicious."

Politely as he could, Ekstrand suggested his client tread lightly. Mark Gottlieb, he knew, would not.

Mark Gottlieb is a fifteen-year veteran of the Durham Police Department, a barrel-chested man known for a get-tough approach to petty crime—especially if the petty criminals were obviously Duke students. A father of three, the forty-three-year-old Gottlieb had worked as a paramedic before becoming a cop in 1991. His peers know him to be "outspoken and sometimes headstrong," according to a profile of him written in the *News & Observer.* The newspaper also noted that in a 2005 court affidavit Gottlieb claimed he had attended a number of community colleges, but never mentioned a degree earned beyond a high school diploma.

Former Durham Assistant District Attorney Freda Black described Gottlieb as "adequate" in cases they worked on.

"There was always going to be some who had a keener intelligence or have a higher education or are just smarter than others," Black said. "He was a willing worker. He would come to court; he would do what I asked him to do. I never had a situation where he had a very complicated task at hand."

Other than that, very little was known about Gottlieb, other than the fact that he took a hard line when it came to dealing with students.

The research done by Sparks and Ekstrand was detailed enough that both the *Raleigh News & Observer* and the *Duke Chronicle* built significant articles around the statistics. Both newspapers agreed that the statistics were clear: During his time patrolling the area near the Duke campus, Gottlieb arrested and jailed Duke students at a much higher rate than he did nonstudents, even when the students were accused of less serious crimes.

The proof was both statistically significant and anecdotally damning.

During a ten-month period in 2005–6 when Gottlieb worked as a patrol shift supervisor in Durham's Police District 2, which includes about a quarter of the city from public housing projects to Duke-area neighborhoods, he arrested twenty-eight people. Twenty were Duke students, including a football quarterback and the sister of a men's lacrosse player. At least fifteen of the Duke students Gottlieb arrested were taken to jail.

All of the Duke student arrests by Gottlieb were for misdemeanor violations such as carrying an open beer on a public sidewalk or violating the city's noise ordinance. Usually, according to the research done by Ekstrand and his staff, such charges earn an offender a "pink ticket," akin to a speeding ticket. But court records show Gottlieb made it a point to arrest Duke students on such charges, taking them to jail in handcuffs.

The statistical data showed Gottlieb's actions were off the chart. During the same ten-month period, the three other squad supervisors working his same district—Sergeant Dale Gunter, John Shelton, and Paul Daye—made a *combined* sixty-four arrests. Two were Duke students, both taken to jail.

Worse, it was apparent that Gottlieb treated Duke students and non-students differently. For example, Gottlieb wrote a citation in 2004 to a young man for illegally carrying a concealed .45-caliber handgun and possessing less than a half-ounce of marijuana, and records indicate he wasn't taken to jail. The man was not a Duke student. On the flip side, several students shared horror stories with the newspapers detailing their jailing for minor crimes by Gottlieb.

"I find this very, very inconsistent," Durham attorney Bill Thomas, who represented a lacrosse player, told the *Chronicle*. "It seems to indicate a real pattern of arresting Duke students on less serious charges while not arresting non-Duke students on much more serious charges. In over twenty-five years of law practice, I have rarely if ever seen someone formally arrested on [noise and open container violations]. I would find this highly unusual and would be very suspicious with respect to an officer who continually, formally arrested people on these two charges."

Yet that was the pattern with Gottlieb. Ask Urosh Tomovich.

A Duke senior in 2006, Tomovich told the *Chronicle* about an October 2005 encounter with the officer. Tomovich and his roommates had thrown a party after the Rolling Stones concert in the area. The party came to an abrupt end when, at three o'clock on the morning after the concert, Gottlieb and nine other police officers burst into the off-campus home and arrested Tomovich and his six housemates for noise ordinance and open-container violations.

"I was still half asleep, and he put me in handcuffs," Tomovich told the student newspaper. "[Gottlieb] said, 'You're going to be in the biggest trouble of your life.' "

Tomovich told the newspaper the police dragged his sleeping housemate Justin Bieber off his bed, causing him to fall on the floor, before dragging him down the stairs. The police then led the housemates outside, handcuffed them, and put them in squad cars.

After they were taken to Durham's police station, Tomovich—a U.S. citizen of Serbian heritage—told the newspaper that Gottlieb threatened to deport him for breaking the law. "He took me to a back room and said, 'Do you need to speak to your consulate? We can deport you.' I said, 'Why would I need to speak to my consulate?' . . . I'm a U.S. citizen. I have a different last name, but I'm a U.S. citizen," Tomovich recounted to the *Chronicle.*

All seven housemates were arrested and taken into custody.

In the same story, the *Chronicle* recounted a separate incident involving two students who asked the newspaper to shield their identities. The students—a man and a woman—told the newspaper they were walking to a local nightclub when Gottlieb and his partner Clayton drove past them. The man was drinking from a water bottle and the woman held a can of vodka-spiked Sprite, but both set their drinks down as the officers slowed. Seeing that, Gottlieb pulled the cruiser up onto the curb.

"Gottlieb drove on the curb to block us," the male, an international student, was quoted as telling the *Chronicle.* "He grabbed me, threw me against the car, and put me in handcuffs."

The student told the newspaper he couldn't believe Gottlieb threw him in handcuffs and pushed him around, especially because, at 130 pounds, he was nearly 80 pounds smaller than Gottlieb. As Gottlieb handcuffed the male student, Clayton did the same to the female. "He yelled at me and said he would let me out if I would admit I was drinking," the woman told the newspaper. "After I said what he wanted me to say, he took me out of the handcuffs."

Finally, as the incident seemed to be winding down, Gottlieb offered a parting shot.

The man told the *Chronicle* that Gottlieb asked him for his identification. When he produced an ID card from his home country, the newspaper quoted Gottlieb as saying, "No, I'm looking for real identification," before threatening to deport him.

Gottlieb's involvement with the lacrosse case became increasingly significant as results from DNA testing showed that there was no scientific evidence that the rape allegations were true. When District Attorney Nifong said he would move on with the case despite the lack of DNA evidence, his linchpin became Gottlieb, who had conducted the interviews with the accuser and had managed the photo lineup that has been roundly criticized because he only showed the accuser pictures of lacrosse players.

And those who were suspicious of Gottlieb from the outset found further grist for the mill.

Gottlieb's case notes, released to the defense, were not written until four months after the night of the party. His typed, single-spaced report was contradicted by the notes of others involved in the case, including both his partner and the nurses at the intake center. In his notes, Gottlieb claimed the nurse who examined Crystal Mangum told Gottlieb that the "blunt-force trauma" seen in the examination "was consistent with the sexual assault that was alleged by the victim."

In fact, that's not what the nurse wrote the night she examined Crystal. To the contrary, the nurse's report stated the only external signs of physical trauma she saw were some superficial scratches on the woman's knee and heel. Nowhere in the twenty-four-page report prepared by the doctors and nurses who examined Crystal is there any mention of "blunt-force trauma."

Gottlieb remained adamant.

His report also contradicted the notes taken by another policeman, Benjamin Himan, on the details from their interview with Crystal. Gottlieb's partner said Crystal described one of her assailants as "chubby." That description fits none of the three lacrosse players who had been arrested by the time Gottlieb turned in his notes.

In Gottlieb's notes, constructed after the indictments, his recollection of Crystal's interview had her describing the same attacker as "baby-faced, tall, lean," a description that could well fit sophomore lacrosse player Collin Finnerty.

Gottlieb was about to turn this case into a national spectacle. "From the very beginning, when we heard he was the lead investigator, we knew this would be trouble," Ekstrand said.

Ekstrand had no idea how right he would be.

CHAPTER SEVEN

1-1 and Done

From the day they started preparing for the 2006 season, everyone associated with the Duke lacrosse program had one week circled on their calendars: March 18–25, 2006. That eight-day span should have been a good week for the Blue Devils. No, make that a great week.

After returning from a trip out West (San Diego) to play Loyola, the poised Blue Devils had three home games over the next eight days against North Carolina, Cornell, and Georgetown. The trio represented a stern test for a team that, nearing the regular season's halfway point, was considered a strong favorite to return to the NCAA title game for the second consecutive year. Little did anyone know what the week had in store for Duke University and its lacrosse program.

On Saturday, March 18, the Blue Devils had a home game against the University of North Carolina and overcame an early 6–0 deficit to win, 11–8. It was considered one of the best comebacks in coach Mike Pressler's sixteen years at Duke. While most Blue Devil players and fans celebrated the emotional victory over their hated rivals, far different emotions surfaced in a cramped, local living room.

That night, after the UNC game, Duke's four captains met at 610 with their parents to discuss what had happened at the team party. Also that weekend, the first accounts of the alleged assault appeared in the local newspapers—police-blotter items that did not mention the Duke connection.

Duke President Richard Brodhead first learned of the incident on Monday, March 20, when the school paper, the *Chronicle*, reported that the scene of the alleged crime was one of the off-campus houses that Duke had recently bought. Brodhead telephoned Larry Moneta, the university's vice president for student affairs, who responded with the now common view of the matter among Duke officials: The accusation wasn't credible, and nothing much was likely to come of it.

"Bob Dean, who is head of our [Duke] police, basically said from his management report that Durham police said there is no credibility to what this woman is saying," said John Burness, Duke's senior vice president for public affairs and government relations. "She had changed her story several times, she was well known to the Durham police. Therefore, he had not paid that much attention to it other than saying he would forward anything else that comes down."

The *Chronicle* and the *Raleigh News & Observer* published stories in the following days reporting that there had been a party at the North Buchanan house and that alcohol had been involved. In both accounts Sergeant Gottlieb made a point of saying that the residents had cooperated with the police. The narrative of the incident to this point, largely shaped by the field cops who had first encountered the accuser, suggested the tenor and the pace of a routine inquiry.

"From day one, they [players] denied that there was any sexual activity that was going on," Burness said. "They acknowledged doing a whole lot of other stuff [underage drinking]. So it stayed sort of at the Student Affairs level, and the Duke police level, and at the athletic level. This was an internal summary of what this cop heard and saw that night. In it he said that he had overheard the Durham police basically saying there was no credible evidence."

Players, returning to classes on Monday, March 20, following spring break, also were surprised by newspaper reports on the alleged assault a week earlier. "Our jaws dropped," junior Tony McDevitt said. "Are you kidding me? That was when it really hit everybody. There really wasn't much grapevine talk about anything having to do with a rape or anything. When we read that article we are like, 'Holy shit. What is going on?' "

Before the week was out, though, Duke would have played its last lacrosse game of the year.

David Evans sat in a chair positioned in the middle of the living room at 610 following the UNC game. Five nights earlier, two strippers had done a five-minute show in that same room that changed their lives. Evans was flanked by roommates Matt Zash and Dan Flannery and fellow captain Bret Thompson. The players' parents were seated on the couch and chairs, waiting to hear what went on during the party, from start to finish. "When we all got together, things were pretty emotional," Evans's father, David, said.

The younger Evans didn't mind speaking to the group. It was only the day before that Evans had telephoned his father and told him for the first time about the party. "The first thing I told my dad was, 'I messed up, I don't need you to tell me, I just need you to listen,' " Evans recalled. "I laid it out for him on that Friday and he immediately started trying to help me make the best decisions going forward." Among those decisions: A meeting with the four captains and their parents at 610 was planned. But not everyone spread the word immediately. One captain didn't tell his parents about the meeting until the team's tailgate following the UNC win.

At the house, Evans told all eight parents what had happened and answered their questions, not wavering and repeating the captains' message: They were surprised by the charges, the alleged assault was a lie, and Duke administrators said the charges would not be taken seriously because the accuser wasn't credible. That did little to soothe the highly charged mood.

Bruce Thompson, Bret's father, repeatedly chastised the boys, calling the party "an incredibly stupid thing to do." Rita Flannery, Dan's mother, feared for the boys' safety, saying they could be shot or harmed by people who might be working with the strippers. Rita, a nurse in New York, said that inviting strippers into their home was "just asking for trouble."

Dan Flannery said he was confident, on the basis of assurances from Dean Sue Wasiolek, that "we have been told everything would be okay and it won't be in the Duke *Chronicle*." (Recalling the story months later, a still angry Flannery said: "We believed, albeit falsely, that these people would look after our best interests. What we didn't realize was that Duke's interests and our interests were diverging rapidly. They wanted us to be guilty.")

At that, Bruce Thompson exploded. "Why are we even talking about the student newspaper," Thompson said in the night's first fateful prediction. "If this gets out, it will be in every newspaper in America."

As cooler heads started to prevail, Bruce Thompson asked David Evans, Sr., a well-regarded Washington, D.C., lawyer, what he thought was going to happen.

"I don't think we can underestimate the fact that this is a black accuser and you've got forty white guys in the house; it would be very difficult for this thing to just go away," the elder Evans said, the words spilling out into a room that was suddenly silent.

As emotions began to settle, the parents developed a plan. "It was, 'Okay, we now have the facts, what are we going to do about it?' " Evans Sr. remembered. "We then planned our next steps."

The elder Evans was asked by the group to telephone Sue Wasiolek and Chris Kennedy (Duke's senior associate director of athletics) the following Monday to discuss the university's stance on the situation and the players' status in school. Evans shared the information with other parents.

"What I got out of the conversations with them [the two Duke administrators] was that our sons had violated no university rules and that no action would be taken by the university against them individually," he said. "They both said they believed all of the players were innocent."

Under normal circumstances, Pressler would have enjoyed the Blue Devils' stirring comeback victory over neighbor North Carolina. But these weren't normal circumstances as Pressler dealt with behind-the-scenes maneuvering by the Durham police and the Duke administration concerning the alleged assault at 610.

On Monday, March 20, Pressler received a morning telephone call from Durham Detective Benjamin Himan. Himan said that he'd like to gather Pressler's team for an informal meeting, at which time he could speak to each of the players who had been at the party. A local attorney, Wes Covington, who had been recommended to the players by Wasiolek and had handled the occasional student brush with the law, told Pressler that he thought the meeting with Himan was a good idea. Pressler talked with Kennedy, who also recommended that players cooperate with police. An appointment was set up for the afternoon of Wednesday, March, 22.

"They said if any of the players were not at the party, they were going to excuse them," Pressler said. "So if Mike Ward and I wasn't there, you're excused. That's what they were telling us. [Ward] was on a job interview up in New York. There were like ten guys who took off that day—the day of the party—and did other things. Brad Ross was in Raleigh visiting his girlfriend at N.C. State. There were guys that I knew of that had talked to me who wanted to go out of town. Six of them were on job interviews."

Players assembled in their bottom-floor meeting room in the Murray Building early Monday afternoon each day before practice. This time the mood was different. Word had started to spread concerning the alleged assault. Despite the uncertainty, the Blue Devils also needed to turn their attention to the next day's game against talented Cornell.

"We get into the meeting room on Monday and obviously we need to talk about it [situation]—now it's out there," McDevitt said. "I remember the guys saying everything is going to take care of itself. Don't worry about this. Let's worry about playing Cornell tomorrow. It's sort of like the people who are involved already are involved, and that's it. I am speaking of Zash, Flannery, and Evans—the guys at the house. So, we are trying to go about business as usual as much as we could."

But it wasn't business as usual.

Favored Duke was awful against Cornell, losing 11–7 on a rainy, cold Tuesday afternoon. Duke wasn't itself that day, far from it. The Blue Devils muffed grounders, and misplayed easy passes. "We were just giving it away," Pressler said. "I ain't Santa Claus. We ain't giving it away. We gave it away."

The dejected Blue Devils trudged into the locker room as their parents mingled in the parking lot and prepared food for the tailgate that's held after each home game. Players expected to hear their coach tell them what they had done wrong on the field. Pressler had no such message. Instead, he revealed for the first time that he and Covington had agreed to send the team to the Duke Police Department the next day for interviews. "We didn't talk about it [game]," Pressler said. "Losing a game was nothing compared with what we're doing now. I said, 'Guys, we will deal with this loss later. Here is what's on our plate today.' "

McDevitt said it was easy to tell Pressler and members of the team, specifically the four captains—Zash, Flannery, Thompson, and Evans—were preoccupied. "What I will never forget, after we played games, we would always get in the meeting room and coach would say a few words about the game and we would leave," McDevitt said. "We play Cornell. We just lost, embarrassingly, too. We get into the meeting room and he didn't mention one thing about Cornell. It was all about what we had to do about this investigation. You could tell Coach P. was waiting for that time. It's like it has been on his mind for a couple of days. And he was like, 'Listen guys, we are going to cooperate to the fullest extent. This is the deal. This is what's happening. This is what Zash, Flannery, and Evans have been through the past couple of days. And this is what we have to do tomorrow afternoon.' "

Pressler, driven by his belief that no rape had occurred on March 13, told his players, point-blank, "Guys, we're doing this. I've talked to Chris Kennedy. I've talked to the administration. We're going to go in there and tell them the truth." Pressler also asked his players to keep their discussions private, a decision later questioned by some parents. "I was told to keep it quiet," Pressler said. "Everybody, Chris Kennedy, Dean Sue, thought it was going to go away. There was no reason to bring more attention to it. So I interpreted that being, 'Hey, guys, it's going to go away, let's keep it in house here. Don't tell your parents yet, don't tell your girlfriends. Keep it in house.' "

By this time, however, a few of the players had told their parents about the incident. Now, faced with the meeting with investigators, one of the players called his father, a Washington attorney; the father insisted that the meeting be postponed, and quickly retained Durham attorney and 2001 Duke law graduate Robert Ekstrand to represent the boys. With the new counsel came a new strategy. Ekstrand disagreed with the plan of sending the players to meet with police without counsel. He told several players that night that, in his opinion, it would be a dangerous choice to walk into the police department "without established ground rules."

Kyle Dowd was returning to his apartment at one-thirty Wednesday morning when he received a telephone call from Ekstrand, asking Dowd to meet him immediately at his office. Ekstrand didn't mince his words. "He called me in and basically told me the worst thing in the world was to go to talk with Wes Covington and then talk to the Durham police," Dowd said. But Dowd was just starting to talk. He telephoned his parents at 2:30 A.M. to inform them about the party and developing situation for the first time. "It wasn't a pleasant experience," Dowd said. "My mom was petrified." Dowd then drove to the Duke campus and alerted some teammates they also needed to meet with Ekstrand.

"I am in my pajamas at three o'clock in the morning and I am like, 'What is going on?' " McDevitt said. "He [Ekstrand] laid it all out to us about we sort of have to wait right now. We all know nothing happened here. But it's a party and all the cops are looking for is some discrepancy. It's just the nature of the situation. He didn't want people having all different stories and the cops are like, boom."

Wednesday morning, Pressler started receiving telephone calls from parents to say their sons would not meet with police later that afternoon without legal representation. Other players who wanted to talk to their parents still had not reached them. Pressler telephoned Kennedy to update him, and the decision was made to postpone the meeting with investigators. Pressler called Covington and asked that the meeting be postponed —not canceled—for at least a week until all players talked to their parents and made preparations.

Pressler believes the decision to postpone the meeting "pissed off" Durham police investigators. A few days later, Pressler was told by an athletic department equipment manager that two Durham plainclothes officers had showed up on Wednesday afternoon at Duke's baseball game against the University of Maryland, Baltimore County (UMBC), looking for the lacrosse team's practice field. The Blue Devils were off that day. "I believe they had every intention to come into our practice to question the guys," Pressler said.

Ekstrand believed the informal meeting scheduled between investigators and the players was a ruse to administer DNA tests. "The fact of the matter was they had the DNA people ready to go, they were going to do just what they did to those three," Ekstrand said of the DNA test administered to Zash, Flannery, and Evans on Thursday, March 16.

"You just cannot look at the situation comfortably," Ekstrand said. "I know it's easy, because we all want police who are honest, and investigators who are always going to do the right thing, and this is not possible. There was no question that anybody could ever seriously say it would have been a good idea to talk to these police without ground rules, and they were going to ask two or three questions and that's it. We know for a fact, and the discovery makes it clear, they had the intention of asking the whole team for DNA. It's unbelievable to ask before they get consent."

Ekstrand also said he never received a telephone call from the Durham Police Department to reschedule the informal meeting with players. "The fact of the matter is that it was nothing magical about Wednesday, we could do this next Tuesday and tell them that," Ekstrand said. "We just are rescheduling so they can tell their parents. That's the truth, that's what the message was. Nobody was saying, 'We're not going in to talk' and to this day we have never refused a request for an interview. They never asked, they never rescheduled."

There was a reason Durham police neither rescheduled nor asked.

On Thursday, March 23, ten days after the party, Himan and Durham Assistant District Attorney David Saacks applied to Judge Ronald L. Stephens for a court order demanding that all members of the lacrosse team except one, who was African-American, submit to photographs and DNA testing. In support of the request, Himan submitted the essential text of his application for the warrant to search 610 several nights earlier:

"Two males, Adam and Matt, pulled the victim into the bathroom," the search warrant read. "Someone closed the door to the bathroom where she was, and said, 'Sweetheart, you can't leave.' The victim stated she tried to leave but the three males (Adam, Bret and Matt) forcefully held her legs and arms and raped and sexually assaulted her anally, vaginally and orally. The victim stated she was hit, kicked and strangled during the assault. As she attempted to defend herself, she was overpowered. The victim reported she was sexually assaulted for an approximate 30-minute time period by the three males."

Saacks said in the application that the DNA samples were crucial. They would "immediately rule out any innocent persons," he wrote, "and show conclusive evidence as to who the suspect(s) are in the alleged violent attack upon this victim."

The phrase would become crucial—"immediately rule out any innocent persons"—and would convince both the players and their lawyers that they needed to submit to the DNA testing as soon as possible. "Everyone saw that and felt good," Pressler remembered of the phrase. "This was a chance to prove innocence quickly. Or so we thought."

Judge Stephens ordered the students to comply.

Pressler received a telephone call that Thursday morning from Covington, explaining that a subpoena was being issued by Durham police to forty-six lacrosse players to give nontestimonial evidence at a facility in downtown Durham later that day.

Unsuspecting players walked into their scheduled meeting at 2:50 P.M. to startling news explained by Covington and Ekstrand. They would leave Duke that afternoon and head to the police station.

As Covington and Ekstrand defined nontestimonial evidence, Pressler peered at his players and searched for reactions, be it guilty eyes or trembling lower lips. "I am going through, row by row, and looking at the faces," Pressler recalled. "Row by row, not one guy flinches. I believed them all along. But if you put yourself in their shoes, you're going downtown via subpoena—cheek swab, picture, all of that—and you did something in that room [at the party], you would be running up to those lawyers right now saying, 'I need an attorney because there is no way I can go down there.' Not one kid flinched. I believed before, and that was just another testament that this didn't happen."

However, Pressler admitted he was scared for the first time, especially after players began to ask about the cuts, lacerations, and bruises they received during their two games following the party. How can police tell the difference between a scratch from an alleged assault and a slash from a lacrosse stick? The lawyers stressed police could tell the difference.

"For the first time, I was scared that this was going to be a full-blown scandal," Pressler remembered. "Now it's going to be leaked, it hasn't gone public yet. This is going to blow wide open—even though we know we didn't do it and the kids are innocent."

Pressler's fax machine hummed at 3:00 P.M. The subpoena arrived with forty-six names on it, the lone exclusion being freshman Devon Sherwood, who did not have to give DNA since the accuser claimed she was assaulted by three white players. Pressler also remembered another important detail from the subpoena: "The phrase about proving innocence became a theme as the conversation went on. You read the subpoena, if the DNA comes back no match, it's over. It's over. Little did we know."

Pressler also instructed his players to take off any Duke apparel they had on. He didn't want them to attract additional attention when they arrived at the downtown facility. Covington telephoned investigators and informed them that the players would arrive voluntarily as a group if it was promised the news would not be leaked to the media. Covington was assured the media would be kept unaware.

As players loaded into their cars, Pressler retreated to his office. Within ten minutes, his telephone rang. A local reporter asked if Pressler wanted to comment on a tip she had received: Duke lacrosse players were headed to a facility in Durham to give nontestimonial evidence. Pressler hung up the telephone without comment. A few minutes later, Pressler's telephone rang again. It was a second reporter from a different newspaper with the same question. Pressler declined to comment and hung up.

It was obvious that the police, still fuming over having been scorned after the Cornell game, had set a media trap, and Duke's players were walking in unprepared.

Pressler's next call was to Kennedy. "I told him, 'This is over,' " Pressler said. "It's going to be a full-blown episode." Pressler couldn't recall Kennedy's exact response, but he knew it was similar to, "Mike, just keep me posted. Thanks for letting me know and we'll deal with this as it moves forward."

It was moving forward . . . and gaining speed. The week that had been marked on everyone's calendars—the week that would prove Duke was a national contender again—would end with the last game Mike Pressler would ever coach as a Blue Devil.

CHAPTER EIGHT

Blue Wall of Silence

The first carload of unsuspecting Duke lacrosse players pulled into the parking lot of the Durham crime lab at 213 Broadway Street in downtown Durham at 4:00 P.M. Before they'd even stepped from their cars, the players realized the same thing their coach had moments earlier—they'd walked right into a trap.

The subpoena stated that pictures of the player's torsos would be taken at the crime lab that day, but those weren't the only pictures to be taken. "As soon as we pulled up, I saw a news photographer pull out his camera," said Matt Zash, a captain who rode in that first car. The photographer from the *Raleigh News & Observer* had received a tip and was waiting to capture images of the men accused of gang-raping a stripper ten days before. The moment the photographer spotted the players, a steady stream of flashes filled the air.

The players walked past him, shaking their heads, and headed up the steps in front of the Durham crime lab, where Bob Ekstrand, the players' lawyer, was waiting. "Only six of us were there by this time," said Zash. "Ekstrand tells us that the door is locked. We'd have to wait outside until someone came to unlock it." The players were being fed to the media on a silver platter. The only thing they could do was try to ignore the lights flashing around them. While they waited impatiently at the door, Ekstrand began offering some typical last-minute advice. "If I'm not in the room, don't talk to police, and don't answer any questions if you are unsure of the answer," he said. A woman with a notepad stood just behind him, recording the group's entire conversation. "I thought it was his secretary or one of his paralegals," Zash later said. As soon as Ekstrand turned around and saw her, he smelled a rat. "Guys, just wait and we'll talk inside," he said, annoyed. They wouldn't know until they read the paper the next morning that she was a reporter from the *News & Observer.*

Police finally opened the doors leading to the crime lab's waiting room, but many team members still hadn't arrived. "Everyone got lost and separated because downtown Durham is so confusing—full of one-way roads and roundabouts," Zash said. The lawyers began to get nervous. While the remaining players slowly trickled in, the crowd of reporters and photographers they had to walk through was quickly multiplying. Ekstrand and Wes Covington, another lawyer who had just arrived, did not want their clients' pictures splashed across front pages, so they made a split-second decision, one that, in the coming days, only served to fuel the fire.

Ekstrand sent a woman from his office to intercept the rest of the players as they arrived. She instructed them to cover their faces, wear hats, and pull their jackets up to conceal their identity. Their intention was to protect the innocent players, but, to the rest of the world, it looked like the grandest of perp walks.

The pictures of these players hiding their faces, paired with the presence of lawyers repeating "no comment," would lead police, protesters and District Attorney Nifong to declare that the team—which several days earlier had been praised for its "cooperation" in the case—was hiding behind a "Blue Wall of Silence." It was an image that confirmed their guilt in the minds of outraged feminists, equal rights and sexual assault victim advocates, and much of the Duke and Durham community.

By 4:30 P.M. all but one member of the lacrosse team was sitting in the waiting room. The group of forty-six waited patiently in a huge lobby that looked as if it belonged in a lawyer's office rather than a crime lab. A counter separating the team from the police was on one side of the room and three individual meeting rooms were on the other. Just as Ekstrand had instructed, they didn't say a word to each other. "It was dead silent," Zash remembers. "If anyone opened their mouth, one of the seniors was telling them to shut up."

After waiting for another fifteen minutes, an officer called the players' names in reverse alphabetical order. One at a time, they entered the first room, where several detectives, including Gottlieb, Clayton, and Himan, sat at a table waiting for them. Each player was briefly questioned about the night of the party, and then asked to verify his name and address in addition to other identification information. When they finished answering the detectives' questions, they individually moved on to the next room, where each player gave a DNA sample in the form of a cheek swab. After the cheek swab, investigators took a picture of each player's face and any wounds he had on his body. "I had an old scab on my elbow and a scrape on my back from another player's helmet," Zash said. "That's what they were taking pictures of." Even though their lawyers told them that police would be able to tell the difference between a scratch from a woman's nails and battle wounds received in games, the players weren't sure they could trust the police anymore.

According to local lawyers, this many men in Durham's crime lab was cause for alarm. "I can't imagine a scenario where this would be reasonable to do so early in the investigation," Durham criminal defense lawyer Alex Charns told the *News & Observer*. "It seems unusual, it seems overbroad, and it seems frightening that they're invading the privacy of so many people." Despite the questionable basis for the request, the players remained cooperative throughout the DNA testing process. They focused on one phrase—"immediately rule out any innocent persons." Soon everyone would know the truth.

By the time Breck Archer, the last player to be tested that evening, took his seat in the lobby with his teammates, a swarm of reporters cluttered the front steps of the crime lab. If the players wanted to get to their cars the same way they came in, they'd have to walk right through the lion's den. "You should just use the back door," someone offered from behind the counter. "It leads to our old parking lot." Within minutes, the boys were out the back door and jumped inside their lawyers' cars, which were waiting for them. "The lawyer I rode with told me and the other players in the car to duck our heads down as we drove past the front of the building," Zash said. "This way, the reporters couldn't get any more pictures. I didn't look up to see how many were out there, but I was told there were a lot of them."

On the way back to campus, Zash and a few other players called Pressler to let him know how the testing had gone and, more important, to inform him that word had been leaked to the media.

Pressler was furious.

He and the team had done everything in their power to cooperate and help with the investigation. "I trusted the police," he said, "and they ended up being the most crooked ones in this whole situation." That was the tip of the iceberg. "The situation was getting out of control," said Pressler. "It had been eleven days since the allegations were made and I still had not spoken to the athletic director, Joe Alleva, so I called his office the next morning, March 24, and demanded a meeting."

"He is still in Atlanta and won't be back until noon," his secretary replied, telling the coach that his boss had not yet returned from a Blue Devils basketball game the night before.

"The captains and I need to meet with him. When is the earliest we can see him?" Pressler asked, with urgency in his voice.

"Two this afternoon."

"We'll be there," he said.

The players had practice at 2:15 P.M., but this meeting—one that Brodhead would later claim he organized—was much more important. Pressler wanted the highest levels of Duke's administration to hear what happened the night of March 13 directly from the captains' mouths.

Alleva, Executive Vice President Tallman Trask, and Senior Associate Athletic Director Chris Kennedy had already gathered inside Alleva's office in Cameron Indoor Stadium when Pressler arrived, alone, at 2:00 P.M. The captains were waiting outside, but Pressler wanted to preface the meeting by telling his colleagues what he already knew. He recounted the version of the story the captains had told him at the bowling alley. "Their story has never changed; each one of them could talk to me at separate times and they [their stories] would be the same," Pressler said. "Two weeks later the story is still the same. That's important," he told them. "They are telling the truth." Then he summoned the captains to join them.

Evans, Flannery, Thompson, and Zash walked into the AD's office with their heads held high; this was their chance to finally iron things out with the administration. They took their seats on an oversized couch across from Alleva's mahogany desk, where he was seated. Kennedy sat in a chair to the left of Alleva, welcoming the boys as they came in, and Trask and Pressler sat on the other side of Alleva's desk.

There was no need to exchange pleasantries. They all knew the purpose of the meeting that afternoon. "Listen, we want to know what happened," Trask told the players. But before Evans could continue the conversation, he had to get something off his chest. "I've been advised by our attorneys that we've got to be careful of what we say to you," he said. Trask told him there was no reason to worry. Whatever they discussed was protected under what he called a "student-administrative privilege." Trask was not a lawyer and "had no right to suggest their conversation was privileged," Pressler said, "but at the time we had no idea, we didn't even suspect that." One by one, each captain proceeded to tell his story—first Evans, then Flannery, then Zash. Their stories all ended with the most important detail: There was no assault, no rape, no one even touched Crystal.

After listening carefully to what each captain said, Alleva told them what all three of the administrators were thinking: "I believe you, but you're stupid." He scolded them for having strippers and underage drinkers at their house in the first place. "We're going to have to punish you for having the party after all of this clears up," Alleva said. The players had expected that much. They apologized for the party and reiterated that they knew it was a stupid decision. When they finished, Pressler told them to head over to the practice field. The team hadn't been able to practice for the past two days and Friday's practice was already halfway over. They would need to fit in as much practice as possible if they expected to beat the number-four team in the country, Georgetown University, the next day.

Trask assured the captains he'd heard all he needed to know "from his side of the university," Zash recalled. As the captains walked out the door, Trask offered them some words of encouragement. He had been through a similar situation in his youth, he told Flannery as he shook his hand. Trask didn't elaborate, but said he had gotten through his challenge and they would, too. "Beat Georgetown!" said Trask, with a smile. They smiled back and headed straight toward the field to meet the rest of their team.

Pressler stayed behind to continue the conversation. "So, what do you think?" he asked his superiors. Kennedy was the first to respond. "I've always believed them," he said. Trask agreed, "I believe them, too." Alleva paused for a moment, then said, "I believe them, but God forbid that DNA comes back positive." *He completely contradicted himself*, Pressler thought. When the conversation shifted to possible punishments for the team, Trask suggested they pick up trash in Trinity Park. "To the senior vice president, that would be sufficient punishment," Pressler said, months later.

The players felt good about the meeting as they walked to practice. "Obviously, the administration was going to deal with this in some way," Flannery thought. "But we were confident they believed our story and our team was still alive, and that's all we cared about at that point. Talk about being naïve!" They had no idea that the next day another authority figure they trusted would betray them. Alleva would prove himself to be as two-faced as the police.

When Bruce Thompson, father of lacrosse captain Bret, unfolded the *News & Observer* the next morning, March 25, he realized his greatest fear had become reality. During the meeting at 610 after the North Carolina game, he had warned the four captains and their parents that this story was going to "blow up."

And there it was.

In black and white.

The front-page headline read: "Dancer Gives Details of Ordeal." An unbelievably sympathetic story followed, portraying Crystal as a single mother of two who was struggling to take care of her family and finish her degree at NCCU. She told Samiha Khanna and Anne Blythe, both writers for the *News & Observer,* that as soon as she and the other stripper started dancing, the more than forty men in the house began shouting racial slurs at them. "We started to cry," she told them. "We were so scared."

Written just below Crystal's concocted sob story was the first public condemnation of the lacrosse players. "We are asking someone from the lacrosse team to come forward," Durham police Corporal David Addison told the newspaper. "We will be relentless in finding out who committed this crime." The police would not stop until they "crack the team's wall of solidarity," he promised.

Crystal's story, which later proved to be filled with half-truths and lies, became the one and only time she actually talked to a reporter.

Before the sun had risen on the morning of March 25, Dick Brodhead stepped outside his president's mansion to find the *News & Observer* waiting on his doorstep. He looked no further than the front page and immediately picked up his phone. He needed to meet with his senior advisors as soon as possible. Within hours, Brodhead was joined in his living room by Senior Vice President John Burness, Trask, university attorney Kate Hendricks, Alleva, chair of Duke's Academic Council Paul Haagen, head of the Athletic Council and biology Professor Kathleen Smith, Provost Peter Lange, and Assistant Vice President for Student Affairs and Dean of Students Sue Wasiolek.

The only familiar face missing was Senior Associate Athletic Director Chris Kennedy. "Kennedy's son, Joe, was our captain in 2005," Pressler said. "I'm convinced they intentionally kept him out of the loop because of his so-called alliance with the lacrosse program." Administrators knew they'd be making some tough decisions regarding the lacrosse team that morning and they did not want Kennedy to "bias" the outcome.

The scandal had just made front-page news and Duke was already receiving threats that protesters would be at the Georgetown game that afternoon. This just added to the pressure building on Duke's administration to react to the situation. "We're all sitting around the table going, 'What the hell do we have here and what the hell do we stand for?' " Burness remembered. "We needed to send a signal that we took seriously what happened in the house, independent of the [sexual assault]."

They needed to punish the students for hiring a stripper and drinking underage at what Duke's leadership agreed was "a team-sanctioned event," Burness would say in a February 2007 interview. Assigning that label to the spring break party did not seem a stretch for administrators, Burness said. The party was held at a house rented by three of the four lacrosse captains, and the majority of partygoers were also members of the team. Burness said there was no accounting for the fact that the coach was unaware of the party or that a number of team members didn't attend because they were away on job interviews or out on dates. This was, he declared, still a "team-sanctioned" event.

"The captains called it, it was a regular event that the team did go to, they just did it in a different way," Burness said, struggling to defend the designation.

The punishment would be the forfeiture of the next two lacrosse games, it was decided that Saturday morning at Brodhead's home. This meant Duke's highly anticipated match against Georgetown, scheduled to begin only hours later, was lost before they ever took the field.

Though the senior advisors felt the punishment fit the crime, many outside Brodhead's living room disagreed. "There's nothing in the handbook that says strippers are against Duke's rules, but the players knew I would never, and could never, condone it," Pressler said. "So how could someone be punished for something they were allowed to do? And what constitutes a team-sanctioned event, anyway? If it was a team-sanctioned event, why wasn't the whole team there?"

Even Burness, when pressed in an interview for this book months later, acknowledged that there was no definition for a team-sanctioned event. It was as if the term had become a way to justify whatever decision the university was going to make and the fact that they wanted to make it immediately.

The only crime some of the players on the team were guilty of that night involved underage drinking. "We would have taken 100 percent responsibility for that," player Tony McDevitt said, "but the team, and everyone else, got the sense that it had nothing to do with that. They were starting to crumble under public pressure."

While Pressler sat in his office, mentally preparing for the big game, he was surprised to see Alleva walk through his door. "He walks into my office at 11:30 A.M.—he never comes in there, never, ever—and he shuts the door and sits down and says, 'Mike, I have some bad news for you.' " Alleva had been sent by his superiors to deliver the "bad news" they had decided on earlier that morning. Pressler remembers Alleva turning toward him and saying, in a stern voice, "We are going to have to forfeit the next two games because of the party." He assured Pressler, "This is a penalty for the party. There will be no further penalties unless charges are brought against the players."

Pressler was mentally prepared for the game. Not for this.

Pressler set aside the initial shock of hearing this news and remembered the team and coach who were already waiting for them on the field. The next step, Alleva said, was to go down to the locker room so Alleva could tell the team. Pressler shot him a disapproving look. "No, you are not," he said. "We are going tell Dave Urick, the Georgetown coach—who is a personal friend of mine—first." Pressler knew he needed to tell his players, but he also knew that that meeting would take a while. Out of respect for a friend and fellow coach, Pressler needed to tell him as soon as possible.

On his way out the door, Pressler spotted his assistant coach, Kevin Cassese, who had come down to his office to discuss their game plan. "I asked him if everything was all right and he wouldn't answer me," Cassese remembers. "Get all the guys in the meeting room right away, we have a mandatory meeting," was all Pressler would say. With that, he and Alleva walked quickly down the hallway and out to the field.

The stands were usually filled with Blue Devil fans and proud parents, but when Pressler looked to them for support this time, he saw a much different crowd. The first of the protesters had shown to express their disapproval of the events they thought had taken place. "I was dismayed at the thought that the lacrosse team was trying to put this behind them and move forward," Francis Conlin, a resident of Trinity Park, told the *Chronicle.* "I am fully aware a crime was committed by someone. It is too bad the rest of the team won't fess up." Other protestors held signs saying: "Shame on Duke. Shame on Pressler. Rapists Should Not Play." and "Men's Lacrosse: Are You All Liars? Do None of You Have Honor?"

Pressler felt abandoned.

They walked down the sidewalk and around to the visiting team's locker room, where they spotted Scott Urick, an assistant coach and Dave Urick's son. Pressler knew him well. "Scott, where's your dad?" he asked. Scott recognized his father's friend. "He's up top," he replied. He was referring to a mezzanine above the two locker rooms. As Pressler and Alleva walked up the stairs, they noticed Coach Urick, "Pacing, walking around." Alleva interrupted the coach's pregame preparation. "Coach, I'm sorry to do this, but we're going to forfeit today's game," he said. Pressler remembers, "That was one of the most humiliating moments in my life." But Coach Urick understood the situation. "When I read the papers this morning, I feared that something like this might happen," he said. He reached to give Pressler a much-needed hug and said, "Mike, if you need anything just give me a call."

Their next stop was the team's meeting room, where the players had already organized themselves. It was one hour before game time and the players tried their best to push the week's events out of their minds and concentrate on the big game. "We are all taped up, eyeblack on, uniforms, everything," McDevitt remembers, "and Joe Alleva walks in." Pressler introduced him, "Guys, this is our athletic director, Joe Alleva." Sadly, this was the first time many players had met him, because he was so disconnected from the lacrosse program.

"Alleva tells us the next two games are canceled because we threw a party and there was underage drinking and strippers," McDevitt said, months later. Alleva reiterated that this was a penalty for the party and that there would be no further punishment. "You can continue to practice," Pressler remembers him saying, "and we'll play the next game, Ohio State, on the road. I believe you didn't do this." But players sensed his insincerity. "The tone he took in that meeting was not one of someone who cared about us as student athletes," player Kyle Dowd said. "Because of that party, he viewed us as a nuisance to him."

The players were stunned by the news, but before they had a chance to react, Alleva was walking out the door. With his hands in his pockets and a nod of his head, he said, "See ya." The line resonated in their minds. He was completely bailing on them. The captains were especially shocked. Just the day before he had said he was in their corner, assuring them that he would take care of everything. He told them no punishments would be handed out until the smoke had settled. Now they were forfeiting games and they hadn't even put out the fire.

The players were livid. Though Pressler was just as angry, he tried to settle them down. "Guys, this is what it is, we're going to have to accept their decision," he said. "We can talk about how much we don't like it or how wrong it is, but it's important we handle this the right way." They usually listened to everything he said, but not this time. Dowd spoke up. "Coach, they're making us look guilty by doing this!" Pressler knew he was right, but there was nothing he could do. "It was a time of great uncertainty," he said later.

Pressler knew the players needed to blow off some steam, so he told his assistants to "get the guys in their workout gear and take them to the track. Just get them out of here." When they opened the doors to leave, a group of enraged parents stood outside. Fans and parents from Georgetown already knew the game had been forfeited, and the news spread like wildfire. Pressler told the team to go to the practice field while he explained to their parents what was happening.

This was one of the biggest games of the season, so every player's parent was there. Within minutes, fifty mothers and fathers were in the meeting room. "Every seat was full, so there were even people standing around the walls of the room," Pressler said. "It was surreal. Parents were sitting in the seats their sons had sat in just ten minutes before." Alleva hadn't gone far, so Pressler summoned him back to the meeting room. "As soon as he walked in, the parents demanded to meet with Dean Sue, Dean Larry Moneta, Trask, and Brodhead," he said. "So Alleva got on the phone to get them all down there."

Everyone showed but Brodhead.

Alleva, Wasiolek, Moneta, and Trask attempted to explain their actions to parents and emphasized that they believed the players' story, but that only served to fuel the fire. "Then why don't you go out and say it?" one of the parents screamed. The parents wondered: If the players had done nothing like what was being alleged by the stripper, and the university believed that, why was the university painting them as guilty in the public eye? The highly charged meeting lasted more than five hours. Parents asked questions. Administrators didn't have answers.

As the gathering came to a close, Bruce Thompson raised his voice and said, "You just moved this story from the back page of the local newspaper to the front page of the *New York Times.*" It all finally hit them. This wasn't going to "blow over," as they'd heard so many times before. This was going to be huge.

Pressler hung behind as the rest of the administration turned their backs and walked out of the room. He stood and watched as the parents continued to talk among themselves, shocked by the day's events and uncertain what to do next. Emotion filled the air. Mothers, and even some fathers, cried as they imagined what the coming days would bring to their falsely accused sons. When the boys were younger and danger lurked, the parents could scoop their sons into their arms and keep them safe. Unfortunately, this was a nightmare the parents couldn't save them from. They felt helpless and distraught.

Though Pressler felt just as powerless, he pulled the parents together. Ever the coach, he reminded them that the key to success is sticking together. The key to success is to make sure that everybody understood that this did not happen. They needed to remain confident, not just in their sons, but in their sons' teammates. "Keep your head up, support your boys, the truth will come out, we will all be vindicated," he told the parents who were now sobbing. Pressler was the rock, as usual.

From a sympathetic newspaper story detailing Crystal's plight to a heated meeting at the president's mansion to the upsetting cancellation of two crucial lacrosse games to tears from parents who watched their sons suffer through all of this—it was impossible to imagine that March 25, 2006, could get any more bizarre. Impossible until you talk to the security manager at Platinum Strip Club, H. P. Thomas, aka "Fats."

Platinum was busier than usual the night of March 25, Fats remembered. The strip club was hosting a promotion party for some local rappers and their event drew a crowd. Though video cameras were never allowed inside, owner Victor Olatoye made an exception that night. A cameraman was supposed to tape the stage where the rappers were performing, but he misunderstood Victor's instructions and set up his camera in front of the dancers' stage. He had no idea he would document such a significant event.

Fats, who was patrolling the crowd, approached the cameraman as soon as he spotted him. "I knew video cameras weren't allowed in the club, but when he told me Victor said it was okay, there was nothing I could do," he said. On the stage in front of him, Crystal proceeded to perform her usual routine.

Just ten days after she claimed she was brutally raped and sodomized, Crystal wildly threw her body from side to side, spread her legs wide open, bounced up and down, and used the pole for balance as she arched her back so far her extensions touched the stage. "She wasn't hurt. She wasn't upset," Fats recalled. "She was completely normal."

It was a far cry from the traumatized image in the *News & Observer* article that morning. The video camera captured this performance, the lap dances she gave afterward, "It even shows her coming out of the VIP room," said Fats, a stunt that would ultimately get her kicked out of the club.

A crowd of protesters who were gathered at a vigil in front of 610 fell to their knees and wept for the poor woman who had been brutally assaulted and damaged for life.

Ironically, Crystal was on her knees at this time, too, but for a much different reason.

After her dance, she wandered into the VIP room searching for the rappers and their entourage. "I walked in and caught her giving some guy a blow job, so I chased her out," said Fats. Police had been keeping a close eye on the club and he didn't want Crystal to jeopardize the business. "She ran out of the room and onto the stage to try and dodge me," he said, but it wasn't long before another manager pulled her down and kicked her out of the club.

In the coming days, Fats would learn the lurid details of Crystal's claim of rape. He decided the video of her dancing was something the district attorney should see, so he contacted an attorney and offered the tape to prove that the woman wasn't as traumatized as she claimed. "I hated seeing what she was doing to those guys," Fats said. "And I was sure that video would tell the DA he needed to worry about her credibility."

The gesture remained only that. District Attorney Mike Nifong told the lawyers he had no interest in the tape.

CHAPTER NINE

Who Is Mike Nifong?

Senator Joseph McCarthy persecuted communists; Pharaoh Ramses II persecuted Hebrews; and District Attorney Mike Nifong, well . . . he persecuted traffic violators. Until, that is, he set his sights on Duke lacrosse players.

In the months after he decided to prosecute the lacrosse players, Nifong managed, like McCarthy, to work himself into history books. His actions have been scrutinized by everyone from scholars to hairdressers.

But long before Nifong's name was used in law classes and judicial decisions, he was nothing but a number-two dog. He worked in the shadows as an assistant DA for twenty-seven years, never having the drive to fight for the number-one spot. When his superior stepped aside in 2005, Nifong accepted the chance to be the Alpha male. Unfortunately, he proved he was incapable of leading the pack.

"Traditionally he's always been number two in a sled dog crew," said Butch Williams, a longtime defense lawyer in Durham. "When Nifong became number one, he still thought like number two. He didn't know how to navigate those curves and took the sled right over the hill."

Williams has worked with prosecutors for nearly three decades, representing more than eighty-seven murder, rape, and drug defendants. He considered his relationship with Nifong to be cordial. He even supported Nifong in his race for district attorney. Williams was hired to defend lacrosse player Dan Flannery in the period when all forty-six white players were considered suspects. During that time, he attempted to reach out to his friend Nifong in an effort "to keep him from going someplace he shouldn't go." Williams and two other lawyers asked for an appointment to see Nifong and present him information that had been gathered about the alleged victim and that they knew to be true about the players suspected.

Sitting in his office opposite the three lawyers, Nifong put his hands over his ears and in a move straight from kindergarten, he repeated, "I can't hear you, I can't hear you."

Mike Nifong may have been the DA, but he was still acting like the number-two dog he always had been. And he was taking a whole sledful of people over the cliff with him.

Nifong was born in the quaint southern beach town of Wilmington, North Carolina. Growing up, he was a nondescript student, never standing out unless he was being picked on. Wilmington was a tight-knit community, but his peers, who walked the same hallways at New Hanover High School, don't seem to remember many details about him.

After graduating high school in 1967, Nifong attended the University of North Carolina at Chapel Hill. His parents were both Duke graduates, so after they had raised their son as a Blue Devil, one can only imagine how they felt when he became a Tar Heel. The rivalry between the two schools is so intense that entire bookshelves have been filled by tomes on the hatred. Nifong was awarded the Herbert W. Jackson scholarship, which traditionally is given to fewer than twenty students a year. He was accepted into Phi Beta Kappa, an honors society whose members include seventeen U.S. presidents (though the society's website doesn't mention Nifong among its "memorable members").

He earned his bachelor's in political science from UNC in 1971, then took a job in Southport as a mathematics teacher and a boys' physical education instructor. Southport was less than an hour away from where he grew up. After a year he left his teaching career and returned to the comforts of his hometown, working three years for the New Hanover County Department of Social Services. The typical Phi Beta Kappa doesn't return home after college to work in a low-paying public service position, but Nifong's life was not marked by many moments of greatness.

Nifong had said from his days in high school that he wanted to become a lawyer, a dream that may have been sparked by one of his favorite books, *To Kill a Mockingbird* by Harper Lee. The irony behind this would catch up to him later in life. Finally, in 1975, Nifong returned to the University of North Carolina Law School. Though there is no record of the fact, rumor has it that he applied to Duke but was not accepted, which some have said would explain his animosity toward Dukies. He graduated law school and was admitted to the North Carolina Bar in 1978.

Even with a law degree, Nifong could not find a job. He took a volunteer position with the Durham district attorney's office. Traditionally, UNC law grads seeking a job in litigation don't have to look hard to find work, but nothing of Nifong's career was typical.

Shortly after Nifong began his volunteer work, then District Attorney Seth Edwards found a way to pay him on a full-time per diem basis. From that moment on Nifong found his comfort zone. In time, his long-term service earned him the spot as chief assistant DA, and he was content to retire there.

"He grew up in Wilmington, the same town as my husband did," *Raleigh News & Observer* columnist Ruth Sheehan said. "My husband's older sister was in some classes with him in high school. They know the family because one of my husband's best friends was married to Susan Nifong, his sister. So though I had no direct experience, I knew a little bit about his family through that. I think it was stunning to those that knew him that he would pull all this [in the lacrosse case]. It seemed very out of character because he has always been sort of the behind-the-scenes guy. Some of these guys are big for wanting the headlines. And he was not one of those."

As time went on, Nifong built a reputation as a competent if unspectacular lawyer. He settled in as a government lawyer where hours don't have to be billed and client development is simply a matter of reading the police blotter. He developed a legendary foul mouth that made many a coworker blush.

Outside the district attorney's office Nifong liked to portray himself as a family man. He has been married twice and has two children, one from each marriage. His daughter Sarah lives in Charlotte, North Carolina, and his son Bryan is still in high school. He has been involved in youth baseball for over three decades, umpiring even after his children were grown. His current wife, Cy Gurney, works as a regional coordinator for the Guardian Ad Litem program, which serves as an advocate in the courtroom for abused and neglected children.

In 1999 Nifong received horrible news when he was diagnosed with prostate cancer. He took some time off for treatment, receiving surgery, radiation, and a year of hormone therapy. When he returned to work he requested easier, less stressful cases and despite his position as the first assistant district attorney, he asked to work traffic court. He spent the next seven years negotiating DWIs and speeding tickets. He refused to go into a courtroom, so he negotiated with lawyers in an office down the hall from Freda Black, the next most senior assistant DA. Black agrees that traffic court was an odd job for someone of Nifong's tenure and salary, but no one was going to come out and say anything, because people understood his health concerns. Of course that didn't keep people from talking.

"A lot of people thought he was being paid too much money to negotiate traffic tickets," Black said. He was making $106,397 a year before he was appointed district attorney. Yet Nifong had served his time, so others didn't voice their concerns.

During his career Nifong was compared to a pit bull, because once he latched on to something he was not going to let it go. He was ruthless in and out of the courtroom. His unwavering convictions drove him to pursue cases that did not have enough supporting evidence. "He had a certain manner about him that was different than others," Black said. "He didn't really like to prepare very much for a case, he found it to be thrilling to just sort of go and do it off the cuff."

It may be thrilling to pursue a legal case off the cuff, but it often left Nifong in the dark about the hard facts that pertained to cases. The *Raleigh*

News & Observer, in a profile of Nifong's legal career, detailed several stories to back Black's claim.

In 1994 Nifong was the prosecutor in a controversial rape case. As with the Duke lacrosse case, Nifong expressed complete confidence that a rape had occurred even though the testimony had many contradictions. And as in the Duke case, all Nifong had was the word of the woman. The defense had actual evidence that a rape did not occur. When the defense asked to delay the trial date Nifong called them "a bunch of chickens," a comment that highlighted Nifong's admitted cockiness. The defendant was Timothy Malloy, a man who worked as a prison guard and a convenience store clerk.

In 1992 the accuser was out partying and drinking with two of her friends when she was left behind at a bar. She walked to a convenience store where Malloy was working to use the phone to try to contact her friends. Despite her multiple attempts she was unable to reach them. After the accuser and Malloy spent time chatting, Malloy propositioned the women to have sex in the storage room. Malloy admits that they had sex, but claims it was not forced.

The accuser called police and reported she was raped, claiming Malloy pulled a gun from his waistband and held it to her head while he raped her both vaginally and anally.

The defense attorneys showed many inconsistencies in the accuser's statements. The first contradiction was in the medical report. It stated that there was no physical evidence consistent with someone who had been anally raped. Another point the defense made was that Malloy could not carry a gun in the flimsy waistband of the sweat pants he was wearing. Then there was the fact the police never found the weapon even after an extensive search of the convenience store and Malloy's car. Also, a newspaper deliveryman testified that he saw the accuser and the defendant talking and he thought they were good friends. Finally, after allegedly being raped, the accuser invited Malloy to come see her at the topless bar where she served drinks.

Despite Nifong's unwavering conviction that Timothy Malloy was guilty, the jury found him not guilty. After the case Malloy told the *News & Observer,* "I guess once Nifong sets his mind that he's going to prosecute, there's nothing you can really do. What could you do?" This was the last rape case Nifong handled until the Duke lacrosse case.

Nifong's lack of preparation and research on cases was overshadowed by his intense and sometimes outrageous courtroom tirades. In 1995 he prosecuted Walter Goldston, who was accused of killing a convenience store owner. Nifong sought the death penalty. Brian Aus was one of Goldston's attorneys who was taken aback by Nifong's unusual tactics during his closing argument. "Nifong started talking to the jury about the angles of the bullets," Aus recalled the incident to the *News & Observer.* "The state believed the defendant fired as he lay on the floor. So Nifong said, 'Well I hate to do this in a suit.' He then flopped on the floor to depict the shooting." Nifong's demonstration helped to convict Goldston.

Despite all his experience in the courtroom, Nifong was still unknown to the greater population. Among other attorneys he was not remembered for his courtroom achievements; instead, when asked, what people remember most about him seems to be his ferocious temper and unpredictability.

Even after requesting a transfer to the more mundane life of traffic court, Nifong maintained his outrageous behavior. Attorneys would anxiously wait outside Nifong's office to negotiate their clients' traffic violations. Often they could hear through the walls as Nifong ripped someone a new one. On October 1, 2006, the *News & Observer* interviewed attorneys about Nifong's vicious personality. "Working with Mike, you never knew from one day to the next who you would be dealing with," said Glen Grey, a lawyer who handled a high volume of traffic cases. "He would curse you, scream at you, and call you names over nothing."

"He'll go off on you like that," said Aus, the veteran lawyer who has known Nifong for two decades. "He's the first one to tell you, 'Don't bother me right now, I'm not in a good mood.' "

"I have seen him lose his temper and berate attorneys in an unprofessional manner," Scot Holmes, a respected Durham lawyer, told the newspaper.

Freda Black, who worked just a few feet away from Nifong's office, recalled one memorable incident. In late February 2005, just months before Nifong was appointed district attorney, a man came into the office during Nifong's lunch break. Every day Nifong would take lunch from one to two o'clock. He would pop some popcorn and lock himself in his office, usually to play solitaire on his computer. He didn't like to be interrupted.

"Well this day, after Nifong had locked his door, this man came in the office to speak to someone about a speeding ticket his child had received in the Durham area," Black remembered. "The gentleman was from Chicago and wanted to see if anything could be done about the ticket before he left to go back home. This way they wouldn't have to travel all the way back to North Carolina to dispute the ticket on the assigned court date. Nifong was the only person who handled traffic tickets, and his secretary knew not to bother him during his lunchtime. The man pleaded with her, asking to talk to somebody, so she gave in and interrupted Nifong. Nifong stormed out of his office and pulled the man to the lobby, where everyone could see and hear them. The man explained his situation to Nifong; he just wanted somebody to look at the citation. Nifong wanted nothing to do with him and said, 'I'm busy; you need to get a lawyer.'

"The father persisted, saying he thought it was a simple matter that could be resolved without people traveling long distances to come to court. This sparked an argument between the two men. Nifong ordered the man to leave or he would call the sheriff's deputy and have him removed from the building for trespassing. That's when the man demanded, 'What is your name and what position do you hold in this office, because I'm going to look further into this?' Mike replied with, 'My name is Mike Nifong and I'm the Chief Asshole of the Durham County district attorney's office.'

"The man looked at Nifong and said, 'That is the only thing you have said that I completely agree with.' He turned around and stomped out of the lobby. There were many witnesses to the incident and it became an ongoing joke that Nifong was the 'Chief Asshole' and he enjoyed the title."

Nifong was not about to cut anyone a break in traffic court, not even a fellow district attorney. Brad Crone, a political campaign consultant who has helped many Democratic political candidates in North Carolina, recalls how one of his clients, District Attorney Seth Edwards, had a similar experience with Nifong. Edwards's niece had received a speeding ticket in Durham, so he called Nifong to see if he would reduce the ticket to the lowest unit rate. This is not an uncommon request, and it would not have been too great an imposition to reduce the ticket so there wouldn't be as many points on her insurance.

Instead, Nifong told his fellow district attorney that his niece had better hire an attorney and show up in district court. Edwards was astonished that Nifong was unwilling to extend the courtesy.

Nifong's pit bull attitude intimidated some, but many local attorneys saw him as a bully and a coward. Joe Cheshire saw through Nifong's intimidation. He represented David Evans, the lacrosse team cocaptain and the third player indicted for rape. Nifong was not too fond of Cheshire because the defense lawyer was so willing to call someone out for their actions. While working Evans's case, Cheshire went to see Judge Ron Stephens for a scheduled meeting. He showed up and got off the elevator to find two women in the lobby who were extremely shaken. The women were Kerry Sutton, another defense lawyer working the lacrosse case, and the judge's secretary, who is an older African-American woman.

Cheshire, seeing how troubled the women were, walked up to them and asked, "What's wrong?" According to Cheshire, the women replied, "You wouldn't believe what just happened . . . Mike Nifong just came up to us and just started screaming and yelling. He was using the f-word and shouting at the top of his lungs that he was going to cut off your balls and shove them down your throat."

Cheshire was not sure what prompted Nifong's tirade so he turned and walked down to Nifong's office. He could see Nifong in his office, so he told Nifong's assistant, "I understand Mr. Nifong has some kind of problem with me. If he's got a problem with me I would appreciate if he'd see me face to face rather than yelling at ladies in the hall." His assistant went into his office and came back out and said, "Mr. Nifong won't see you."

Cheshire is five-nine, sixty years old, and weighs 175 pounds. He's not a terrifying figure by any means, but Nifong refused to come out of his office. "He didn't have the nerve to say anything to my face," Cheshire said. "He's a bully and a coward."

On April 18, 2005, Governor Mike Easley appointed Nifong as the Durham district attorney when Jim Hardin became a judge. Nifong was sworn in on April 27, and on April 28 the first thing he did was change the letterhead and force Assistant DA Black to resign. Black, a single parent who had worked in the DA's office for more than fourteen years, was told by Nifong that if she signed the resignation letter and left quietly she could receive one additional month's pay. Like any single parent looking out for her children, Black signed the letter and packed all the things in her office. She left without a fight and without an explanation.

"He told me if I kept my mouth shut, he would quote, 'Pay me for another month so you can feed your girls,' " Black said. "He knew what I would do."

Nifong was finally the number-one dog and, as "Chief Asshole," he could do as he pleased. Nifong is "aloof, arrogant, and very standoffish. He's not the type of guy that you would want to go to have a beer with. And he enjoys being a prick," said Crone.

These personality traits, combined with his inability to admit it when he is wrong, would be Nifong's undoing. As Butch Williams said, "Nifong didn't know how to be a true leader." The Duke lacrosse case was Nifong's chance to step out of the shadows and prove to the world that he was number one.

Instead it shone light on all his worst characteristics.

CHAPTER TEN

Press Hound

In all the years Freda Black worked with Mike Nifong as assistant district attorney, she seldom saw him grant a reporter an interview. But after he announced he'd be taking the reins of the Duke case he began a media spree that would put a presidential candidate to shame.

"Suddenly he was Mr. Press Guy," said Black, who would later oppose Nifong in the Democratic primary for district attorney. "The press loved him. They were everywhere. He was, too. You should have seen it." Black recalled a Democratic debate that was held at the end of March 2006. "We finished up and I came out of the auditorium. There were TV cameras everywhere. Suddenly, I heard Nifong talking about the Duke lacrosse case. It caused such a frenzy somebody got knocked down by one of the cameras being shoved in Nifong's face. Mike smiled the whole time."

Nifong jumped on his media opportunity like a fat kid on a cake. He made sure to take full advantage of his newfound rock star status, hogging center stage every chance he got. Between March 24 and April 11 he granted increasingly outlandish interviews to everyone from the *Wilmington Herald* to *Good Morning America.*

The eighteen-day media marathon was played out in print, television broadcast, and the radio airwaves. Nifong redefined the title "Mouth of the South" as he repeatedly expressed his opinions about the lacrosse players, his certainty of the rape allegations, and his commitment to seeking justice on behalf of the accuser.

"The information that I have does lead me to conclude that a rape did occur," Nifong said. "I'm making a statement to the Durham community and, as a citizen of Durham, I am making a statement for the Durham community," Nifong said on *NBC 17 News.* "This is not the kind of activity we condone, and it must be dealt with quickly and harshly."

His critics said it was as if he inexplicably suffered from lockjaw with his mouth in the open position. By March 31, Nifong told the *Raleigh News & Observer,* he'd given "in excess of fifty interviews," and estimated that they consumed forty hours of his time. But Nifong's interviews didn't slow down for a couple of more weeks. It has been estimated that he granted up to seventy interviews in rapid succession.

Nifong began his media onslaught by declaring that he would take the case and prosecute everyone in his path. He threatened the lacrosse party's bystanders, claiming they could be charged because they did nothing to stop the rape. "There's a good chance, if someone had spoken up and said 'You can't do this,' it might not have happened," Nifong told a reporter at WRAL News.

Though he had not stepped into a courtroom in more than a year, he was personally handling this for the good of the Durham community, he said repeatedly. "I felt that this was a case that we needed to make a statement, as a community, that we would not tolerate this kind of behavior here in Durham," Nifong said on MSNBC's *Rita Cosby Live & Direct.* "And I felt that the best way to make that statement was to take this case myself."

He attempted to use the press to pressure the players and attack their character, telling the *News & Observer,* "I would like to think that somebody who was not in the bathroom has the human decency to call up and say, 'What am I doing covering up for a bunch of hooligans?' I'd like to be able to think that there were some people in that house that were not involved in this and were as horrified by it as the rest of us are."

His reference to the Duke lacrosse players as "hooligans" was only one of many low blows Nifong took at the accused players. He even used their allegedly privileged upbringing against them. "There's been a feeling in the past that Duke students are treated differently by the court system," Nifong told *USA Today.* "There was a feeling that Duke students' daddies could buy them expensive lawyers and that they knew the right people. It's discouraging when people feel that way, and we try not to make that the case."

In every interview, Nifong avoided facts that discredited his case. Instead he focused on his opinions and suspicions, tearing the players apart. "One would wonder why one needs an attorney if one was not charged and had not done anything wrong," Nifong said suggestively to a reporter for ESPN. (The irony of that statement became apparent when Nifong himself had to hire lawyers nine months later to defend his actions.)

"There are three people who went into the bathroom with the young lady, and whether the other people there knew what was going on at the time, they do now and have not come forward," Nifong told the *New York Times.* "I'm disappointed that no one has been enough of a man to come forward. And if they would have spoken up at the time, this may never have happened," he said. The possibility that the accuser was not telling the truth apparently never entered Nifong's mind. Certainly it never came out of his mouth.

Though the majority of reporters and the public ate up every word Nifong said, there were others who began to notice his blatant disregard for the lies surrounding Crystal's allegations. Nifong stood at a candidates' forum, in Durham, to answer a question about how he had handled the lacrosse case. His voice grew louder and his finger pointed vigorously as he said with confidence, "I'm not going to allow Durham's view in the minds of the world to be a bunch of lacrosse players at Duke raping a black girl from Durham."

At a forum held at North Carolina Central University on April 11, he announced, "In 75 percent to 80 percent of sexual assault cases, there is no DNA evidence . . ." Nifong quoted NCCU student Tiffany Evans, who had responded to the DNA results, "It doesn't mean nothing happened, it just means nothing was left behind." Nifong went on to discuss how he had been doing his job for a long time, "And for most of the years I've been doing this, we had to deal with sexual assault cases the good old-fashioned way. Witnesses got on the stand and told what happened to them. . . . The fact is any time you have a victim who can identify her assailant, then what you have is a case a judge must let go to the jury. In this situation, I would suspect that a jury will get to evaluate the evidence." Students at the forum cheered in support of Nifong and on behalf of their fellow student, the alleged victim.

His remarks didn't just add fuel to the fire of public opinion that was already burning hot; Nifong opened up a whole oil well to keep the flames ablaze. "There is evidence of trauma in the victim's vaginal area that was noted when she was examined by a nurse at the hospital. And her general demeanor was suggestive of the fact that she had been through a traumatic situation," Nifong said on *The Abrams Report*. Ironically, he followed with, "Well, I don't want to go into a lot of the details of the evidence right now, but obviously, the story that these people were hired to dance and were asked to leave is the alternate story."

Because the lacrosse players wouldn't admit to a crime they didn't commit, Nifong said on CBS's *The Early Show*, "The lacrosse team, clearly, has not been fully cooperative in the investigation."

To ensure that his quotations were completely incendiary, Nifong seldom failed to mention the racial implications of the case: "The circumstances of the rape indicated a deep racial motivation for some of the things that were done," Nifong said on *NBC 17 News*. "It makes a crime that is by its nature one of the most offensive and invasive even more so."

"The thing that most of us found so abhorrent, and the reason I decided to take it over myself, was the combination ganglike rape activity accompanied by the racial slurs and general racial hostility," he said in a telephone interview with the *New York Times*.

"Certainly I have heard the criticism that if the situation were reversed, it's usually said that if this was a white girl and the focus was on the NC Central basketball team, they would all be in jail right now, and I understand that is a sentiment in the community, but I just want you to know, that's not the way I conduct business," Nifong told *USA Today*.

"I still think that the racial slurs that were involved are relevant to show the mind-set, I guess, that was involved in this particular attack, and obviously, to make what is already an extremely reprehensible attack even more reprehensible," Nifong said to Harry Smith of CBS's *The Early Show.*

"This is the type of case that because of the—on top of the rape, which is already an abhorrent crime enough, you have the additional racial animus and hostility that just seems totally out of place for this community in this day and age," Nifong said on MSNBC's *Rita Cosby Live & Direct.*

Though Crystal's fellow stripper admitted to *60 Minutes*' Ed Bradley that she was the first to shout a racial slur that fateful night, Nifong placed the blame for the racial tension on the shoulders of the lacrosse players. And each time he played the race card, he effectively gave credibility to an accuser whose story was in complete flux. His painting of Crystal as a poor damsel in distress allowed Nifong to be seen as her knight in shining armor.

This was a two-way street. The media took advantage of Nifong, granting him prime media spots and taking his words as divine information. After all, he was the district attorney; a credible position by most standards. But Nifong's statements continued to be a slushy combination of alleged facts and opinions, and no one attempted to sort one from the other. Even after the accuser stated that no condoms were used in the sexual assault, Nifong suggested on more than one occasion that if no DNA was found matching the lacrosse players it must be due to the use of condoms.

In a March interview with the *Charlotte Observer,* Nifong said, "I would not be surprised if condoms were used. Probably an exotic dancer would not be your first choice for unprotected sex."

"Well, if you are being forced to have sex against your will, you may not necessarily notice whether or not somebody behind you is using a condom. This was not a consensual sex situation. This was a struggle, wherein she was struggling just to be able to breathe," Nifong explained on *The Abrams Report.*

"So I'm not sure that she would really have much way of knowing whether a condom was being used."

"How does DNA exonerate you? It's either a match or there's not a match," Nifong told the *News & Observer*. "If the only thing that we ever have in this case is DNA, then we wouldn't have a case."

Nifong even implied that date rape drugs had been used. In April, *Newsweek* reported that "Nifong had 'hinted' that a date rape drug may have been used in the alleged gang rape of the woman by three Duke lacrosse players at a March party."

Toxicology reports later proved this suggestion false, but the damage, from this and all his other comments, had already been done. Nifong might as well have pinned a scarlet letter on the chests of Duke's lacrosse players. They could do nothing but sit back and watch in disbelief, as the district attorney ran their names through the mud.

During his March 31 interview on *The Abrams Report*, Nifong took it upon himself to dramatically demonstrate how the victim was choked during the rape. He elaborated on how she was grabbed from behind and struggled to breathe. One fact Nifong failed to mention before this interview was that he had not discussed the facts of the case with the victim. He claimed it was because her experience was so traumatizing he did not want her to have to recount what happened. So Nifong's choking performance on national TV was his own personal version. It helped to further blur the lines between fact and fiction in this case.

Nifong continued to display incredible, if not brazen, confidence and conviction that this crime had occurred. His mind was like a runaway train . . . heading the wrong way on a one-way track. "The contempt that was shown for the victim, based on her race, was totally abhorrent," Nifong told ABC TV. "My guess is that some of this stone wall of silence that we had seen may tend to crumble once charges start to come out."

Nifong told *The Abrams Report*, "I am convinced there was a rape, yes, sir."

"There's no doubt in my mind that she was raped and assaulted at this location," Nifong told Bill O'Reilly on *The O'Reilly Factor*.

"My reading of the report of the emergency room nurse would indicate that some type of sexual assault did in fact take place," Nifong said on WRAL.

In early April, Nifong discovered how to say "no comment" to the media, though that didn't mean they would disappear. Nifong had fed them enough information to keep them talking for a lifetime.

Still, at his July 28 press conference he declared, "I have not backed down from my initial assessments of the case. . . . There were things we hoped to have in terms of evidence that we ended up not having. . . . My handling of the media coverage of this case has occasioned substantial criticism, some of which is undoubtedly justified. I both underestimated the level of media attention this case would draw and misjudged the effect that my words would have."

Mike Nifong had forgotten the most basic law of physics: For every action there is an equal and opposite reaction. His scores of headlines and one-liners would eventually come back to haunt him.

CHAPTER ELEVEN

THE PRESIDENT

Back in the summer of 2003, when Duke began searching for its next president, nobody at Yale University would have believed that Richard Brodhead, beloved dean and English professor, would soon leave New Haven for Durham—not even the man himself. After all, he had spent his entire adult life at Yale, forty years walking the same paths to the same Gothic buildings.

The campus would become the backdrop of his life, where he'd grow from a somewhat shy but enviably smart seventeen-year-old freshman to a renowned lecturer and professor to arguably the most popular dean the university has ever seen.

So, when Brodhead was offered the presidency at Duke, it would have been easy for him to decline, to stay at Yale where he had built his career and his life. He had done so a handful of other times—kindly declining a position or an offer of interest from schools across the country—but there was something about Duke that intrigued him, a sense of youthful ambition and inspiration absent from the well-established and esteemed Ivy League.

He joked at the press conference about a comment one of his students made upon hearing he would leave Yale for Duke: "How typical. You're leaving us for someone younger and more athletic." But in reality, here was his chance to be part of a school that was on its way up, and for Duke, here was its chance to climb up the Ivy-covered ladder by welcoming someone from the top.

"He may be the smartest person I've ever met," said John Burness, Duke's senior vice president for public affairs and government relations.

"He is a really deep thinker and it's fascinating to watch how he thinks and how he talks because he starts with the big picture and he works his way down to the points. He is so fast with his wit you just do a double-take sometimes. He has a Mr. Chips quality to him; he's this much-beloved faculty type who students really like. They loved him at Yale."

But would they love him at Duke?

Even as an adolescent, Brodhead displayed the intellectual curiosity and passion that made him famous at Yale. Born in Dayton, Ohio, in 1947, Richard (or Dick, as he is known) was the second of three children. He lost his older brother a few years after a tragic car accident had left him paralyzed, and he has a sister who is currently a nurse.

After attending public school in Fairfield, Connecticut, where his family moved when he was six, he enrolled in the prestigious Phillips Andover Academy in Massachusetts, an all-boys boarding school that boasts alumni like Frederick Law Olmsted, JFK, Jr., and the presidents George H. W. and George W. Bush—the latter was a classmate of Brodhead's both at Andover and then later at Yale. In his commencement address to the Yale Class of 2001, President George W. Bush quipped about his interactions with Brodhead in the library, "We had a mutual understanding—Dick wouldn't read aloud, and I wouldn't snore."

Andover was a relatively small school—the class of 1964 had 231 people—and has often been seen as a symbol of the white male privileged world that would be so central to the debate over the lacrosse scandal at Duke years later. Brodhead made friends of all kinds while at Andover, athletes and academics alike. This boarding school, a half hour north of Boston, carried with it a definite air of privilege, and yet to its students it was also democratic. "Certainly there were lots of people there from important families and histories and money and so on, but you absolutely didn't know it," said William Stowe, a classmate of Brodhead's who enrolled at Andover on scholarship as a junior. "It was just not cool to show off."

The boys at Andover, all in the requisite coat and tie and wearing similar haircuts, would meander the idyllic campus together from early morning chapel to classes and dinner. Among them, Brodhead was by no means an imposing physical figure. His father, Stanley, played lacrosse for Cornell in the 1940s, and the two even watched the Duke-Cornell game in 2005 together, each wearing their respective jerseys. But Brodhead himself was not much of an athlete, sticking mostly to intramural sports such as soccer and squash to fulfill the school's athletic requirement. Instead, it was his mind that was his most remarkable asset as a young student.

"What struck me the most about him before I knew him from class was his absolutely phenomenal memory," said Stowe, who would later become his teaching assistant when Brodhead was an assistant professor at Yale. "He could remember everything he ever read, and it was pretty intimidating. Even back then."

To learn about Sigmund Freud, he'd read *The Interpretation of Dreams*; to learn about Chinese philosophy, he'd read the *Tao Te Ching*. It was at Andover where he learned to appreciate and learn straight from the source. And for many years, that intellectual curiosity and memory would be his trademark. His speeches and lectures were filled with allusions to Faulkner, to Homer; he can draw from any great work of literature with effortless ease. But this sometimes-intimidating intelligence was never a factor that Brodhead boasted; he was as modest and personable as he was smart. Ironically, he didn't give much thought to selecting a college; Andover was Yale's feeder school, and Yale was undoubtedly one of the most prestigious universities in the country. It made perfect sense to further his education there.

Entering Yale in the fall of 1964, Brodhead quickly found his calling. He took a couple of American literature courses taught by Yale's most renowned English professors early on and soon decided to study "intensive English," a major that went beyond mere literature into the realms of economics and politics. He graduated from Yale in 1968 with an immaculate academic record—summa cum laude with exceptional distinction in English.

He immediately continued his graduate studies at Yale, earning both his master's and Ph.D. degrees in English within four years. It was during his first year as a graduate student that Brodhead met fellow English grad student Cynthia Degnan, who came to Yale after graduating from Syracuse University. The two began dating, and by the end of their second year (in 1970), they were married. Cindy opted not to finish her Ph.D., but became a book editor for the Yale University Press. And when Dick earned his Ph.D. in 1972, he promptly accepted a job as an assistant professor of English at his alma mater.

Although he wouldn't receive tenure until 1980 and wouldn't be named a full professor until 1985, Brodhead was still making a name for himself as an untenured assistant professor in the seventies. He taught a nineteenth-century American literature course that quickly became enormously popular. As a lecturer, Brodhead became famous for his wit, intelligence, and warmth. But perhaps more inspiring to his students was witnessing his passion, hearing it in his deep and resonant yet Kermit-the-Frog-esque voice. It was a kind of class that made students think—or rather, he was the kind of professor to make students think.

Brodhead's classrooms were consistently packed at every meeting. "It wasn't a class that people skipped, because they all really wanted to come," said Stowe, who assisted the American literature course as a graduate student at Yale. Stowe, who had graduated Andover with Brodhead, recalled his admiration for his onetime classmate and later professorial role model: "I found myself completely unconsciously—until someone pointed it out—imitating the way he would talk and gesture because I was so impressed by how well it worked. I don't think it was even an illusion. I think he was lecturing and thinking at the same time, so that it was a thoughtful presentation."

Brodhead has always had a unique public-speaking style, which became his most famous characteristic and continues to draw countless impersonations from students and colleagues. Most imitate his voice, which is surprisingly deep for the five-foot-ten man, and his tendency to enunciate—perhaps even overenunciate—every word. "He's not an intimidating guy," Duke lacrosse captain Matt Zash said. "He's like Mr. Burns from the Simpsons."

But what strikes most who see and listen to Brodhead are the erudite and scholarly allusions he inserts all the time just off the top of his head.

With absolute ease, he can conjure up the Shakespearean sonnet that best describes the situation. He'll explain how he feels by drawing parallels to characters in a Hawthorne short story. And whether he is standing at a lectern or sitting in a cozy chair, he speaks just as much from his hands as he does from his mouth.

A few years after earning the title of full professor at Yale, Brodhead became the chair of the English department, a role he kept for many years before being appointed dean of Yale College in 1993. He became a well-known figure in academia. He participated in several external review committees for university English departments, and even chaired Duke's review in 1991. Through these activities and other administrative duties he was given at Yale, Brodhead began to understand more deeply the workings of a university, and they ultimately helped him prepare for his role as dean and later president of Duke University.

The dean of Yale College more or less oversees the entire undergraduate experience at the university—from academics to student life to managing faculty. For eleven years, the third-longest tenure of a dean in Yale's history, Brodhead was dean, administrator, and advisor.

"You'd be hard-pressed to find anybody with anything negative to say about Dick [at Yale]," said Richard Levin, who became president of Yale about the same time Brodhead became dean.

At Yale, he was universally respected, admired, and loved as a person but also as an administrator. In times of crisis, Brodhead was one of the few people called upon to handle any situation, especially when it concerned the undergraduate community.

In the waning hours of December 4, 1998, Brodhead and several of the other top administrators had received troubling news. Suzanne Jovin, a senior and political science major, had been brutally murdered, stabbed seventeen times in the back, neck, and head, about two miles off campus.

"When we heard of the tragedy, he was in my living room immediately at 2:00 A.M. to sort out how to proceed," said Yale Vice President and Secretary Linda Lorimer, who, with Brodhead, made up a sort of "crisis team." "You have to try and locate the parents, you have to contact the parents, you then have to plan on communicating this to the college community, which is sound asleep but when they arrive in the morning, they will confront the fact that one of their number has been murdered off-campus."

The murder came as a massive shock to the community, and Brodhead helped bring solace to those grieving the loss of this promising student. The incident, however, gained a great deal of media attention as more and more questions arose and very few were answered. Early on, the media and New Haven police seemed to focus its collective suspicion on James Van de Velde—a Yale lecturer and Jovin's senior thesis advisor—who was portrayed as a mysterious man with a nebulous military past. Yale maintained that it considered Van de Velde innocent until proven otherwise. But on the Sunday before spring semester classes were to start in January 1999, Brodhead called Van de Velde to his office. There, Brodhead told the lecturer that his classes that semester would be cancelled, and he could pursue research or other scholarly projects instead.

Yale believed that "under these circumstances, it is inevitable that [Van de Velde's] classroom presence would be accompanied by continuing speculation about events outside the classroom that would constitute a major distraction for students and impair their educational experience." Even though he was never charged with any crime, and only named by police as one in a pool of suspects they investigated, Van de Velde and his reputation bore the brunt of what turned out to be shoddy police work.

In March of that year, he asked Brodhead to write him a reference as he searched for other jobs. Van de Velde said that the dean replied that he'd gladly write one, but that he would have to at least mention the Jovin incident and how it pertained to him. Van de Velde filed suit against the

New Haven police commissioner and Yale's top administrators, including Levin, Lorimer, and Brodhead, but his lawsuit was thrown out in 2006 (he's still in the process of appealing that decision).

The story, Jovin's tragic murder, the unanswered questions surrounding it, and the unsubstantiated suspicion of Van de Velde, his firing by Yale and the civil suits that followed appeared in *Vanity Fair*, the *New York Times Magazine*, and on *20/20*, and were covered by a host of local media organizations.

No charges were ever filed, and in 2006, the case was handed over to the cold case unit. It remains unsolved to this day.

For a man who had spent nearly forty years in the same place, the prospect of leaving it all behind to start somewhere altogether new was almost unthinkable. Brodhead went back and forth on what to do for several weeks. At one point, he even called Robert K. Steel, vice chairman of the board of trustees, who led the nineteen-member search committee of trustees, faculty, students, staff, and alumni, to decline the offer, but Steel persuaded him to reconsider.

"He was very torn, and it was truly up in the air. It took him a little while to make the decision," Levin recalls. "But I will say that once he took it, he was absolutely committed and truly excited about it." For six months after he accepted the job, Brodhead traveled to and from Durham for many weekends to start getting a feel for the campus he'd soon be leading.

"It was striking to us how closely Dick's background and interests match the values and aspirations of Duke University," Steel said of Brodhead. Those who read the quotation often wondered if Steel had it backward.

Brodhead couldn't have imagined that his first major decision as president would present itself so quickly. On July 1, 2004, his first day on the job, Duke Athletic Director Joe Alleva came to Brodhead with news that the Los Angeles Lakers were wooing iconic basketball coach Mike Krzyzewski with a contract for $40 million over five years. On this July Fourth weekend, Brodhead would have to do whatever he could to keep Coach K in Durham.

Making a cameo appearance in Krzyzewskiville, legendary grassy knoll where students camp out in line for a spot in Cameron Indoor Stadium, Brodhead sported a white DUKE headband as he joined students at the impromptu rally chanting, "Coach K, No L.A.!" For some, especially the Cameron Crazies, it showed that Brodhead would be in tune with Duke.

Once basketball season began, the fans would salute Brodhead and his presence at just about every game with his very own cheer. But others saw the image of Brodhead in K-ville that night as something almost troubling. "What you saw there was the lay of the land," Orin Starn, a Duke professor who specializes in the anthropology of sports, told *The New Yorker.* "The fact is that it's the basketball coach, Coach K, who's the most powerful person at Duke, and in Durham, and maybe in North Carolina, much more powerful than the college president himself. I mean, there was almost this kind of ritual humiliation, this ritual obeisance, or fealty, that was required of him."

Nevertheless, it wasn't your typical first day on the job. "It wasn't the week I'd been expecting," Brodhead told the student newspaper, the *Chronicle.* "And yet, I have had university administrative jobs for years, and the main thing you know about them is that you never can know on any given day what's going to happen."

Ultimately, Coach K turned down the Lakers' offer because, he says, a letter from a student moved him and his wife to tears and convinced them to stay. While the Lakers scare may have been Brodhead's first surprise at Duke and first major concern with any athletic department, it certainly would not be his last.

Coming from Yale, not exactly an athletic powerhouse even within the Ivy League, Brodhead had to acclimate to a different kind of university, one where sports is a big part of business, not just something to watch over the weekends. At Duke, where 10 percent of the undergraduate body are Division I athletes, sports even plays a part in recruiting nonathletes to the school.

"I can tell you that I would probably not be here without Duke's basketball team," *Chronicle* sports columnist Alex Fanaroff wrote in October 2006. "I can tell you that many, if not all, of my friends (most of them non-athletes, some of them student leaders) would not be here without the allure of Duke's athletic program. I would estimate that at least a quarter of Duke's undergrads feel the same way, and I think that is an extraordinarily conservative estimate. Duke's all-star professors and nationally-renowned academic programs are great, but lots of schools have all that. There is just one school in the entire country where you can get a top-10 education, cheer for a top-five basketball team, watch Florida State and Miami football come to campus on back-to-back weekends and attend some of the highest-quality competitions in basically any sport."

Even though men's basketball put Duke on the proverbial college sports map, the Blue Devils have for the past few years become a perennial contender in the Director's Cup, which ranks overall athletic departments. Duke placed fourth in the 2006 standings behind top-ranked Stanford.

Despite that all-around athletic success, Brodhead entered a Duke that was deliberately looking to reinvent itself and prove that it offered far more than a basketball team and crazy fans. It was only quite recently that Krzyzewski didn't grace the covers of all the prospective student pamphlets. By 2000, with Duke's brand firmly established by way of Coach K and company, the university began to shift its focus to the classrooms and labs. Previous President Nan Keohane sought to build Duke's future as a leading research institution with capital campaign after capital campaign, and new state-of-the-art facilities began popping up all over campus.

So what Duke needed to continue to beef up its scholarly credentials was an academic heavyweight, and Brodhead, in Steel's mind, was the perfect contender because he offered even more than a massively impressive CV. He was also an eloquent and charming man with more than enough wit and personality to help in fundraising efforts.

The fundraising and building was by no means exclusive to the academic side of Duke. During the same period, most of the athletic facilities on campus were upgraded as well—from fields to training facilities to sports medicine. Just about everything got a facelift during the last five years of the Keohane era. These physical improvements translated to better success in recruiting, so in reality, the growth of Duke as school and Duke as team went very much hand in hand.

For Brodhead, athletics had always been just a fun experience, a leisurely activity on campus, but it rarely ever raised serious questions or concerns while he was at Yale. At Duke, though, he'd be playing in a whole new ballgame, faced with an athletics controversy in a league of its own.

"This guy has got a vision of where he wants to take the place, and miraculously these big, big, big things are actually happening," Burness said. "He's resilient. I don't know how he deals with the resiliency issue given everything he's had to deal with. The shots that have come because of lacrosse, the personal attacks, all that stuff. This isn't a politician or a guy running for public office. This is the president of the university trying to be president of the university. He has these qualities in him that are awesome. I'm not saying this because I'm the PR guy. The guy has some awesome qualities, this intelligence and vision.

"His understanding of undergraduate education is, for me, so far superior to anybody I've ever heard talk about it before. It goes back to a piece of what I think of who he is and why he understands it, which is he has so enjoyed learning. He loves the kids, the students. He wants them to be able to have the wonderful experiences he's had. He wants them to create their own Duke. He wants them to explore just about anything. It's how he thinks."

Burness was asked why, if Brodhead loves students as deeply as he said, he was not more supportive of the lacrosse team when a stripper alleged that those players had brutalized her.

"You asked the fundamental question, if he loves students so much, why didn't he wrap his arms around them?" Burness said. "There's a paradox there, but it's also true he's having to deal with what he was dealt with at the moment he was dealt with it and put out the principles that were going to guide his behavior and the institution's behavior."

Burness struggled with the follow-up question as well. Did Brodhead believe his students after looking them in the eyes and hearing what did—or didn't—happen that night?

"You know, I don't know the answer to that. I honestly don't. My guess is he probably did. The issue that I think is there is if he says that we need to have the truth emerge from the judicial process and people should be making their own judgments, you need to let the truth emerge from this process because this is how we do it, then he couldn't just say I'm going to make my decision and announce where I am."

Effusive in his defense of his boss, Burness made one thing clear: In the days after the lacrosse party, as a district attorney made one outrageous claim after another about the Duke athletes, Dick Brodhead found himself in a bind like never before. And no experience, no education, no event in his forty years at Yale or his three at Duke could have helped him.

As Brodhead learned on that first day as president, he would never supplant basketball coach Mike Krzyzewski as the man most linked to Duke. The three-time national championship coach *is* the face of the university, and his statesman's stature could have provided the president a place to turn as the lacrosse crisis spun wildly out of control.

But, in a move no one has yet understood, Brodhead chose to leave Krzyzewski on the sidelines, leaning instead on an inner circle that obviously was overmatched by the moment. Krzyzewski, who remained largely silent during the lacrosse controversy, offered his first extended comments about the case to sportscaster Bob Costas on the HBO sports program *Costas Now* on March 13, 2007—a year after the party at 610.

"I met with my college president, and I told Dick Brodhead if you need me—if *you* need me—you tell me and then put me in a position where I am not the basketball coach but I am that special assistant to you," Krzyzewski said. "Dick Brodhead did not bring me in."

When Costas asked Krzyzewski if the university acted with too much haste—Costas pointed out that the initial pressure on the university caused it to suspend the program and "Pressler lost his job"—Coach K responded, "The one thing that I wish we would have done is just publicly say, 'Look, those are our kids and we're going to support them because they are still our kids.' That's what I wished we would have done . . . I don't think we did a good job of that."

Krzyzewski also was critical of faculty members who denounced the defendants. "We had almost one hundred professors come out publicly against certain things in athletics and I was a little bit shocked at that," he said. "But it shows that there is a latent hostility—or whatever you want to say—toward sports on campus. I thought it was inappropriate, to be quite frank with you."

Krzyzewski agreed with Costas and said the lacrosse players' behavior, though not criminal, was questionable. But Krzyzewski pointed out there "were frat parties and kegs on campus and things like that for years. Kids misbehave in college. They were doing it forty years ago and they will still do it." Krzyzewski also admitted the lacrosse controversy has bruised Duke's image. "It's hurt Duke's image. I think a lot of people feel that we left the kids unsupported."

CHAPTER TWELVE

Perfect Offenders, Perfect Victim

It is one of America's worst-kept secrets: College campuses are a breeding ground for radical left-leaning faculty. They are often anti-American, anti-white male, and anti any other facet of our society that has enjoyed "privilege" at one time or another. Duke's campus was no exception. In fact, its "academic freedom movement" may arguably place it as one of the leading universities blazing the trail toward an even more extreme campus culture.

With members of the lacrosse team accused of raping a black stripper, those who were predisposed to abhor privilege were provided a platform from which to rail against all that they loathed.

Stephen Miller, a conservative columnist for the *Chronicle*, explained the behavior of these radicals. "Basically you have these people who have dedicated years of their lives to this notion of a deeply oppressive society. So for them, this is just the case to get their social agenda going."

Proof? Take a look at this web posting about "the incident" written by Wahneema Lubiano, an associate professor of literature and African-American Studies at Duke, on newblackman.blogspot.com on April 13, 2006:

> Within the terms of the responses to the incident, I understand the impulse of those outraged and who see the alleged offenders as the exemplars of the upper end of the class hierarchy, the politically dominant race and ethnicity, the dominant gender, the dominant sexuality, and the dominant social group on campus. Further, this group has been responsible for extended social violence against the neighborhood in which they

> reside. In short, by a combination of their behaviors and what they represent in terms of social facts, and by virtue of their relation to the alleged victim, for those who are defenders of the victim, the members of the team are almost perfect offenders.

Division between economic class, race, ethnicity, sex, sexuality, social status, violence; Lubiano hit on them all. And in her opinion, the lacrosse players reigned dominant in each, the epitome of the "perfect offender." Her post continued:

> As more information circulates and the stakes are raised by virtue of considerations of Duke's and the nation's long-standing class, race, and gender disparities, they are increasingly "perfected" as offenders. As part of this dynamic, the young woman, black and non-wealthy, made even more vulnerable by virtue of being employed by the perfect offenders and outnumbered, approaches the state of perfect victim.

This was one of the many commentaries Lubiano would pen concerning the lacrosse case, but it would not be her most noteworthy.

What began as an email from Lubiano was transformed into the infamous ad that would appear in the *Chronicle* for just one day. However, this one-page ad in the student publication would put Lubiano, and more than seven dozen other Duke professors who endorsed it, front and center in the debate over the role of Duke's faculty in stirring emotions. It was a debate over the rush to judgment; a debate over the responsibility of a faculty to support its students; a debate over what happens when members of the academic community begin eating their own.

On April 6, 2006, a collection of eighty-eight professors came forward, voicing their outrage at what they perceived as "a social disaster." Specifically, they were naming themselves as backers of a full-page notice, referred to as the "We're Listening" ad, which appeared in the student newspaper. "We are listening to our students," the text begins. "We're also listening to the Durham community, to the Duke staff, and to each other.

Regardless of the results of the police investigations, what is apparent everyday now is the anger and fear of many students who know themselves to be objects of racism and sexism, who see illuminated in this moment's extraordinary spotlight what they live with everyday. . . . These students are shouting and whispering about what happened to this young woman and to themselves." The ad insisted that the undersigned faculty members were listening to these concerns, but it soon became apparent that the so-called Group of 88 was more interested in listening to themselves than in listening to the facts.

Karla FC Holloway, an English and African-American Studies professor at Duke, first conceived the idea for the ad at an African and African-American Studies program forum on March 29, shortly after the lacrosse party story made national headlines. Students were invited to voice their frustration with the current situation and, it became apparent, with the university as a whole. Numerous complaints were made about perceived racism and sexism in the university's social and political structure.

Lubiano wrote down many of the students' remarks during the proceedings, and it was from these notes that she composed the ad, at Holloway's urging. The statements, which ranged from complaints about female students' being groped at parties to accusations of African-American male students being singled out by campus police, appeared in varying fonts, staggered across the body of the ad, while a large black text box stretched across the center, bearing the question: "What Does a Social Disaster Sound Like?" Several of the statements referred specifically to the current legal situation. One quotation contained the remark, "I am only comfortable talking about this event in my room with close friends. I am actually afraid to bring it up in public." Another comment alleged, "No one is really talking about how to keep the young woman herself central to this conversation, how to keep her humanity before us." Evident in all of the statements is anger, dissatisfaction, and a pervading malaise about the ethnic and sexual lines at Duke.

Although Lubiano took her own notes at the forum and used some comments she documented in the ad, she also used three quotations from an article in the *Independent Weekly*—a local alternative newspaper with low circulation and unimpressive journalism—from March 29 entitled "Not Your Video Ho." Although the sources were named in the article, Lubiano inexplicably decided to keep their quotations anonymous, a choice that would later call into question the credibility and intended message of the ad.

When later questioned by numerous reporters about the implications of the ad, Lubiano stood by her original work, adamant that the text made no implicit pronunciation of guilt about any party, and instead insisted that the ad was merely intended to give voice to the varied frustrations of many female and minority members of the student body.

Across the bottom of the text ran the lines "We thank the following departments and programs for signing onto this ad with African & African American Studies; Romance Studies; Psychology; Social and Health Sciences; Franklin Humanities Institute; Critical U.S. Studies; Art, Art History and Visual Studies; Classical Studies; Asian & African Languages and Literature; Women's Studies; Latino/a Studies; Latin American and Caribbean Studies; Medieval and Renaissance Studies; European Studies; Program in Education; and the Center for Documentary Studies." Though the ad then mentioned that the names of the individual signers were available on the African and African-American Studies program's website, the implication in thanking the various departments was that the endorsement was a departmentally backed, and, therefore, university-sanctioned action—something that was never the case.

These radical professors who signed on with Lubiano and Holloway saw this as the quintessential opportunity to make their statement, but they rushed it. In order to meet the *Chronicle* deadline, they were forced to turn the ad in quickly. They weren't waiting on the facts; they couldn't. Time would not allow it.

The signatures they needed to endorse their ad were solicited with haste. Those professors who were approached to sign on could not have grasped the effect this tiny statement would have on them, and on their reputations as respected academics.

Few could have imagined it would create the tsunami that it did. Few could have known this ad would wipe out some of the trust that many Duke alumni and others had in the university. Although their ad was only printed one time in the *Chronicle,* it would remain on the African-American Studies website for months afterward. Thanks to their encouraging words, they would get the answer to the question they so boldly asked, dead center in the middle of their ad.

They would get to hear exactly what a social disaster sounded like.

Although that number of professors signing the ad may seem insignificant, eighty-eight professors is nearly 20 percent of Duke's total undergraduate faculty, a sizable enough number that though they came from the most liberal disciplines, to many, it appeared they spoke for all Duke faculty—especially when no one stood up against them.

Although many within the Group of 88 stuck to the common themes of privileged white versus poor black, empowered male versus subservient female—and any combination in between—when explaining why they signed the ad, there were some outliers even within these radicals. For example, Philosophy Professor Alex Rosenberg said his reason for signing the ad was his concern with alcohol abuse on Duke's campus, although that theme, or anything related to it is mentioned nowhere in the ad. More specifically, Rosenberg was bothered by "affluent kids violating the law to get exploited women to take their clothes off when they could get as much hookup as they wanted from rich and attractive Duke coeds," as he told the *New York Sun* on March 27.

Mark Anthony Neal, an associate professor of African-American Studies at Duke, posted this commentary on a blog entitled "A Social Disaster"; Voices from Durham. (White) Male Privilege, Black Respectability, and Black Women's Bodies:

> When a young black woman was allegedly raped, sodomized, robbed and beaten by members of the Duke University Lacrosse team of March 13 of this year, it was initially treated as little more than another case of

> "(privileged) boys gone wild." . . . Thus in all likelihood, regardless of what happened inside of 610 N. Buchanan Blvd, the young men were hoping to consume something that they felt that a black woman uniquely possessed. If these young men did in fact rape, sodomize, rob, and beat this young woman, it wasn't simply because she was a woman, but because she was a black woman.

Clearly, Neal felt these white "privileged boys gone wild" were searching for something only a black woman could provide.

Neal's scholarly merit was displayed at its finest in an interview with *Duke* magazine in the 2006 July–August edition. When asked about his alter ego, he responded with, "My intellectual alter ego is thugniggerintellectual—one word." He also explained his theory of "intellectual thuggery" as, "I wanted to embody this figure that comes into intellectual spaces like a thug, who literally is fearful and menacing."

Neal's theory should have been well received by his fellow colleagues in the Group of 88; it seemed they had no problem creating a menace all their own.

The personal outrage felt by many within the Group of 88 was not directed only at the lacrosse team. Peter Lange, Duke University's provost, would receive a scalding letter of disgust concerning the university's handling of the case from English and African-American Studies Professor Houston A. Baker. Highlights from his letter made clear Baker's anger with the university, and the extreme nature of his radical beliefs:

> How is a Duke community citizen to respond to such a national embarrassment from under the cloud of a "culture of silence" that seeks to protect white, male, athletic, violence. . . . It is virtually inconceivable that representatives of Duke University's Athletic Department would allow its lacrosse team to engage in regular underage drinking and out-of-control bacchanalia. . . . Young, white violent, drunk men among us—implicitly boated by our athletic directors and administrators—have injured lives. . . . What is precipitously teetering in the balance at this

> point, during weeks marked by inaction and duck-and-cover from our designated leaders is, well, confidence. . . . There can be no confidence in an administration that believes suspending a lacrosse season and removing pictures of Duke lacrosse players from a web page is a dutifully moral response to abhorrent sexual assault, verbal racial violence, and drunken white male privileged loosed amongst us.

Baker now teaches at Vanderbilt University.

While Baker was outraged and embarrassed by the lack of action from the Duke administration, suggesting they fostered such "abhorrent" behavior, Professor Orin Starn had a solution. As a sports-anthropology professor at Duke, his solution was simple; pull Duke out of Division I athletic competition altogether, and adopt club teams in its place. He was quoted in a *New Yorker* article written by Peter Boyer: " 'I think it would be a huge mistake to go back to business as usual,' he said. 'Now what happened, or didn't happen, I'm not sure we'll ever know. But at the very minimum we know that we have guys hiring strippers, a record of underage drinking, and pretty strong evidence of the use of racial slurs.' "

Starn believes that Duke University is trying to feed two opposing university stereotypes; the athletic powerhouse versus the academically elite. In the *New Yorker* article he states, "On the one hand, you have a university that wants to be first-class liberal arts university, with a cutting-edge university press, these great programs in literature and history and African-American studies, that's really done some amazing things over the last twenty years, building itself from a kind of regional school mostly for the Southern elite into a really global university with first-class scholarship. But then you have another university. That's a university of partying and getting drunk, hiring strippers, frats, big-time college athletics."

According to Starn, these two universities should not coexist. Athletics needed to be the first of these extraneous elements to get axed, and all of that time, money, and effort could then be redistributed toward the more beneficial aspects of the university.

• • •

Another Group of 88 member decided the most effective way "to put into context what occurred in Durham" was to compare it to historical racial injustices our society has previously witnessed. In his guest column for the *Chronicle*, entitled "Sex and Race," William Chafe, history professor and former arts and sciences dean at Duke, wrote:

> Sex and race have always interacted in a vicious chemistry of power, privilege, and control. Emmett Till was brutalized and lynched in Mississippi in 1954 for allegedly speaking with too easy familiarity to a white woman storekeeper. . . . What has all this to do with America today, and with Duke? Among other things, it helps to put into context what occurred in Durham two weeks ago. The mixture of race and sex that transpired on Buchanan Boulevard is not new.

Chafe's choice to compare the alleged rape to one of the most violent racial crimes documented in American history, in addition to the outlandish allegations from his fellow colleagues, brought a whole new definition to the word "radical."

Karla FC Holloway would also target her anger at the very university where she worked, but for a different reason than Baker. Where he became enraged because of the inaction of Duke's administration in regard to the lacrosse case, Holloway would become frustrated with the action that was taken by the administration; more specifically, by President Brodhead. When Brodhead decided to invite indicted players Reade Seligmann and Collin Finnerty back to school, she promptly resigned her role as subgroup chair of the Campus Culture Initiative Committee. Her reason: She "could no longer work in good faith with this breach of common trust."

Despite Holloway's decision to leave the CCI, her opinions on the lacrosse case were not silenced. In her article entitled "Coda: Bodies of Evidence," published in the *Scholar and Feminist Online Journal*, she provides a graphic description of the injustice the victim endured:

> At Duke University this past spring, the bodies left to the trauma of a campus brought to its knees by members of Duke University's lacrosse team were African-American and women. I use the kneeling metaphor with deliberate intent. It was precisely this demeanor towards women and girls that mattered here. The lacrosse team's notion of who was in service of whom and the presumption of privilege that their elite sports' performance had earned seemed their entitlement as well to behaving badly and without concern for consequence.

Holloway's outspoken condemnation of the players placed her comfortably among fellow radicals within the Group of 88. However, this article struck a chord with one specific person who was closely related to the lacrosse team, for one specific reason. Patricia Dowd, mother to player Kyle Dowd, could not dismiss the critical statements from Holloway because her personal circumstances differentiated her from the many others who slandered her son and his teammate's names'. Holloway was a mother. Holloway's son had been convicted of rape and attempted murder.

The *News and Observer* published an email exchange between Patricia Dowd and Holloway, at Dowd's request. Dowd explained in her email to Holloway that after she read the article listed above in September, she "penned a response," hoping her rage would cool and it would remain unsent. However, her anger did not subside, and the letter was sent.

In her letter to Holloway, Dowd writes, "How could any woman be so cruel and callous, and judge a whole class of individuals without any facts? What was more puzzling and definitely more alarming was that you had a son convicted of rape and attempted murder, and who was going to be tried for the murder of two others." She continues to ask Holloway a series of vicious questions, trying to understand how a fellow mother could feel justified in her actions. "Do you attack our sons because you feel guilt for your own failure as a mother? . . . Do you attack our sons to justify your own son's shortcomings? Do you attack our sons because they are innocent and your son was not?"

Although the article in the *News & Observer* did explain that Holloway's son was adopted and "was abused in a series of foster homes," as well as having a "mental illness," for Dowd, that served as no justification. She described Holloway as "a pathetic, heartless individual, . . . a sad, bitter, resentful woman, attempting to squash the dreams of others."

Although, as she told the newspaper, this may not have been one of Patricia Dowd's "finest moments," the response she received from Holloway gave more merit to her criticisms.

> *Dear Patricia Dowd,*
> *Indeed, you should have held off sending it. Your letter reflects nothing so much as an impoverished spirit and intellect. What a shame, for you, and your family.*
> *Karla FC Holloway*

The condemnation aimed at the players from members of the Duke faculty was not limited to blogs, ads, and guest columns in the school paper. These lacrosse players were students. Some of those eighty-eight professors were their professors. If the players did not want to jeopardize their academic careers—and if some senior players wanted to graduate—they had to face these professors in the classroom.

Devon Sherwood, the lone African-American player on the team, recounts a situation in which one of his professors resorted to the lacrosse case for a discussion topic when the class came unprepared. "It was my cultural anthropology class, a big lecture class, about 130 people," said Sherwood. "During this whole trial, I guess no one did the reading assignment, and she kind of recognized that, no one's answering their questions. She was like, so, 'Okay, anybody want to talk about the lacrosse case?' "

Another professor, Peter Wood, a member of the Group of 88, teaches Native American history at Duke. Based on the reviews Wood had received from previous students on the website ratemyprofessor.com, his class was popular. "The comment was something along the lines of you will be able to get by as long as you preach every liberal view in class," Matt Zash said.

It seemed Wood was also the type of professor who was not fond of the idea of teaching every day class was scheduled to meet. "On Friday, all he did was put in a movie that you can get at the school library, instead of lecturing," Zash said. "He never quizzed us on it. He never tested us on it."

However, Wood's seemingly lackadaisical teaching style would shift when lacrosse players who enrolled in the class explained they would have to miss a Friday session because they would be traveling to play in Virginia. "He was very upset about the fact that we weren't taking our studies seriously. That we would miss one of his classes for a game," recalls Zash.

It seemed the players did not realize how much they angered their tenured professor.

When it came time for Wood's students to fill out the anonymous teacher evaluations, a response from one of his sixty-five students in this same Native American history class caught his attention. It read: "I wish all the Indians had died; then we wouldn't have to study them."

Some may call it a hunch, but Wood made it clear he was convinced that this comment came from a lacrosse player. After all, there were ten of them enrolled in his class that semester. It didn't matter that the evaluations were anonymous.

Despite the fact that the fallout from the ad would spawn letters from parents, draw thousands of blog posts and ultimately produce at least one lawsuit, Duke's leadership seemed oblivious or, worse, uncaring. "It didn't catch a whole lot of attention," said John Burness, Duke's senior vice president for public affairs and government relations. "It was an ad, it had its one day. Nobody paid any attention to that ever. I didn't see it for three days. I was so busy doing my own stuff."

Burness also said Duke would do nothing to prevent its faculty from making ill-timed statements, no matter how troubling. According to Burness, statements such as this made by the faculty happen often, and it is not the duty of Duke's administration to hinder their expression in any way.

Apparently, Burness has not read the first paragraph of Chapter 6 of the Duke Faculty Handbook. Under the title "Faculty Responsibilities with Respect to Students," it states, "students are fellow members of the university community, deserving of respect and consideration in their dealings with the faculty." Through the actions taken against the professors in this case—or lack of action—Duke made clear that professors who violate their very own faculty code of conduct do not deserve condemnation.

For this group of professors, images continued to change as the story progressed. Suddenly, the intended impact of this simple ad to draw people to their political opinions—like so many other aspects of this case—had boomeranged. This change was clear just in the subtlety of the phrasing used to describe them. The term used to describe them, "Group of 88," had shifted by midsummer; they became known as the "Gang of 88."

CHAPTER THIRTEEN

AGENDAS ALL AROUND

A popular theme in the news media after the stripper party at 610 was that the lacrosse team was a pack of wolves who roamed Duke's campus, leaving a wake of doom and destruction. And they were all the rage. In fact, several reporters described the lacrosse players as "the most popular guys on campus." If that were true—and some doubt that it was—it was hard to imagine that so many people could think the worst about them so quickly. But they did.

The immediate backlash facing the team was threefold. It came equally from their peers, the Duke faculty, and the surrounding Durham community. Without question, nearly everyone believed these forty-seven lacrosse players were capable of the most heinous of crimes.

"It's pretty tough to be one of fifty people who believe in one truth," Coach Mike Pressler would say, "when fifty million people believe something else."

Staying off Duke's campus and avoiding the protests in front of 610 did not give the players an escape from those who instantly assumed their guilt. New websites popped up daily, some focusing on the players individually. Devon Sherwood was especially targeted, being the only African-American on the team.

"There were comments about how I'm letting down my forefathers, basically reversing what we were striving for, blaming everything on me," Sherwood recalled months later. "A bunch of them wrote that 'this is your aunt, this is your mother that was raped.' They wrote that if I did know this happened, I should rot and burn in hell."

• • •

Every faction within the community had an opinion about the events that had allegedly transpired and they wanted the lacrosse players—and the rest of the world—to hear it. This was the time to voice their opinions, and to voice them loudly. The demonstrations were numerous.

It began with an all-night candlelight vigil on Saturday, March 25.

"More than 250 protestors attended two demonstrations Saturday night and Sunday morning in front of the residence where three members of the men's lacrosse team allegedly raped a local woman," reported the *Chronicle*. "The demonstration was intended to be both a 'wake-up call' to raise awareness about sexual assault and a sign of support for the alleged victims."

As the flames from the protesters' candles burned out, and the rising sun brought a new day, the vigil would continue with the infamous "pot-bangers."

They came wielding pots and pans and anything else made of tin or metal that would make plenty of noise. Some were armed with megaphones, chanting phrases like, "You can't run, you can't hide." Others held signs with slogans reading: "Get a Conscience, Not a Lawyer."

The largest banner read: "Give Them Equal Measure. CASTRATE!"

A circle of protesters posted in front of 610, beating on drums like a school marching band. They filled the air with an uptempo beat while repeating one single phrase: "We say no more."

These "pot-bangers" ranged from black to white, young to old, affluent to poor, Duke student to Durham resident, even including some faculty members. "Those are the Trinity Park folks," Pressler described them. "The liberal side of Durham lives over there." They did not discriminate against anyone who had something to say.

Lacrosse player William Wolcott did not live at 610, but he still lived close enough to feel the wrath of the pot-bangers. When there was no response at 610, they made their way to his front door instead; they knew a lacrosse teammate lived nearby.

"K. J. Sauer [another Duke player] and I lived around the corner from 610," Wolcott said. "We were sitting in our house and K.J. comes running into my room. He's scared and he's frightened. There's a mob outside our house, banging pots and pans. We went to the front and there were people banging on our windows, people screaming, 'Time to confess.' I like to think that I've faced some pretty scary things; going one on one with Reade Seligmann in practice—he's a hell of a player—is a daunting task, but that was the most scared I've been in my whole life. We had to sneak out the back door."

The pot-bangers' outrage was impossible to ignore. "The community consequences for this action, I guarantee, will range far beyond the legal consequences you will face." These words thundered through a megaphone, screamed by one of the passionate pot-bangers.

Preachers from the community positioned themselves in front of 610 in crisp white suits, preaching to all who would listen. They were determined to find justice for their poor "sister" who they believed had been beaten, raped, and sodomized by this team of brutish white men.

Next came the "wanted" poster and its more appalling offspring—the "vigilante" poster.

The original "wanted" poster came from the Durham Police Department CrimeStoppers program. Although DPD claims CrimeStoppers is independently managed, there is a DPD liaison, Corporal David Addison, who is in charge of producing these wanted posters. His original version displayed text only. It read:

> On Monday, March 13, 2006 about 11:00pm, the Duke University Lacrosse Team solicited a local escort service for entertainment. The victim was paid to dance at the residence located at 610 Buchanan. The Duke Lacrosse Team was hosting a party at the residence. The victim was sodomized, raped, assaulted and robbed. This horrific crime sent shock waves throughout our community.

> Durham Police needs your assistance in solving this case. We are asking anyone who has any information related to this case, please contact Inv. Himan.
>
> Information can also be provided anonymously through Durham CrimeStoppers. (Please use an anonymous email account.) Durham CrimeStoppers will pay *cash* for any information which leads to an arrest in this case.

On March 29, another poster was distributed. This one had pictures. With the headline PLEASE COME FORWARD, this "vigilante" poster displayed headshots of forty-three of the forty-six white lacrosse players, with their names printed below the photos. All forty-six were not displayed only because the pictures were pulled from Duke's website before every white player's photo could be retrieved, a fact explained on the bottom of the poster.

This protestor-produced vigilante poster quoted Addison's previous comment to ABC News: "We're not saying that all 46 were involved. But we do know that some of the players inside that house on that evening knew what transpired and we need them to come forward."

As if one wanted poster was not condemning enough for the players, two of them made an obvious statement.

The New Black Panthers also planned a trip to Duke; it seemed they didn't want to miss out on the action. They marched through campus on May 1, "Dressed in fatigues, combat boots and flak jackets—some sporting knives on their belts," as described in the *Raleigh News & Observer.* They were outfitted to fight another battle in their war against racial injustice, even coming with a set of eight "demands" for "justice." Duke would do very little to stand in their way.

Sue Pressler remembers her exact reaction when she heard of this planned demonstration: "The New Black Panthers come to town and you have Duke saying, 'We're going to let them walk through campus quietly,' even when their intentions were clear. The *News & Observer* that day reported that the Panthers said, 'We are conducting an independent investigation, and we intend to enter the campus and interview lacrosse players. We seek to ensure an adequate, strong, and vigorous prosecution.' How scary is that? How could these kids be safe, in class and on campus? It tells you how out of control the thinking was, how crazy the moment was."

Then there were the emails and anonymous threats. The emails to players were often thoughtless and cruel and, in some cases, threatening. The players weren't the only ones targeted. Mike Pressler would become a mark, as well.

Caught in the middle of this whirlwind, Pressler tried to stand strong. His head was spinning as everything he had built unraveled before his eyes. The one thing he still had was his family. That was the glue that held him together.

On March 27, 2006, at 1:59 P.M., a young African-American student from Duke sent Pressler two emails that nearly sent him spiraling out of control. The first message that appeared made it clear to Pressler that this student was one of the fifty million who assumed his lacrosse players were guilty. It read:

> RE: SOME THINGS ARE MORE IMPORTANT THAN WINNING A FEW GAMES. END THE SEASON UNTIL THE ALLEGED RAPISTS ARE FOUND! YOU'LL BE A MUCH BETTER COACH FOR IT.

Although this message made a bold statement, it was the next email, which Pressler received just two minutes later from this same student, that would absolutely infuriate him. Only six words were in the subject line, but those six words shot rage through every bone in Pressler's body:

> RE: WHAT IF JANET LYNN WERE NEXT???

As any father of a teenage daughter could imagine, this crossed a line that far exceeded what Pressler was prepared to handle.

The sender's name was Chauncey Nartey. He was only a junior at Duke and had developed a reputation for being a vocal African-American activist on campus.

"I turned the email over to my attorney and he said you could have him arrested," Pressler said. "We chose not to do that. We chose to report it to the dean of students, Larry Moneta, and have him deal with it."

Pressler's outrage only intensified when he learned how the Duke administration dealt with Nartey. "This is what they did," said Pressler. "They said, 'Chauncey, don't do it again. Okay? And you should write the coach an apology.' "

That was it. Nothing more than a mere slap on the wrist.

Unbeknownst to Pressler at the time, the exposure of another email from one of his own players would be treated very differently by that same Duke administration. This player would be immediately suspended for the distasteful content of his email, and it would ultimately end Pressler's coaching career at Duke. That player was Ryan McFadyen. "Look at the standard, a black junior threatens my daughter and he gets a slap on the wrist. A white lacrosse player, Ryan McFadyen, threatens nobody by name and writes an email that is a parody of *American Psycho,* and he gets suspended indefinitely."

The double standard became blazingly apparent.

When Pressler handed the Nartey emails to Duke, the university made sure to fill out a police report detailing the coach's concern. Still, no action was taken against Nartey. In fact, when President Brodhead appointed a committee, the Campus Cultural Initiative, to study the "culture" at Duke in the wake of the lacrosse case, among those selected to the committee was . . . Nartey.

To his credit, Nartey realized the error of his ways . . . two months later. He contacted Pressler again, this time mailing a letter directly to Pressler's home address. This was a letter of apology. Although Nartey's repentant attempt spilled over onto two pages, no sentence in this letter matched the effect of those six words he sent to Pressler shortly after the rape allegations became public.

Nartey's letter to Pressler seemed sincere, but excerpts from his six lengthy paragraphs can summarize his thoughts in a condensed version. "I wholeheartedly apologize for referencing your daughter" in the "ostensibly threatening email" to "a family that did not deserve such treatment." He tried to explain his intentions. "I simply wanted you to perhaps make the connection between how the families of the alleged victim might feel, especially when it appears as though the ALLEGED perpetrators were so insensitive as to continue forward with activities as though a national scandal were not occurring underneath their noses," he wrote.

And, as any true apology letter should conclude, Nartey made sure to suck up to the former coach, commenting on his character. He wrote, "From the moment you assumed your position until the day of your resignation, you personified leadership and helped elevate the lacrosse team to a position among the elite."

When asked in an interview for this book to clarify his actions, Nartey was less than enthusiastic, even threatening a lawsuit if his words were mischaracterized. Before refusing further comment, he did explain why he believed his emails should not have been considered "a threat." "The email I sent—I sent two—I sent them from my Duke email address," Nartey said, explaining his twisted logic. "I sent them with my name attached. It wasn't like any anonymous thing. I knew I was going to be attached to it, so it wasn't any sort of threat."

Nartey also admitted that it was "a mistake" to bring Pressler's daughter into the mix "just because I didn't think it would be so heavily misconstrued." He went on say, "It was a stupid thing to mention his daughter, in retrospect, but at the time I thought if somebody can't see why it's inappropriate to move forward with athletics in this sort of situation then perhaps that parallel could be drawn by incorporating somebody near and dear to him. And again, foolish, but the rationale was that you can draw the parallel."

Sincere or not, it seemed even the most radical among the activists were beginning to realize the backlash aimed at the Duke lacrosse team and their coach might have been unjustified.

How much did this event divide Duke? John Burness, Duke's vice president, told a story of one student he encountered during the tumultuous days following the rape allegations.

"I talked to an African-American kid earlier this year and I asked her what her life has been like," Burness said. "This was a kid from New York. Her parents had no money. When she came down to look at Duke, she applied and was admitted. When she came down, she and her mother came down on a bus for fourteen hours or whatever the bus ride was, attended that day, and then turned around and went back on the bus because they didn't have enough money to stay down. She gets in, she gets her financial aid, she does study abroad, she's taking advantage of this place exactly the way you'd want to do. She only had positive things to say about this place.

"And I said to her, 'What about last spring [2006]?' There was a long pause and she said, 'You know, we all had to take a side. I never felt at any time in my time at Duke that I was being discriminated against, all I saw was the positive, and then last spring.' And she was one of those who started talking about discrimination because folks had to take a side. That's what happens in white-heat environments like that. The mood on this campus, the ambiguity, the people feeling threatened, all that stuff was for many people incredibly real."

The frenzy was so out of control everyone, even people without an opinion of their own, felt pressured to pick a side.

North Carolina Central University, a historically African-American college in Durham, was pulled into the fray when reports surfaced that Crystal attended school there. While the case reverberated through Duke's Gothic halls, raising questions about divisions in race and class, NCCU chancellor James Ammons also understood the seriousness of the situation. Ammons, along with Durham Mayor Bill Bell and several of the city's African-American leaders, met with Duke President Richard Brodhead on Thursday, March 30, 2006, to discuss the case.

"I guess one of the best ways to describe this is we have the potential for a perfect storm," Ammons told Fox News. "You have all of these issues that we're going to have to discuss. He [Brodhead] wanted to feel the pulse of the community and he wanted our help in sharing information and our thoughts to help Duke deal with this situation."

Attorney Joe Cheshire credited Ammons, who was named Florida A&M University's tenth president on February 1, 2007, as a calming influence in the Duke case. "The guy that probably made the most impassioned plea for sanity and reason was Chancellor Ammons," Cheshire said. "He's the guy who first used words like, 'Don't rush to judgment . . . the presumption of innocence' and all these kind of things. While Brodhead and his crew were just acting like those were dirty words and this was a done deal."

Not everyone at NCCU was as reserved as Ammons. Law Professor Irving Joyner, whom the NAACP designated as "case monitor" on April 19, 2006, was repeatedly quoted by local and national media. Joyner welcomed it when the case shifted to state Attorney General Roy Cooper after Nifong asked to be relieved while he faced charges from the North Carolina Bar Association.

"I think people may be surprised," Joyner told the *Washington Post.* "They are not going to bow to public sentiment."

Father Joe Vetter, sixty, Duke's Catholic chaplain, walked down from the altar and stood in the center aisle between the pews and began his homily to parishioners on Sunday, March 26, 2006. As he referred to the day's Scripture readings, Father Vetter commented on how people, including himself, had become "desensitized" due to cultural trends. "Things that were really shocking to me not very long ago, I find kind of normal now," the bespectacled and balding Vetter said.

It wasn't a normal Sunday morning at 610.

Father Vetter, who lives in a townhouse a few blocks from North Buchanan Boulevard, drove past 610 to White Auditorium on Duke's East Campus for 11:00 A.M. Mass. There was a large crowd in front of the house—it was the infamous Sunday morning vigil, where pot-bangers and protesters carried "castrate" and "measure for measure" banners. Six minutes into his sermon, Father Vetter mentioned the lacrosse case, possibly becoming the first respected authority on the Duke campus to publicly share his opinion on the situation. The lacrosse team's home game against Georgetown a day earlier had been canceled, and the story had begun to take on a dangerous, twisted life of its own.

"I always try to talk about a current topic and how it relates to the Scripture readings, and everyone was talking about the lacrosse situation—it was in the newspaper and on the news," Father Vetter said nearly a year later. "I have been concerned with the rumor that several Duke lacrosse parents have been upset about what I said, but they are not talking with me about it directly, other than the few parents I either talked with or heard from after Mass."

Father Vetter said in his homily that "we don't fully yet know what happened, and no one is guilty—everybody is innocent until they're proven guilty—but it seems pretty apparent something was going on there that was pretty bad the other night." He continued, "Apparently something happened the other night where it really got out of control. At least the person claims that she was raped, that she was beaten, that she had racial slurs used against her. And if all that's true, and if the people that were involved are convicted, then some young people are going to jail and pay some really serious penalties for those crimes. That's really tragic, because I am sure that none of those people involved in that incident had any idea that something like that was going to happen. Nobody would set that up. Nobody wanted that to turn bad—but it did."

Father Vetter continued his homily and cited other examples of how people had become desensitized. While he did not mention the lacrosse case again, his comments directed at the team offended Bob and Donna Wellington—their son, Rob, who attended that Mass with them, was a sophomore midfielder on the team. Bob Wellington approached Father Vetter following Mass and reminded him of the presumption of innocence and said part of a priest's job was to minister to Catholic players on the team.

"His basic assumption was, of course, that the worst-case scenario had happened, and that these boys are prone to this sort of behavior anyway," Donna Wellington said. "A casual listener might have concluded that he had more facts than even the DA at that point. It was very humiliating for my son, who was sitting next to me. We were absolutely furious. My husband was fuming . . . he [Father Vetter] was already condemning these boys without knowing any of the facts, and my husband told him that he would deeply regret this when the real facts did get revealed."

Father Vetter said he heard from two or three other lacrosse parents, including Duke Coach John Danowski, within a couple of days following Mass and said the conversations were cordial. Father Vetter said he understood their concerns, but believed his homily message was misunderstood. His hope was to get "young people to understand their decisions to drink and party can carry serious consequences if not careful."

Donna Wellington wasn't in a forgiving mood.

"If a priest is going to rush to judgment, where can anyone go for support and counsel about surviving the inevitable barrage of false accusations, and finding spiritual strength and solace in God's eventual justice and truth?" she said. "I didn't know what to say to him other than to point out that this was a man with obvious human frailties and prejudices, and that he was very misguided."

No Duke athletic team offered a stronger show of solidarity with the men's lacrosse team than members of the school's women's team. The Blue Devils wore sweatbands with the numbers of the indicted players in their NCAA semifinal game against Northwestern on May 26, 2006.

Coach Kerstin Kimel, whose office was at the opposite end of the hall from that of Coach Mike Pressler in the Murray Building, actively supported her players' choice to show their support despite media criticism.

The women also had Pressler speak to the team a month after his forced resignation.

"I think Mike has shown incredible restraint, personal strength, and fortitude to not allow his emotions override good judgment," said Kimel, voted the 2006 ACC Coach of the Year after she led her team to a school-record eighteen wins and the third trip to the NCAA Final Four in school history—the Blue Devils lost 11–10 in double overtime to Northwestern.

"To me, it's unbelievable," Kimel said. "Of all the adults who have been caught up in this tangled web, the person who was most affected was Mike. But Mike has shown just an incredible ability to deal and stay level-headed and be smart and careful of what he said, unlike a lot of other adults who have not been very careful about what they've said and therefore have opened themselves up to be target of criticism or potential liability."

Kimel also was one of the friends and athletic department officials who hosted an August 2006 shindig for Pressler before he left for Bryant University in Rhode Island, held at Duke's University Club. Many in attendance wore Bryant Bulldog T-shirts that were purchased by Pressler's coaching replacement at Duke, John Danowski. Kimel said Pressler—reluctantly—gave a speech. But it demonstrated his resolve to remain firmly but quietly behind his players.

"I don't know if I could have done that if the roles had been reversed—I really, really don't know," Kimel said. "But the anger and the hurt—the hurt that is there—is so profound. I understand. You saw it every day here in these offices."

Kimel also had harsh words for administrators and faculty who refused to support the men's program as scandal engulfed it, saying, "There was not a whole lot of courage displayed during this time. The thing that surprised me the most was how unprofessional the adults on this campus were, particularly faculty. The thing to me that was so hypocritical about all of it, you have these left-leaning faculty and they champion left-leaning causes and are, a lot of times, sticking up for people who are wrongly accused. They protest against the death penalty and all this stuff—injustice. And it was happening and unfolding right before their eyes and they didn't do anything about it.

"There are other people, and they are not sorry. I think they're a disgrace. I can't believe they call themselves or consider themselves educators. I am an educator. I would never treat . . . they are an educator and to them educating is their research and their focus. It's not the kids. For us, our whole mantra is we're in the kids business. We're here to educate them, prepare them for the real world. We are not on the same page that way. They don't really embrace that as part of what their responsibility is as an educator."

The *Chronicle* recounted what the campus climate was like during the month after the charges became public:

> Surrounded on the quad in the middle of Duke's West Campus, lacrosse player [Bo Carrington] wanted to convince protestors that neither he nor any of his teammates were rapists. But Carrington, a sophomore, couldn't muster a word.
>
> "You know what happened that night!" shouted one member of the crowd. "Why aren't you saying anything?" . . . During those weeks in early April, Carrington and his teammates encountered pictures of themselves plastered around campus like WANTED posters. Posters that, in their minds, conveyed a predetermined judgment: guilty.

The players had had enough. How much longer were they expected to remain in hiding, to take the lashings from fellow students, their professors, and community members? Action needed to be taken to combat the growing public opinion that they were undoubtedly guilty. After the forfeiture of the Georgetown game, with hopes of saving the remainder of their season, Pressler demanded a meeting with the one man he thought would be able to help: President Brodhead.

Unbelievably, a crisis was ripping his campus apart, and Brodhead had yet to meet with the very people who sat at its epicenter. As Pressler and the captains were preparing to walk across campus to meet with Brodhead, the athletic director called, telling Pressler he was not invited to join the players at the meeting. Stunned, he sent his four captains to meet Brodhead without him.

Only Brodhead, his senior staff, and the four captains were privy to the information discussed at this meeting. Zash explains the reason for the meeting months later. "We wanted to meet with him to look us in the eyes," he said. "We wanted to reassure him that nothing happened."

And that is exactly what they did. Although they repeatedly denied the allegations to Brodhead face to face, the captains were not asking him to pardon them for their irresponsible behavior "but to reserve judgment," Zash said.

"I remember him saying at some point in the meeting something along the lines of, 'I hope for all of our sakes you guys are telling the truth,' " recalled Dan Flannery. "But he never specifically said, 'I believe your story.' "

The captains offered more than their apologies to Brodhead that morning. They knew that until the DNA results came back, the cloud hanging over them would not pass. To prove they understood the seriousness of the allegations and the distress it brought to the university and the community, they offered to voluntarily suspend further competitive play until the DNA results were revealed. In their minds, the DNA would provide the tangible evidence they needed to prove their innocence. Brodhead graciously accepted their offer and announced it in a press release.

However, despite Brodhead's emotional, and seemingly sincere, responses in the meeting, his statements in a press conference hours later would prove Flannery was right. He did not believe their story. In what Brodhead called "a slight modification" to the offer made by the captains, he said, "I have decided that future games should be suspended *until there is a clearer resolution of the legal situation.*"

The minor change Brodhead was referring to was not minor at all. It made it clear that in his mind, the DNA results would not prove anything.

They would not be the deciding factor for the future of the lacrosse team as the captains had hoped. "No match" would not exonerate anyone.

Zash describes Brodhead's comments as "very vague in wording that basically left the ball in their court. It was just another thing that played into their hands."

Though his job was to defend Brodhead, Vice President John Burness admitted several months later that he was not sure whether the university president ever *really* believed the lacrosse players. Brodhead, Burness said repeatedly, was in a tough spot, trying to react to "information he knew," and the statements of the lacrosse players were not placed by the president in the "fact" category.

Nifong, on the other hand, was given the highest credibility by Brodhead. The result: The president chose to believe a district attorney he barely knew over student athletes at his own university—and he made every decision accordingly.

"When somebody else [like the district attorney] is strong, it gives you a reason to believe that maybe they have a reason they're that strong," Burness said in an interview for this book. "You say to yourself, I'm looking back at it, too, I'm saying to myself you have the district attorney of this county, who was a reasonably well-respected guy, who was not known as being a wild man. He didn't, that wasn't his reputation, as being a pretty thoughtful hard-nosed guy. He was so far out there in the things he was saying about the certainty that a rape had occurred and the knowledge that it had occurred by some of these kids. You have to then say, 'He's just making it up?' I don't think a lot of people were saying that right off the bat.

"Nifong and the police were so incredibly strong in what they were saying," Burness continued. "He [Nifong] hadn't been a whack job throughout his career. He had a fairly good rep in this town . . . The judges thought he was a solid, plodding sort of guy. Nobody had a sense that his integrity was in question."

Through their words and actions, Brodhead and Burness made it clear the integrity of the players *was* in question. They picked a side, choosing to believe Nifong. It would prove to be a horrible choice.

One of the ways the lacrosse team held itself together was by gathering a list of names of those who were targeting them. The list became known as the Grail.

It was the ultimate cathartic exercise for the players. Keeping this running tally of all the people who slandered their names and reputations was their way of saying that one day, when all of this was over, these people would be held accountable. Then, they would be forced, the lacrosse players believed, to ask for some level of forgiveness. But the players need to make sure they remembered who these people were.

Professors, students, activists, public officials, the media; the Grail spared no one.

One player, one of the smartest on the team, was charged with the grave responsibility of keeping this list. His name was Erik Henkelman. He would become the "Keeper of the Grail."

Every time they had practice or a team meeting, each player would be given the chance to report in. After each name was identified, Pressler would look at Henkelman and ask with a smile, "On the Grail?" The keeper would reply without haste, "Got it, Coach."

The first ten to make the list included Alleva, campus activists, several reporters, Gottlieb, and a few pot-bangers. But the name written atop the Grail made it clear who the players felt was the first to betray them: "Dick Brodhead."

Athletes are notorious for making up opponents. However, in this particular case, these were not faux opponents at all. They were very real.

This was the lacrosse team's way of keeping score.

CHAPTER FOURTEEN

The Media

Dan Okrent saw it coming. When Okrent, who served as the *New York Times'* ombudsman until 2005, saw the front page of the *Times* on March 29, 2006, he felt a national story brewing. "It had everything that would excite the right-thinking New York journalist: It was white over black, it was male over female, it was jocks over a nonstudent, it was rich over poor," said Okrent, a longtime player among New York's media elite.

Under the headline "Rape Allegation Against Athletes Is Roiling Duke," the nation's most influential newspaper announced the lacrosse scandal to the world.

The decision by Duke President Richard Brodhead the day before to "suspend" the lacrosse season "until there is a clearer resolution of the legal situation" ensured that the story would leap from the sports pages. Brodhead had been responding to local reporters as he moved quickly to punish the athletes, but by doing so, he "practically invited the *Times* to take up camp at Duke Chapel," one longtime media analyst said. And once the *Times* reserved a spot for this story on A-1, the national media genie was definitely out of the bottle.

That same morning, NBC's *Today* show would open with "France on edge . . . millions of protesters took to the streets closing down the Eiffel Tower. . . . On the sidelines, prestigious Duke University suspends its entire men's lacrosse team amid allegations of a gang rape." Both CNN and Fox News would begin months of daily coverage of the Duke case, and satellite trucks began streaming to the Durham campus. *Newsweek* would devote a cover to the story and, according to Duke Vice President John

Burness, more than one hundred thousand stories would be written mentioning the words Duke, lacrosse, and rape.

The *Times* would also set up shop at Duke, pumping out nearly two dozen stories in the next two weeks—written by reporters from the newspaper's news, sports, education, science, and editorial departments. Okrent, in a speech to the Neiman Fellows at Harvard on April 13, 2006, made it clear that the power of the *New York Times* had turned the lacrosse story into a national event, and that he was a little concerned.

"Had the *Times* not pounded that drum so much in the first several weeks—if they had reported the charges, run the story on A-11, and dropped it—it wouldn't have become a national media story," Okrent said, taking a look at the coverage nearly a year later. "The *Times* put it on the cover of *Newsweek*. The *Times* made it a lead in the evening news broadcasts. In nearly every American newsroom of any size, if you see the *Times* running something as prominently and as repeatedly as they did this story, you say 'This is important.' Then you try to figure out how you can top it, how you can find something the *Times* didn't have. The competitive nature of journalism being what it is, if you're not first, you'd better have something new, something that distinguishes you. But in the twenty-four-hour news cycle, getting something better finishes a distant second behind getting something fast."

As reporters flooded the Duke campus they found more than enough to fill their notebooks. Faculty, students, community activists, even the New Black Panther Party followed reporters to the story, all looking for their fifteen minutes of fame. Protesters banging pots, waving signs emblazoned with "Confess" and calling for the castration of players, chanting, "They must be rapists," and singing spirituals understood that the moment needed them, and they needed the moment.

"It's like these fringe lunatics who were around the campus around Durham, that's who the media went after," said Debbie Krzyzewski Savarino, a Duke fundraiser and the daughter of celebrated basketball coach Mike Krzyzewski. "If you had an intelligent, knowledgeable, calm opinion of the whole situation, you were not to be interviewed. The media looked at those people and said, 'We would like for you to be hysterical, preferably carrying some form of kitchen equipment, yelling, going nutty. If you can do that, then you will be on TV today. But if you would like to say something that's calm, we'll move on to the next person holding a spoon and a pot. Everyone that was on TV was hysterical.

"You hated coming to work," said Savarino, who proudly calls Sue Pressler her close friend. "You hated it. It was awful. There is a love for this school that is . . . you bleed true blue. It's just so deep. I've been this way since I was nine. People hate us because we're good. And you have to sit here and watch all these lies being told about our school, about your athletic program, and all these people are jumping on the bandwagon nationally that Duke is elitist, that we are racists, that we have so much money that we are buying people off and . . . it was awful."

Yes, this was everything a New York reporter loved, and cable news reporters, too.

It would be an obvious low point if there wasn't so much competition. On April 10, 2006, the day it was announced that the DNA samples taken from each of the forty-six lacrosse players had yielded no evidence that any player had raped the alleged victim, CNN's Nancy Grace turned to the equally outrageous Wendy Murphy to engage in a Duke lacrosse hate fest. Murphy, a former prosecutor who runs a Boston-based victims' advocacy group, is a regular on the talking-head circuit, ensuring repeat invitations by making sure to be the most bombastic guest in the mix.

Grace had already let her feelings on the case be well known, calling the players "rapists" in nearly every show in which the lacrosse case was mentioned. On March 31, when she learned that the team had played two games since the night in question, she mentioned this fact on her program and snapped, "I'm so glad they didn't miss a lacrosse game over a little thing like gang rape!"

Later in that same broadcast she raved about the forthcoming DNA evidence and the unquestionable convictions it would surely bring: "The first line of defense is, 'I didn't do it.' The second line of defense is,

'I did it, but it was consensual.' The third line of defense is, 'She's a hooker.' Now, let's just say we get DNA back. They'll immediately claim consensual."

The stage was already set for an attack on the team, and on April 10, Grace opened her show with an announcement of the "No DNA" press conference, but didn't take a breath before offering, "Did the perpetrators use condoms?" The rhetorical question would become part of that night's theme even though defense lawyers had made the point during the press conference that the alleged victim had told police her attackers had not, in fact, worn condoms.

One of her guests that night was Larry Kobilinsky, a forensic scientist. He offered an answer to Grace's question, suggesting, "It's not the latex that we look for. We look for the condom lubricant. Most condoms have some sort of lubrication, and we do have tests for that. Failure to find that would indicate that condoms were not used." He then proposed two other possibilities that might account for the lack of DNA evidence from even one of the alleged attackers. Either they had all undergone vasectomies or they were all sterile.

Grace immediately jumped upon the point, demanding to know if such tests had been run to determine if traces of a lubricant had been found. When she was told that the tests had been conducted and had come back negative, she quickly diverted the line of questioning to a towel that was found outside one of the players' bathrooms, on which DNA matching a player had been detected. Though the towel was found to contain DNA from a player who lived in the home and an unidentified person who was not present at the party, several of Grace's guests—led by Murphy—seized the opportunity to turn the towel into a smoking gun, presented their own speculations as fact, and ironically, pointed the finger of blame at the defense team by accusing them of withholding information.

"The most telling statement is what they didn't do, Nancy," Murphy insisted. "[The defense] didn't just turn over the results. Isn't that interesting, that the only thing they would give us was their characterization of what the report said.

"And I think you absolutely hit the nail on the head when you challenged Dr. Kobilinsky about the significance of the negative findings because I think about 90 percent of rape cases involve no DNA at all, even with the available technology. And frankly, that towel, the towel in the bathroom, the deafening silence from the defense attorneys about what was found on the towel in the bathroom—how do you explain that? And I think Dr. Kobilinsky just didn't tell us an honest answer, frankly, to your question, which is that the reason there was no DNA found in her body is because they finished the act, if I could be polite for a second here—they finished the act outside of her body, on the towel. That's damning evidence!"

Grace went along with this speculation, and as the show progressed, it became increasingly clear that Murphy was the only guest to whom Grace would give free rein to spout her theories. As Penny Douglass Furr, a criminal defense attorney, spoke up to remind the panel that the crimes were only still alleged at this point, the following exchange about the towel took place.

Furr: Well, Nancy, to me, it says they do live there. I mean, their DNA will be in the towel, all over the bathroom and all over the house. My concern is, if this woman did make this up, she's ruined a lot of lives, and there needs to be some—

Grace: I'm asking you about the towel.

Furr:—type of punishment for her.

Grace: Before we start preaching . . .

Furr: The towel? They live there. They live there. They're going to—

Grace: Oh, okay.

Furr:—have their DNA on the towel, in the bathroom, in the bedroom. That is their bedroom.

Grace: You don't think it's pretty—a little bit of a coinky-dink—a coincidence—that her torn-off nails are there? She says that's where she was attacked. And then you've got a towel with possible ejaculate in it. That doesn't, like, strike you as disturbing?

Grace's accusations of "preaching" were hurled later in the program at another guest, defense attorney Lauren Lake, who attempted to voice a similar reminder that the players were only suspected and not convicted—or even charged, at this point—with the crime.

Lake: Nancy, what's killing me right now we just had the prosecution bandwagon raring up and somebody is already saying these guys are rapists. No, what they are, are alleged rapists.

And you better believe I'd be the first one if they raped this young girl like, well, be done with you, go ahead and go. But we know right now that they are alleged rapists, and we should treat it as such.

Grace: Okay. All right. Thank you for the sermon, Lauren. I've got a question for you.

Lake: It's not a sermon.

Grace: I have a question about the evidence. Can we try to get back to the evidence?

Lake: I was just talking about DNA.

Grace was clearly seeking to establish unquestionable guilt regarding the players' actions while she continually badgered her dissenting guests. Meanwhile, Grace allowed Murphy uninterrupted, incendiary monologues that painted wild speculation as truth and laid out imagined scenarios as if they were documented fact.

"I mean, look, it's the fact that they take an awful long time for the defense to come out and say anything meaningful," Murphy said. "And the silence is deafening in terms of why they didn't come forward right away and say, 'Look, we're all innocent.' What they did was clam up and say, 'Let's stick together so we can get away with this.'

"Look, I think the real key here is that these guys, like so many rapists—and I'm going to say it because, at this point, she's entitled to the respect that she is a crime victim. These guys watch *CSI*, and they know it's a really bad idea to ejaculate on or in the victim. And maybe what she said, which makes her particularly credible, is, These guys didn't ejaculate on or inside of my body, which means she deserves extra credibility because no one's suggesting that she lied about whether there would be DNA found on her person.

"And Nancy, look, you know, why? Why do we live in a culture people are so willing to assume women are masochist enough to not only do all the things you describe but strangle themselves and tear their own vaginas to make, what, a false claim look good? We would let women be perceived as hysterical masochists rather than believe that if it walks like a duck and quacks like a duck, it's a duck? Can we use a little bit of common sense here?

"Forget respect and disrespect for a minute! How about common sense and decency? A DA who was not born yesterday has said, after two weeks of investigation, I believe this woman was brutally raped and attacked. And now, because of DNA—which never tells the whole story, ever—somehow, we're going to just abandon the case and celebrate the boys as, you know, having had a bad night?"

Common sense? Unfortunately, no one on the show forced Murphy to use just that. Every significant "fact" she shared that night was completely incorrect.

By the end of spring 2006, Grace had established a pattern of provocative and unsubstantiated statements regarding this case. She insisted that the accuser had never changed her story, despite police records to the contrary. She misunderstood and misrepresented the details of the case, at one point accounting for the lack of witnesses by explaining, "You've got to keep into account that a lot of the guys were probably downstairs." Several critics would later point out that the Buchanan street house is only one story.

On June 9, Grace had an especially spiteful rant at the very beginning of her show. One guest, Kevin Miller, a reporter with WPTF radio in the Durham area, pointed out that public opinion on the case was shifting, noting that "on the street in Durham, or in North Carolina, wherever, there's a high degree of skepticism, not only there within the community, but throughout it, everybody is wondering what Mike Nifong has. People are talking about a silver bullet. The bottom line is, I've talked to defense sources, I've talked to everybody. Nobody knows what he has and it's starting to get very troubling on why this case is continuing. They seem to answer everything—these recent court documents, Nancy, pretty much answer all of the allegations and barring anything else, reasonable doubt is there."

Grace pounced, seething: "Well, I'm glad you have already decided the outcome of the case, based on all of the defense filings. Why don't we just all move to Nazi Germany, where we don't have a justice system and a jury of one's peers? What about it, Joe Lawless? Why can you imagine would the defense put these allegations into court documents? It sounds like a little bit of trial by ambush."

As the Duke case progressed and the tide of undeniable facts flooded the scene, Grace quietly dropped the subject, no longer featured Murphy on her program, and maintained a growing silence and lack of interest in the matter.

Ruth Sheehan is no Nancy Grace. For that, the *Raleigh News & Observer* is grateful. Sheehan, a twice-a-week columnist for the region's largest daily, was among the first to opine on the story.

"When the story initially broke, everyone had a reaction to it," Sheehan recalled in an interview eleven months later. "I think on Saturday [March 25] we had the interview with the alleged victim. It was on Sunday I called into the office. I already had a column in the can because I run on Mondays. But I called in about this story and they told me that there was another story with Nifong talking about how there was this wall of silence. That's when I decided on that Sunday to write my first column about the case. I try to write off the news as often as possible, especially when there's something big going on that people are really talking about. So I said I am going to try to put together a column for tomorrow and send it in. I have to write a column about what people are talking about. And everybody was talking about it. It was so outrageous, the stuff that was in the paper. Her story, Nifong's recounting of it. Oh, my God. It was just like . . . you couldn't even believe it."

Under the headline "Team's Silence Is Sickening," Sheehan excoriated the lacrosse team for failing to cooperate with police—unaware that they had already done just that.

"Members of the Duke men's lacrosse team: You know," Sheehan wrote. "We know you know. Whatever happened in the bathroom at the stripper party gone terribly, terribly bad, you know who was involved. Every one of you does. And one of you needs to come forward and tell the police. Do not be afraid of retribution on the team. Do not be persuaded that somehow this 'happened' to one or more 'good guys.' If what the strippers say is true—that one of them was raped, sodomized, beaten and strangled—the guys responsible are not 'good.' "

Sheehan continued: "I can see the team going down this path, justifying its silence. And it makes me sick . . . I don't know what happened in that house, and in that bathroom, over in Durham. Ultimately, that will be a matter for the court system to decide. But who was in that room is something the police need to know. Now. They shouldn't have to wait for 46 DNA samples to be returned. Every member of the men's lacrosse team knows who was involved, whether it was gang rape or not. Until the team members come forward with that information, forfeiting games isn't enough. Shut down the team."

As she wrote, Sheehan made clear that in her mind the stories bubbling up from Nifong's office and the Durham Police Department were true. She was not alone.

"Back during that period, no one was telling us that the players had been cooperative," she said in a January 2007 interview. "I know now that that was not true. If I had known that then, I would have never written what I did. I would have thought what is Nifong talking about? That's not a wall of silence then. How is that a wall of silence?

"When I first wrote that column, hundreds and hundreds and hundreds of emails from people who thought the same way flooded my mailbox. I laugh now. Please understand I am only laughing at myself because the tide has definitely turned. I did have a conversation with [Duke Vice President] John Burness about the university's role in the case at some point and asked why when all of this was coming out that they [the university] didn't help us understand the truth, why they didn't spin the other side to us. They could have helped us, that's for sure. One thing he did say to me at that time, which is a convenient excuse but also true, was that they also have to be really careful how they handle student information. That caution, I think, made things worse."

A few days later, Sheehan would write about the lacrosse team's history of "out-of-control" behavior, a theme that was regularly being struck by Burness in off-the-record conversations with reporters. At the end of that column, Sheehan wrote that Burness had told her that "upholding Duke's standard" for player behavior was Pressler's responsibility.

"So dump him," she wrote, two days before Duke did just that. At the time she was among the first to suggest in print that the coach be fired.

As the case dragged on, Sheehan would write another half dozen columns about the case. Finally, on New Year's Day 2007, Sheehan reached the point where her view on the case had taken a complete turn.

"Every time I think the Duke lacrosse case cannot get any more excruciating to watch—it does," Sheehan wrote in her column. "There was a moment of hope right before Christmas, when we got word that Durham District Attorney Mike Nifong was dropping charges. Finally! I thought. Nifong has come to his senses and is putting us all out of our misery—from the three men charged in the alleged sexual assault of a dancer at their stripper party to the alleged victim herself.

"But as it turned out, Nifong dropped only one of the charges in the case—rape—leaving the sexual assault and kidnapping charges to stand. These are charges, like rape, that could put the men behind bars for life. Nifong's explanation for dropping the rape charge only added to the excruciation factor: The accuser said she now cannot remember whether a penis was involved in the alleged attack.

"I cringe just typing the words. As the victim of a date rape more than twenty years ago myself, I can attest that there are some details you can train your mind to glance over. Whether a penis was involved is a detail one is unlikely to forget."

Sheehan wondered: "What kind of dimwitted fools does Nifong believe us, and the potential jurors, to be? I ask this, of course, from some experience. I was one of the hopelessly naive who fell—hard—for Nifong's original depiction of the case."

At that point, Sheehan accomplished another major first: she was among the few journalists who put in writing what everyone was then saying—I was wrong. Further, Sheehan told her readers she was sorry for not having been more critical of Nifong's version of events.

"My thoughts on this case have evolved over time as many of our readers have," Sheehan said. "And I've written about that. I've tried to be as honest about that as possible. I am not sorry I wrote about it, but, yeah, I was suckered. I bought into his take of the case from the beginning. I also feel like I should have known better. I should have understood a prosecutor can be suspect and this one certainly has been.

"I am in a position to acknowledge my mistake because I am in an ongoing conversation with readers here. This is the community where I live. This is our little world, and it's a wonderful one. So, at times I've screwed some things up . . . I've had a couple times where I've had to apologize for things in my column, and that's really hard. But that's what you have to do. Because that's what you do if you were in a conversation with your loved one, or your friend, your neighbor."

Sheehan's early work drew the attention of another group that played an integral role in this story's development and its eventual outcome. Bloggers, a twenty-first-century new-media power, took to the Duke lacrosse case early, often, and with a vengeance.

The power of the blogger is slowly being acknowledged by the mainstream media. Their influence, on rare occasions, has actually outreached that of the media. One of the most notable examples of this is the now-infamous National Guard letter disparaging George W. Bush's service during the 1970s. Dan Rather broke the story on CBS News, hailing it as a major scandal that was sure to turn the tide of the 2004 election against Bush. Bloggers quickly picked up the story and soon proved that the documents were, in fact, forgeries.

Bloggers were likewise responsible for exposing the untrue allegations, reported by CNN chief news executive Eason Jordan, that the U.S. military was killing journalists in the Middle East. The blogging efforts brought the situation into the national spotlight and the resulting outcry against such journalistic misconduct eventually caused Jordan to resign.

As the *New York Times* and Nancy Grace proved, there weren't many highlights for those analyzing the media's performance in coverage of the Duke lacrosse team case. But as the story played out, two did become apparent: the work of several bloggers and the consistent effort of the smallest newspaper on the beat—the student-run *Duke Chronicle.*

Many news outlets, recognizing the online trend, were beginning to start developing blogs of their own on their official websites. Sheehan recalled how the timing of the Duke story coincided with this upswing of interest: "The story broke right when we were getting our blogs off the ground. Newspapers are trying in their own way to be a more significant presence with up-to-the-minute news online. We just reorganized our entire newsroom to do this."

Unfortunately, some bloggers used the anonymity offered by their medium to make outrageous claims and vitriolic accusations. Sheehan witnessed the trend firsthand. "When we first started really communicating more by email," she said, "a lot, especially in the South, of the niceties of person-to-person conversation kind of flew out the window because people can just blast you by email. Even today people are stunned when I respond and I am like a nice person and say, thanks for your note. Then they often reply back, 'Oh, my God, I am so sorry.' I think the blogosphere, especially these guys, I don't know if it's a test of their manhood, but the more extreme, the more they can challenge the people who they think are the bad guys in this, the better. And there's plenty of bad guys, so there's plenty of people to go after. They try to get as far out there on that as they can; I think it increases their blog traffic.

"I will be curious to see what happens to some of these guys," she continued. "I am always very tempted to reply back to some of them and ask what exactly are you going to do in two months when the criminal charges are resolved? When we put the whole thing to bed? Whenever, however many months it is. Or, I guess, eventually when the civil cases are resolved, they will be able to eke some more out of that. K. C. Johnson is the most even-handed of them. And he actually has done a little bit of reporting of his own. I think that is one value of the blogosphere. There are times they've been embedded in all the attacks, there are some times they actually break some news."

K. C. Johnson, a history professor at Brooklyn College in New York, is, indeed, a notable exception. Few would expect this Matthew Broderick lookalike, bow-tie-wearing academic, living five hundred miles away from Durham, to take a special interest in a case involving athletics, rape, and local politics. Johnson, however, would disagree.

He was blogging on a site called Cliopatria, with the History News Network, in March 2006 when the story broke. Immediately, he recognized it as a headline-grabbing case that would have staying power in the national news, no matter the outcome. And he saw the role of faculty in the Durham debacle. So his blog entries began, and in July, he started his own online forum dedicated to the case, calling it Durham-in-Wonderland. He anticipated that the blog would remain active for two to three months, receiving up to a thousand visitors a day while the case resolved itself in the national spotlight. His first post on the subject received zero comments.

But things changed rapidly. The site was soon seeing more than fifteen thousand hits per day and the comments regularly topped several hundred on each posting. In fact, by the start of 2007, Durham-in-Wonderland was approaching the daily readership of the local newspaper, the *Durham Herald-Sun.* "My early goal was to give a place for people with no voice to express their anger and opinions," he told a class of communications students at Florida State in January 2007. "The further this went, the more I wanted to reach a goal of beating the readership of the *Herald-Sun.* They were doing such a terrible job of covering this story, I thought it would be great to be able to be their counter."

To many interested in the Duke case, Johnson's blog became required morning reading. The site was often the first to offer commentary on breaking stories and new developments. Unencumbered by the twenty-four-hour news cycle of print or the broadcast restrictions of network taping, the blog could be updated almost instantly, offering fresh discussion on the latest in a constantly changing case.

Durham-in-Wonderland also offered readers a well-organized and easily accessible cache of articles, links, timelines, photos, and commentaries on every aspect of the case. His organizing topics included media, faculty, administration, Nifong, politics, police, procedure, and medical. The blog provided visitors the opportunity to evaluate the evidence themselves, read reports and quotations, and learn about actions of local groups that went largely ignored in the national press. Many credit Johnson's reporting on the faculty conduct as one of the main reasons that syndicated news outlets began to finally pay attention to the irrational behavior of many within the university's power structure.

Johnson's blog was not the only outlet for these otherwise overlooked and under-represented in the call for real justice. United by a common cause, Durham-in-Wonderland offered links to such other like-minded sites as Liestoppers and Duke Students for an Ethical Durham. These sites helped to raise public awareness and understanding of the case to a new level that was independent of the news controlled by the traditional media, and it was instrumental in creating a new demand for broader coverage.

There was another small but loud voice offering up alternative coverage of the story, and that was the *Chronicle,* Duke's own student newspaper.

Stephen Miller, a student columnist, led the charge. He published a series of articles challenging the handling of the case by both the Durham DA's office and the school's administration.

On August 28, 2006, he published an article entitled "Persecution" in which he outlined in detail several of the many intentional misrepresentations of the case by Nifong, many of the Duke faculty, and members of the media. Then Miller appealed to his fellow students, "Now, take a breath and remind yourself that this isn't fiction. The madness is real and the stakes enormous. Lives, futures, hopes—all on the line.

"As the story unfolds a national magnifying glass will continue to be held over our campus and as a student body we have a moral duty to act with dignity and to demand fair and just treatment for our peers—no slander, no abuse, no prejudice tolerated.

"And lastly, if you find yourself in the presence of a student who insists the lacrosse players are a bunch of racist criminals and that the players are guilty no matter what the evidence says—put them in their place.

"If you don't, I will." And he did.

Throughout the summer and fall, Miller appeared on several national television programs, calling for unbiased reporting on the case and fair representation of the players. Some hosts, like Bill O'Reilly from Fox News, were receptive to the call and allied with Miller's cause. "It really began escalating the pressure about that ad," Miller said about his interview with O'Reilly regarding the Group of 88's "We're Listening" ad. "I think that's the thing—it was always apparent that at the beginning the people turned it from an issue about a specific charge about a specific situation into all-out class and race and gender warfare."

Nancy Grace, he recalled, was among the least gracious hosts he encountered. She "flipped out" when Miller suggested that the players should be regarded as innocent until proven guilty.

The *Chronicle* continued its campaign for fair coverage into the following school year, running a February 12, 2007, article by Miller entitled "Alums: Withhold Your Support." Miller offered the following plea to donors: "If we truly love Duke, and truly support its students, then we will take action to repair the University we love and to protect all its students present and future. If we truly love Duke, then we will demand that it live up to its ideals.

"What sense is it for alumni to criticize Duke, see Duke be totally unresponsive to their criticisms and then to keep the checks rolling in? Is it any wonder Duke perpetually ignores the grievances of its students and alumni? . . .

"The faculty handbook, which lays out some very basic professional standards to which professors must adhere, forbids attacks on students such as those we saw in the wake of the lacrosse allegations. The ad from the Group of 88 goes against almost every tenet of what it means to be a professor. Yet Brodhead refuses to issue even a verbal condemnation. . . .

"The best thing we can do for the students of Duke, and our many great professors, is to use the power of alumni support to institute changes for the good of all and to propel Duke beyond every other major university in the nation that suffers the crippling problem of radical faculty and weak administrators."

Miller was only one student reporter with a cause; there were many others who shared his passion.

During the summer of 2006, the *Chronicle* ran a story called "Living the Nightmare." Student reporter John Taddei offered personal stories and narratives from the lives of not only the indicted lacrosse players, but other members of the team whose lives had been thrown into chaos by the accusations. It was an important piece in reminding his readers that there were more than just three men on trial—there was an entire team whose lives and reputations had been sullied in front of the entire nation by charges that had already been shown to be largely unfounded.

In January 2007, the *Chronicle* ran an interview that student Rob Copeland had conducted with President Brodhead in which he respectfully but pointedly posed the questions that had been on the mind of many students. "If you were Reade Seligmann and Collin Finnerty," he asked, "would you want to come back to a campus where professors have denounced them and where students have held protests against them personally?"

Copeland confronted the actions of the faculty, too: "Let's talk about the attention Duke's faculty has received in this case, in particular the members of the so-called Group of 88. Do you hold the faculty to a higher standard? Should they understand the legal process, and recognize that it's not appropriate to speak about their individual students to the national press?"

President Brodhead's responses were calculated, but not always on target. In fact, he completely avoided some of the more direct challenges. The university paper ran the exchange, recognizing the importance of highlighting the administration's questionable conduct, even if very few other media outlets would.

In fact, many of the student newspaper's reporters wrote aggressively about the case, conducting interviews and voicing displeasure at the manner in which their school was being portrayed as an elitist, racist institution . . . and frustration with the faculty conduct that was allowing it to be portrayed that way.

It was one of the many ironies of the case that the nationally credentialed media and practicing attorneys had to be reminded by bloggers and a group of students that "due process" and "innocent until proven guilty" were more than just textbook phrases.

The vicious cycle of media coverage quickly grew into a self-perpetuating monster. Nifong needed the media and they proved to be willing participants in his little circus. When he spoke, they listened. When he ranted, they rubbed their hands excitedly and greedily consumed his every word. The reporters teased out every sordid detail that they knew the audience would lap up and came back asking for more, and Nifong was happy to dish it out again.

Even some among the faculty recognized the buzz this case had generated and jumped at the opportunity for their own moment in the spotlight. It was a chance to create a name for themselves outside the insular, specialty-specific window of fame they currently enjoyed in academia.

And as the media orgy progressed, few—very few—dissenting voices dared to question the trend. Joe Neff and Benjamin Niolet of the *Raleigh News & Observer* had offered responsible reporting, but their reasoned voices were easily drowned out by the shouts for more scandalous details during the early days of the case. The bloggers and the student reporters were largely ignored at first, as well.

But as the media began the gradual shift of its sympathies away from Nifong, it became clear that he was none too pleased by his loss of the spotlight. On June 19, 2006, *Newsweek* printed part of an angry email he sent to a reporter who had dared to run an article questioning the validity of the case. "None of the 'facts' I know at this time, indeed, none of the evidence I have seen from any source, has changed the opinion that I expressed initially," he stormed. ". . . The only people I have to persuade will be the twelve sitting on the jury, and if you want to know how I am going to do that, you will need to attend the trial. If in the meantime, you and other 'journalists' want to continue your speculations in the competition to come up with the most sellable story . . . then please spare me the recriminations when you get things wrong, as you inevitably will."

The damage had been done, though. Even as the charges dissolved, the social sentence had already been handed down to the accused and the rest of the lacrosse team.

"Until a year ago," Mike Pressler lamented in early 2007, "if you looked my name up you found stories about good lacrosse. Now, if you Google the words "Mike Pressler," "Duke," and "rape" you'll come up with more than one hundred thousand hits. Those stories will be out there forever."

Perhaps Okrent best encapsulated the sentiment that the players and their families felt in surveying the damage that his former paper, among many others, had helped to cause. "I'm reminded of Reagan's labor secretary Ray Donovan," he said, "who asked, after he was acquitted of whatever he'd been accused of, 'Which office do I go to to get my reputation back?' That's the question I have for the *Times*. What are they going to say to these three young men or their families? It incenses me, because I believe in fairness, and it saddens me, because I believe in the *Times*."

CHAPTER FIFTEEN

"It's Not About the Truth Anymore"

Mike Pressler can't tell you what time he awoke on April 5. Mostly that's because he can't remember if he went to sleep the night before. Day by day, the press had been getting worse. And despite the fact he was sure—absolutely positively sure—that his players had not committed the crime they were being accused of, he wasn't sure how many outside his household shared his confidence.

After pacing the living room of his dream home of fifteen years in the Duke Forest neighborhood all night, Pressler dressed and "headed in for another day of battle." As Pressler pulled on his jacket, his wife, Sue, gave him a kiss and a hug. This morning, the hug lasted a little longer.

At 10:00 A.M., Pressler got the first clue that his day was headed downhill. Athletic Director Joe Alleva summoned the coach to his office, where Senior Associate Athletic Director Chris Kennedy and Alleva waited.

"Alleva said the situation has gotten out of hand and they must cancel the season immediately," Pressler said. "I was shocked. I respond by saying, 'You promised the players to their face there would be no more forfeiture of games unless charges were brought. What new has happened? Joe, you told the players and the parents you believed their story, you believed in them, you believed that they were telling the truth. It's all about the truth; we must stand for the truth.'

"Alleva looked right at me and made the statement I'll never forget as long as I live: 'It's not about the truth anymore,' he said. 'It's about the integrity of the university, it's about the faculty, the city, the NAACP, the protesters, and the other interest groups.'

"I was dumbfounded. I told him that if he was worried about the players' safety from the protesters on game day, he should hire a thousand security guards. If it was football or basketball that is exactly what he would do. But it is lacrosse and we are expendable. I said, 'We are educators first and foremost. Now we are saying to the players the truth only matters when it is convenient.' "

Then Pressler pleaded: "Joe, the DNA results are imminent and you know that there will be no match. Just wait a few more days and we will have verification of what we all believe. Just a few more days."

The words hung out there. Just a few more days.

After forty-five minutes, Alleva agreed. "Okay, we will wait," he told Pressler. "You can continue to practice and prepare to go to Ohio State on Saturday."

The coach walked out of Alleva's office in Cameron Indoor Stadium and quickly called his wife. "I feel like we had won a stay of execution," he told Sue.

The stay didn't last long. Forty-five minutes later, Sue Pressler called her husband. A local television station was running a promo for its noon broadcast. Startling news in the lacrosse case was promised.

"Sue called to tell me that the noon news was going to include release of an email from Ryan McFadyen," Pressler said. "She said I should come home to watch the news. I had heard about the email, knew that the police had gone to Ryan's dorm room (at Eden Hall) and taken his computer. I heard the email wasn't good, but truthfully I didn't focus on it because that seemed to be the least of our worries."

A reporter standing there live with Duke Chapel in the background read from a search warrant unsealed by a judge that morning. "Tomorrow night, after tonight's show, I've decided to have some strippers over to Eden 2C," McFadyen wrote in the email, which was sent at 1:48 A.M. on March 14, about an hour after the party at 610 had ended. "All are welcome. However there will be no nudity. I plan on killing the bitches as soon as they walk in and proceeding to cut their skin off while cumming in my Duke issue spandex."

"The news station reported the wording of McFadyen's email straight from a document given to them," Pressler said. "What the reporters didn't know—and I wouldn't learn for some time—was that someone had edited Ryan's email leaving no context for it." The reference in McFadyen's email is from *American Psycho,* required reading in several Duke classes.

"All I knew at that moment," the coach said, "was that I had to find Ryan. The reporter had shown his picture from our media guide and I had to make sure he was safe."

Pressler didn't stay to discuss the story's ramifications with his wife. He raced out of the house and back toward campus, furiously dialing McFadyen's cell number. "I was worried about his well-being," Pressler said. "I was worried that they had shown his picture and in the craziness that something could happen to him."

At 1:00 P.M. McFadyen finally returned Pressler's call. He was sitting in the office of his attorney, Bob Ekstrand. He was safe, but admitted to being a little scared. "I went immediately to see him," Pressler said. "He started to explain the email, but I let him know that wasn't important. His well-being was the priority. Ekstrand and I agreed that Ryan should stay there for the time being."

On his way to Ekstrand's office, Pressler's constantly buzzing cell phone showed an incoming call from the athletic director. The words were short. "Mike, I need to see you immediately," Alleva said. Pressler promised he would get there after he checked on McFadyen, a delay that didn't sit well with the AD.

"I walked into Alleva's office about one-thirty-five," Pressler recalled. "It was just him, me, and Chris Kennedy."

No pleasantries were exchanged. Kennedy, who takes daily four-mile jogs around campus, was dressed in his running gear but, for some unknown reason, had decided not to take his run that day. The professional execution that Pressler had stayed three hours earlier was almost assuredly at hand.

"Alleva immediately said the email was very bad," Pressler read from his diary. "He said our season was immediately canceled and I had to resign by 4:30 P.M. that day or take an interim suspension until a committee report on the program is furnished to the president—which is the investigation of the program. He told me the president will be holding a press conference at four-thirty announcing the season's end and my resignation. It was a kick in the gut. I asked Joe who was firing me, him or Brodhead? He hesitated and said, 'I am firing you.' In my mind, I thought, 'Even at the very end he can't tell me the truth.' I wasn't sure what to say, so I emotionally blurted out what I estimated my total compensation was worth.

"I looked directly at Joe and reminded him he had told the players he believed them. I said, 'Joe, if I knew this was true and my players had not turned themselves in, I would have turned them in to the police immediately, I would have offered my resignation, and I would have encouraged you to end the program. I would have done so in a New York minute. But with the *same zeal*, I am telling you they didn't do it. They didn't touch that person.' I have said from the very beginning of this that if you believe, you stand all the way—you can't have it both ways—if you believe, you stand.

"I knew the minute I stood up and said I believed the players that this could cost me in the end. To this day, if you asked me, I would do the same thing again. I could have not supported the players and probably saved my job, just as Alleva and the administration were doing—condemn those guys and distance myself from them. I wasn't doing that because we as coaches boil it down to the bottom line, we are bottom-line guys, right?

"And in times of adversity, you have to be a bottom-line guy, and you have to take a stand. What do you stand for here? Like my daughter Janet said, 'If you believe in the truth, why do you need a good memory?' And that's what it came down to: the truth. If you are to build anything in this life, you can talk about loyalty, honesty, trust, all that—it comes down to the truth. If you base everything on the truth and doing the right thing, everything else is secondary. Joe Alleva wasn't hearing a word I said.

"My head was spinning. I walked out of there and headed to my office and called Sue at home. I asked her to fax me my contract immediately, largely because I wasn't really sure what I earned. The previous year, coming off the national championship game, Alleva had offered me a three-year extension. There was a substantial raise, a car allowance, and security when he said to me, 'Mike, as long as I'm athletic director, you're my lacrosse coach.' Sue and I were so confident we'd be at Duke forever that we built an extension on our home, the home we always dreamed of. It was unprecedented for a nonrevenue coach, unprecedented. For sports other than football and basketball, all coaches have one-year contracts.

"As Sue was looking for the contract, I called my lawyer, Eddie Falcone, and left an urgent message. No one could find Eddie. They told me he must be in court. I asked my assistants Kevin Cassese and John Lantzy to get the players together immediately, that I was calling an emergency meeting at 4:30 P.M. No questions asked. Everyone knew this was the low point.

"I knew that Brodhead's press conference was scheduled for four-thirty—he would announce my 'resignation' to the world, the creation of a handful of committees to study every aspect of this thing, and finally that Duke was suspending the lacrosse program. With that bomb coming out of the president's office, the players had to hear it from me first.

"At the same time, I had to settle my contract question and I basically had ninety minutes to do so. Once I got hold of my lawyer, he raced over. We went back to talk to Alleva. I had come up with some numbers in my head and I said, 'Joe, if you want me to resign this is what I believe I'm owed.' Joe said, 'Okay, I think we can do this.' While Eddie and I left and went back to my office, Alleva called up to the administration building. He called us back to his office in twenty minutes shaking his head and said, 'Mike, you are not going to be happy with this. They [the administration] are not going to give you what you asked for, what we agreed upon. The university counsel has said we can fire you with cause.' I lost it.

"What? What cause? What did I do?" I said, my voice rising.

"This is about your players and their past disciplinary problems," he said.

"Joe, that's bullshit and you know it. You knew about all of those incidents two years ago. We dealt with those. You also know that majority of those problems [player citations for open containers, and so on] I was never aware of because the dean of students office did not make me aware of them. Joe, you are holding me accountable for things I didn't know. You know that, and I know that."

Alleva sat silent.

"They basically gave me no choice," Pressler said. "Either I had to take a less than fair, unsatisfactory settlement or get fired with cause. My only other option was to accept an 'interim suspension' and wait until a report on my program was done by a committee of the president's choosing. I had no option. At that time, I said to myself, 'If I resign, I get severance of some kind. If I roll the dice and take the suspension until the end of June, they rule that I am at fault for some reason, they fire me in June and I get nothing.' With a wife and children, I couldn't risk being fired with cause and having no severance and no benefits.

"But maybe the part of this that bothers me most is that after sixteen years building a program for Duke, sixteen very loyal years, I was being given an hour and a half to decide my future."

As Duke knew he would, Pressler "resigned." Then, as he prepared to walk the two hundred yards from Alleva's office to the meeting room at the Murray Building where the players awaited his announcement, Alleva threw one last curve. "Do you want me to go?" Alleva asked Pressler. "I can help handle this for you or talk to the team myself."

"Are you fucking kidding me?" Pressler said to himself.

"I smiled because it told me how out of touch the man was," Pressler recalled months later. "I told him, 'I got it, I want the players to hear from me exactly what went on today.' But I was saying to myself, 'If he goes over there with me, this guy will not make it out of that room alive.'

"On the short walk over I noticed reporters out of the corner of my eye. They were snapping pictures and racing toward Chris Kennedy and me as we headed in for the worst meeting of my life. My youngest brother died three years ago of a heart attack at age forty-one. I had to eulogize him and that doesn't even compare to what I was getting ready to do.

"When I walked into the building, the assistant coaches were there. I pulled them aside and told them what was happening. Then we walked in to the meeting room. All forty-six players were present—everyone except Ryan McFadyen, who was suspended that afternoon by the dean of students and told he could not step back on campus. The coaches were there, our trainer, sports information, Chris Kennedy, and myself.

"I start the meeting by looking right into the eyes of the seniors, who were sitting in the front row as usual. 'Gentlemen, our darkest hour has arrived.' I paused and I could see their eyes welling up. 'The season has been canceled and I am resigning, effective immediately, as the head men's lacrosse coach at Duke.' Within seconds mass hysteria broke out. I continued to speak to the team, emotional myself. I said to the guys, 'You are not responsible for this, you did not do this. It is not Ryan McFadyen's fault. It is the administration that did this to us. It is the prosecutor who did this to us. We have paid our price for that evening of March 13, all that has occurred after that is not your fault, guys. You didn't get me fired. You didn't cancel the season.' I wanted to try to make it a very, very positive spin—I am not sure they heard a word I said because of the anguish, the emotion—and I've never—I'm crying my eyes out and trying to hold it together.

"Gentlemen," I said, 'Someday we will have our day. Someday I will tell the world the truth. I promise you all the lies, all the myths, all the injustice will be made right. Someday we will tell the world the truth. I promise you.' "

Players began begging Pressler not to resign, missing that the choice was not his. They asked questions, most of which he could not answer. The pendulum of emotion swung from fear to anger, from pain to guilt. Even good friend Kennedy felt remorse. Kennedy had recommended to Pressler earlier that day that Pressler resign. "It's the one piece of bad advice I game him," said Kennedy, who regretted his words for many months.

Despite Pressler's constant assurance, players felt guilty that their party had cost him his career. The coach attempted to end the meeting on as positive a note as possible.

One by one, each player came forward. Coach and player hugged and Pressler quietly whispered in each young man's ear a few words of encouragement. Mostly, he told his team to remain just that, a team. "Stick together and always stand up for the truth."

As the players ran from the meeting room, reporters descended. "It was sick," the coach said of watching each player head into the media maelstrom.

Pressler turned to Chris Kennedy. Voice cracking, the proud coach asked simply, "Dr. K., how did I do?"

"The most amazing thing I have ever heard in my life," Kennedy said. The two couldn't hold back their tears.

According to his players, Pressler was a rock during the darkest days.

"Sometimes you ask yourself what you learn from people," Dan Flannery said. "I don't have to ask what I learned from Coach Pressler. He showed more class, more strength, and more dignity than anyone in this whole situation. I can confidently say that the meeting on April 5, when coach resigned, that was the worst meeting of my life and will be the worst meeting of my life. Duke took his livelihood away for something we did. And he was a complete stand-up man. I will keep that the rest of my life."

"Coach P. was the one person who was keeping it all together," defenseman Tony McDevitt said. "None of us really suspected that Coach P. was going to get fired. We walked in that day thinking we are going for another meeting. Coach looked exhausted. He did his best to stay strong. He was at a loss for words. Everyone was crying and he was being strong, doing it for us. It felt so wrong. I remember leaving the meeting, tears in my eyes because I was watching a guy I looked up to in so many ways and a guy who took a chance on me, my coach, a friend, a mentor, everything. And everything has just been taken from him. I remember calling my mom, she was at work, and I remember telling her this is so wrong what happened to this poor guy. That was the climax of the disaster. It was April 5. It couldn't get worse than that day.

"The one thing Coach reassured us of several times in that meeting was that we would get through this. 'I am going to be here for you guys, I am not going anywhere,' he said. 'Duke has decided to go the way they wanted to go, but I am not part of that. I am still here for you guys. You are my kids. You are my students, my athletes, and I am going to be here.' It was amazing. He could have been screw you, I am gone. F-u, Duke. That's not his way. He had too much loyalty to his players. He was big in those next coming weeks because it only got harder for us. It only got harder. And he was there for us."

But as strong as Pressler was on campus, his time at home was more challenging.

While Mike Pressler faced the daunting task of explaining the day's events to his players, Sue Pressler had a challenge that was just as great: telling their children.

"At about four-forty that day, our oldest daughter, Janet, came home," Sue said. "I had called the mother of her best friend, Billy Zarzour, and had asked if he could come over so that Janet had someone in addition to us when she got home. When she walked in, I told Janet, 'Daddy's resigned. He's not working at Duke anymore.' She cried, was very emotional with me, and hugged me, and she said, 'Can I go tell Billy?' He had gone up to her room to play Playstation, and I said, 'You can tell Billy because that's why he's here.'

"She went upstairs and they disappeared and I don't really know all that they discussed. What she told me later was that Billy 'cried with me and he got on my computer and deleted my MySpace and Facebook pages so no one would write things.' That was thoughtful. It was interesting that Billy took the initiative that day to withdraw Facebook. Smart kid.

"A hundred plus people would ultimately come to our house that night and I think there was something really good in it for Janet. The next day, she said, 'I saw people cry that I had no idea knew how to cry!' That day, and I think there's people that can relate to this, Janet was able to see what her dad meant to people, and what he did for people. It was really a cool gift. Being a teenager and seeing that and gaining a different level of appreciation for her parent. I might be looking for a silver lining, but that's a pretty valuable one."

After the team meeting, Pressler, his coaches, Sports Information Director Art Chase, trainers, and administrative staff had retreated to an upstairs office for a few minutes together when Chase's cell phone rang. It was Sue calling: "Art, don't let Mike come home right now," Sue said. "The TV trucks and reporters are everywhere in our front yard. Please stay away until they leave."

Mike had other ideas. "I met with the staff and briefly exchanged a few final words and hugs," he said. "Then I decided I was going home to be with my family. I was not going to let anyone—especially reporters—keep me away. Art offered to drive me the two miles to my house."

Unbeknownst to Mike, Sue had called her best friend, Debbie Krzyzewski Savarino, a Duke fundraiser and the daughter of legendary basketball coach Mike Krzyzewski.

"Debbie dropped what she was doing, left work, and was at our house ten minutes later," Sue said. "She saw that I was struggling to manage the phone and she just took over. It was one of the great gifts we received that day."

"When Sue called," Savarino said, "I could barely even recognize her voice she was so shaken. All she said was, 'Well, it's over.' I drove straight to her house. There were TV cameras outside. Not a lot, but there were some. I thought 'This is crazy. My girlfriend is inside upset. Her husband has lost his job, and there are TV cameras in their yard? What is the world coming to?'

"I drove straight up into her driveway," Savarino said. "I can remember Sue saying, 'You don't have to pull into the driveway if you don't want anybody to see your car.' I asked, 'What the hell are you talking about?' She said,

'It's okay. If you want to park in Sheryl's driveway that would be fine.' She thought I might not want to be seen, which was absurd. I am proud to have Mike and Sue Pressler as my friends. I drove up with my big old Duke license plate, parked in the driveway, and walked into the house. I hugged her really tight and I started to cry. I didn't know the details but I didn't ask. I just figured they would come out when they needed to. I should stand there, I should just be there. As I started to cry, Sue said, 'It's all right. It's going to be all right. Those boys are the focus. That's why we need to be strong. That's what this is about.' She was right. It's about them. It wasn't about a job. We would fix that later. It was about the players."

One by one, coaches and others from the athletic department followed Savarino to the Pressler house. Soon, much of Duke's athletic staff was there, as were neighbors, friends, and others.

"All of a sudden it's like a party," Savarino said. "It was a celebration of the undying loyalty Mike and Sue had for their players. It was beautiful. If you could have seen these grown men from the athletic department and all of them crying, all of them, it was . . . it's what I was saying before, this mutual admiration society.

"Sue's phone is ringing off the hook. Home phone. Her cell. All phones are ringing off the hook. I said to her, 'Stop. You are not answering the phone anymore. I am answering it.' So I took out a pad of paper and I sat my butt down at the kitchen table and I started answering the phone and taking messages. Oh, my gosh, everyone from former coaches from other schools, ACC coaches who are in the league now, friends of Mike's in the lacrosse world, to Larry King called. I answered the phone, 'Presslers' residence.' 'Hello, this is Larry King calling. Yes, I wanted to know if I could speak to Mike Pressler.' 'No, you can't talk to him.' He said, 'Well, we are on live.' I said, 'That's great, but I am sorry, he's unavailable right now, may I take a message for him.' Barbara Walters. It was craziness. I filled up two pages, single-spaced on a yellow legal pad. And that was without writing down a lot of reporters who were calling. It got to be funny. You laugh when things are getting so tough.

"Finally I asked Sue who she would talk to. Who do you feel like talking to? Sue said, 'Oprah. If Oprah calls . . . ' and we just laughed. I was like, if Oprah calls we're going. Are you kidding? I am with you. I want it to be on the dream day at Oprah when gifts are under the seats. That's when we're going. She was like, yes. That was the only person Sue would speak to. But Oprah didn't call."

About that time, Mike made it home. "When we arrived, TV trucks were everywhere," Mike said. "There was a helicopter, a TV helicopter, hovering over the house. It was a media circus outside my door, microphones in my face, reporters talking to my neighbors. My neighbors actually formed a gauntlet so I could get up my driveway to my front door without any harassment."

"When Mike walked in," Savarino recalled, "he looked right at me. He always calls me Debbie K. Always. He looked me right in the eyes and said, 'Debbie K., I took a hard one today.' Tears welled up in my eyes and I said, 'Yes you did. *Yes, you did.*' And this man, this big, burly, bearded hunter man, was hugging me in his kitchen and was crying. It was awful."

"In a way, it turned into something like an Irish wake," Mike said. "The party went on until about midnight. Finally the media was gone, the house was empty, and it was just me, Sue, and our oldest daughter, Janet. I wished Maggie could have been with me, too, but out of concern for her safety, we had sent her to be with her grandmother in Illinois. What a day."

CHAPTER SIXTEEN

No Match

In its request for nontestimonial evidence, Mike Nifong's own office made it clear they were betting the prosecutorial farm on the DNA tests taken from the forty-six players on March 23. So convinced was he that DNA would connect the players and the accuser that he personally committed to prosecuting the case and proudly smiled for every camera in sight. As he charged ahead—still making no arrests and no formal charges, but continually attacking the entire men's lacrosse team in the national media—Nifong seemed as concerned with talking about the situation as he did with pursuing it.

Other than maintaining their innocence, the team had little to say and acted as innocents should, the team banding together, supporting one another. But their comparative silence stood in stark contrast to Nifong's near-constant chatter, and their failure to strike back after his barrages and outrageous statements hardly improved their public image. After all, the initial evidence that Nifong fed to the news outlets indicated that the prosecution had an open-and-shut case. According to court records, a medical examination of the woman found injuries consistent with sexual assault. All that was needed was a positive identification of the alleged assailants and a DNA match to back it up, and that would be the end of the argument.

In reality, it was just the beginning.

Nifong's team, led by Sergeant Mark Gottlieb and Assistant District Attorney Tracey Cline—who handles sex crimes—had convinced him that he was going to have all the physical evidence he needed once the DNA samples taken from the players were analyzed.

DNA testing is a precise, extremely involved process that yields virtually indisputable results. However, those results are actually more indisputable as exculpatory evidence; in other words, they can give investigators a better idea of who most definitely did *not* commit the crime than who actually did. As Dr. Brian Meehan, whose private lab later analyzed the players' samples, would testify in a December 15 hearing: "We were asked to determine if any of the evidence items match any of the reference specimens or really, can we exclude any of these references? Who can we exclude from this reference group? That's what we do. We exclude suspects. That's the best way to approach this work. And that's what we were asked to do, to find out if we can exclude everybody or offer anybody as a match." When asked if a weak "no match" conclusion can exist, Meehan confirmed that it does not exist in DNA testing: "Either you're excluded or you're not."

The lacrosse players received a similar explanation from their lawyers. One player, William Wolcott, explained, "When we went to give our DNA, all forty-six of us, that should have been a pretty powerful indication of innocence. We read that order. We are all pretty smart guys. We saw that for what it was. That was an absolute crock that we all had to go give our DNA. But we thought, hey, we'll go give our DNA and it will immediately rule us all out and we can go play again. And Coach Pressler can coach again. It didn't work out that way."

Collin Finnerty told *60 Minutes*: "We were told it would help clear everything up, so we were happy to go." Reade Seligmann agreed, noting, "It's so frustrating because it was an opportunity for us to exonerate ourselves. And we were told that. If we cooperated, those that were innocent would be shown to be innocent." Dave Evans had already voluntarily given a DNA sample on March 16 after cooperating with the police when they showed up at his house that night with the search warrant. Having been assured that a failure to produce a match would mean that they would no longer be suspect, all forty-six white members of the lacrosse team submitted cheek swab samples to the police.

On March 27, Agent Rachel Winn of the State Bureau of Investigation lab received those DNA samples as well as the samples from the rape kit and prepared to examine them for possible matches. The following day, Agent Winn conducted a series of tests on all of the specimens collected from the victim, including the vaginal, oral, and rectal swabs, as well as the underwear submitted in the rape kit. There was no semen, blood, or saliva found on any of those items. Further DNA tests on the fingernails conducted by Agent Jennifer Leyn determined that, beyond the DNA of the accuser, there was not enough material present to make any identifications, despite Crystal's claims that they had been torn off as she clawed at her attackers in self-defense.

Bad news was quietly coming at Nifong a little at a time. For several days in late March and early April, the SBI lab was returning batches of results, letting Nifong's team know that there was "no match" from anyone in that batch to any evidence taken from the accuser. Each day, the SBI was telling Nifong that his decision to bet on the DNA could soon leave him holding a handful of Jokers.

Unhappy with SBI's results, Nifong went shopping for a second firm to review the DNA. That's when he contacted Meehan at DNA Security, a private testing firm in Burlington, North Carolina. He wanted further analysis, and as documents submitted to the Durham County Court would testify, "Dr. Meehan indicated that DNA Security would be willing to work with the State on pricing, because 'they would really like to be involved in [the] case.' "

By April 5, it had become clear that the SBI labs could find no incriminating samples on any of the items taken from the house. However, analysis showed that the sample from the confiscated towel did, in fact contain a variety of DNA types from Dave Evans as well as from one other, unknown person who did not match any of the team profiles or the accuser's. In other words, there was material on the towel from the individual who lived in the house and who owned the towel, and from another person who must have used it at some point—and that person was not the stripper.

That was the DNA evidence provided to Mike Nifong from the State

Bureau of Investigation. It was not what he had bet on. The rape kit and players' DNA samples were all transferred to DNA Security the following day.

Strangely, as this information was trickling into the prosecutor's office, the previously loose-lipped Nifong suddenly became virtually silent in the media, significantly curtailing his public comments from April 3 onward.

On April 10, after receiving word that the state's DNA tests had produced no link between any of the players and the accuser, the lawyers for the defense announced the findings and continued the fight back in the public arena that had started in Joe Cheshire's law office when he held the first press conference on behalf of the players on March 30. The team's lacrosse season might have been canceled, but they were now up against a new series of matches, and this was, without a doubt, the first decisive win for their side.

The Associated Press issued a news alert that same afternoon, stating, "Attorneys for the players say DNA test results find no match between Duke lacrosse players and a woman who says she was raped at a team party." *All Things Considered* on NPR announced, "Duke Players' Lawyer Say DNA Doesn't Match." The *Charlotte Observer* ran the headline, "No Match in Duke DNA Tests."

The following day, the *Raleigh News & Observer* blared, "DNA clears players, lawyers say; DA vows to continue inquiry: Attorneys for Duke lacrosse players say the tests show they did not assault woman." The *New York Times* had a headline stating, "Lawyers for Duke Players Say DNA Evidence Clears the Team", and the *L.A. Times* ran a front-page article titled "No DNA Match in Duke Case." While the story was already a national sensation, the most recent twist made it even more compelling—surely now, with the prosecution's strongest evidence proven a bust, the charges would be dropped.

Three stories also ran in the *Duke Chronicle* on April 11, all pertaining to the lack of DNA evidence. The front-page headline consisted of two words: "NO MATCH." The subhead blared, "Lawyers say DNA tests exonerate lax players." The main article relayed the announcement from the previous day. Another article chronicled the reactions from the Durham community, including that of one anonymous resident, who said, "From what I understand, the DNA results aren't necessarily proving anything. The neighborhood would like to see something—one or more found guilty." There was also a piece that interviewed several lawyers not attached to the case to ask what the results might mean and their possible impact on the case. The lack of a match was, without question, the hottest news in both local and national media outlets.

The vindication felt by the team was short-lived, however, as Nifong quickly made clear that he would persist in doing what the DNA results could not—pinning the blame on the suspected players. It may have been an early high point as the defense held its press conference, but the players were quickly deflated. Within hours, Nifong announced to a predominantly African-American audience that he was still going to pursue the case, and Duke's hierarchy—which had already fired Coach Pressler and suspended the season—announced that it was similarly unmoved.

Months later, Vice President John Burness explained the university's actions: "No charges have been filed. People are presumed innocent until proven guilty. We know that some of the people that were asked for DNA weren't even at the party. So we've got to cooperate and here we go again. That's the basis on which we were trying to do this. Let's see what the statement is. . . . What [President Brodhead] said is, 'I'm not going to just let it be on the DNA, I need to have it based on the whole legal cloud.' And all we were saying is, we need to have the legal cloud lifted from this team. That is the variable; it isn't just the DNA test. The DNA test may lift the cloud, but it may not. As it turned out it didn't, did it?"

The reaction from the team, however, was not the joy than many might have expected. Coach Pressler described his personal reaction to the news: "People called me and asked, 'Are you relieved, are you overjoyed?' And I said, 'Overjoyed?' I'm out of my tree. It's not joy here, it's absolute anger because we've known from day one that no DNA would be found, that nothing happened. I was absolutely enraged. We knew the truth, and this just helped prove it. I remember when it came on the TV I was at my desk at home, and I just walked out the door. I got my walking stick and I walked about seven miles, turned my cell phone off, and I said 'fuck you' to the world on that day when that happened. I couldn't take it anymore. . . . In athletics when you say you believe somebody you stand by them all the way. It cost me my job, it could have cost me my career. I would change nothing. I believe them."

The outrage the now-former coach felt was shared, and it would only grow because there was more—much more—to the lab findings, but no one would learn about it for several more months.

With the university still withholding its support, the lacrosse team was now facing its biggest setback thus far, following on the heels of what should have been their greatest victory. Even if there was no DNA, Nifong insisted that the physical evidence was on his side, as the emergency room staff who treated the alleged victim in the early morning hours of March 14 had noted that the woman's genitals showed evidence of recent trauma. So, on April 18, sophomores Collin Finnerty and Reade Seligmann were taken into custody and charged with rape, kidnapping, and sexual offense—indictments based solely upon the accuser's identifications made from a botched photo lineup.

Almost one month later, on May 15, senior cocaptain Dave Evans was also indicted by a grand jury, who, according to normal court proceedings, heard only from the prosecuting team. Three days after Evans's indictment, on May 18, six weeks after DNA Security received the samples, the defendants were given the final analysis of findings from the private firm, confirming that there were no matches with the three players.

The DNA findings, which promised to mark the end of the legal nightmare for the team, were instead cast aside as Nifong turned to "other evidence," in a desperate attempt to support his rapidly disintegrating case. And it was becoming increasingly obvious which side had something to hide.

CHAPTER SEVENTEEN

Politics of Race

Mike Nifong was a political virgin. He had never run for office, never put his name on a ballot. Although he had spent twenty-seven years in the district attorney's office, he hadn't held a position that required the Durham electorate's approval. Even Nifong recognized his lack of name recognition within the community when he introduced himself to the boisterous, largely African-American crowd at a North Carolina Central University forum on April 11, 2006.

"Good morning, I am Mike Nifong. I am the district attorney for Durham. I am somebody who probably most of you didn't know before a few weeks ago and now everywhere I go I have newspaper men following me around and television cameras."

The day before defense lawyers held a press conference to announce "no match" of the DNA taken from the forty-six players. But Nifong did not skip a beat. "A lot has been said in the press, particularly by some attorneys yesterday, about this case should go away. I hope that you will understand by the fact that I am here this morning that my presence here means that this case is not going away."

Nifong, who had been appointed district attorney when his boss became a judge, received a thundering round of applause. He was playing to the audience and he knew it.

A division was becoming more and more apparent in Durham as many whites began to believe Nifong's case had been weakened by the news released just twenty-four hours earlier. Many African-Americans were still convinced that a rape had occurred. It seemed as though Nifong stood dead center in this division and continued to push each side further from the other as he ignored the lack of DNA evidence. Why would any district attorney continue prosecution of a case without solid evidence or a credible witness? The question spawned national debate.

If he wanted to remain as district attorney, the people in Durham needed to know who he was. The Democratic primary was only six weeks away. His one shot for victory required him to gain name recognition and to gain it quickly. Pandering to the African-American community seemed like a great place to start. Using the media attention this case was guaranteed to receive seemed like a great way to do it.

On the fifth floor of the Durham County courthouse, Nifong turned to his campaign manager, Jackie Brown, and with a blank stare said to her, "This is like a million dollars' worth of free advertisement."

Nifong may have been a political virgin, but he did know something about being a whore.

Brad Crone has been involved in North Carolina politics since 1980. Sixteen years ago, he had started his company, Campaign Connections, out of Raleigh, North Carolina. In the fifteen years he has run judicial and district attorney races, he has never lost a race. Not one. Until the 2006 Democratic primary. The candidate he represented was Freda Black. She would prove to be Nifong's most formidable opponent.

When it became apparent that Nifong would indeed run for office, it took some coercion from other concerned public officials to persuade Freda Black to get into the race. "Based on the phone calls I received from judges, clerks, people in the community, my final decision was I live in Durham," Black said. "Nifong would end up being my district attorney. I might be the only one that can change this to keep him from being district attorney because I knew of problems that he had, some that I wouldn't even discuss publicly. I thought I might be the only one that could do something about it, that had the name recognition that could defeat him."

Her prediction was dead-on.

Black was fortunate to come well equipped with noteworthy name recognition, thanks to the work she had done while she served under DA

Hardin. During his term, he asked her to assist with the successful prosecution of Michael Peterson, a novelist charged with murdering his wife, Kathleen. Because Peterson was a high-profile suspect, the investigation received media attention. Throughout the trial coverage, Black's aggressive approach proved to be a valuable contrast to Hardin's more passive style. As she said, "People comment on how our personalities were such that we complemented each other. Fire and ice is what they used to call us; I was the fire." Crone admitted this was one of the main reasons he took Black on as a client. "I was impressed with her on the way she handled the Peterson case," he said. "The public's perception was that she was one mean, tough, prosecutor—no bullshit—who cut to the chase."

Some speculated that Hardin's choice to work with Black on the Peterson trial, and not Nifong, may have fostered the jealousy between the pair. However, although it was unusual for the DA to ask the second assistant to help with prosecuting a case in place of the chief assistant, Black was not surprised. "Mike Nifong and Jim had never tried a case together," Black said. And even after she was chosen, she said, "Mike really didn't seem like he cared."

With Crone's experience in running successful campaigns, teamed with Black's established reputation and name recognition, it seemed that defeating this obscure incumbent DA would be a cakewalk.

The polling data suggested the same thing. On March 27, a poll conducted by Black's campaign phoned more than nine thousand registered voters in Durham County. Of the voters who responded, 37 percent said they supported Black. Only 20 percent of the respondents chose Mike Nifong. Five weeks before the election, Nifong's flagging campaign trailed by an astounding seventeen points. More significantly, Black was polling right near the 40 percent mark required to win a three-way primary in North Carolina. (A third candidate, African-American lawyer Keith Bishop, was chosen by a mere 3 percent of voters queried.)

These polling results made it clear Nifong was in a bad spot. Trailing so significantly—but with 39 percent of respondents still undecided—Nifong needed help.

• • •

It wasn't the first time Nifong had understood how poorly he was doing in a head-to-head contest with Black. Months earlier, knowing he was falling further and further behind his nemesis, Nifong had reached out to local political legend Jackie Brown.

Brown is a loving mother and grandmother, with three children and three grandsons. She has been married to her husband, Richard, for over forty years, and was born and raised in Durham. However, Brown's roles were not merely those of housewife and mother. Her number is not listed because her services are not public. Brown is trying to, as she said, "Make Durham a better place, one person at a time." She does this through Durham County politics. Her name is never found on the ballot, but her role is to ensure the right person is elected to the right position.

Brown's selection process is simple and her services are free. "I must know the person or know what the person's done in the community," before she will agree to help with a campaign, she said. She didn't know Mike Nifong. In fact, she said, "If I had ever heard his name, I didn't know it." So, around Thanksgiving time, when Jackie's unlisted phone rang, she was surprised to hear the current DA's voice on the other end of the line. Nifong told her he had decided to run and needed her help. He had enough sense to know his experience in politics and running a campaign was nonexistent. That's where Brown came in.

The holiday season was not all eggnog and cheers for Brown. She began to get more phone calls, but these were from Nifong's employees. Many of these people were Brown's longtime friends. These friends had held their jobs at the DA's office for twelve and fifteen years and told Brown they feared losing those jobs if Nifong lost. She was told rumors had begun to circulate that if Black won the election, as it was projected, "They're saying they're going to bring in the big broom and they're going to scoop us out." Although she didn't know the man running for district attorney, his work could help people she knew very well.

Jackie decided to enlist the help of her contacts at Durham's major political committees—the People's Alliance, Friends of Durham, Durham Committee on the Affairs of Black People—asking their opinions on this Nifong character. The responses she received were unanimous. "Everyone told me the same thing," she said. "He is the ultimate asshole, but he is the best qualified for the job. He was the lesser of two evils."

On January 2, around eleven-thirty in the morning, Jackie walked into the lobby of the downtown Marriott hotel to meet Nifong for the first time. Surprisingly, he had beaten her there. As she approached the table, she noticed that he was not alone. Sitting beside him was a lady, a lady she had never met before either. Nifong stood up and shook Jackie's hand, and then politely introduced the woman who sat beside him. Her name was Cy Gurney. She was Mike Nifong's wife.

As Jackie said, this was something that "should have been my first yield sign. I had never met with anybody who brought their spouse with them at the first meeting." It quickly became apparent Cy was not there to merely listen. "As we sit down, she pulls out a legal pad," Jackie said. "So, Nifong began to talk and explains that if Jackie agrees to do this, he said, 'I am a one-term candidate. I need three years and seven or eight months to finish out my retirement.' If only that could have been Nifong's campaign slogan, everyone could have had a clearer understanding of his motives."

Despite Brown's reservations about Nifong, she agreed to answer his SOS. She told him—and his wife—that she does not charge anything. That brought a sigh of relief because money was one of the many things their campaign was lacking. "The only thing I ask is that Mike acknowledge that I am his campaign manager," Jackie recalled. "No problem," they both replied.

The agreement had been made. Now action needed to be taken. If Nifong was going to get elected, the ball needed to be set in motion right away and Brown needed to be the one laying out its path. However, the thing that caught Brown off guard when she first met Nifong would continue to grow into a much larger problem. Brown soon realized Cy was the one in control; she was the one making the decisions. "He had to have her approval on everything and that's where the tension came from between me, her, and him," Brown said.

Brown knew what needed to be done to win an election in Durham, but unfortunately Cy's approval took precedence over her experience. "At some point in the campaign, I really wondered who the candidate was," Brown said. "Was the candidate Michael or was it her?"

Brown found herself in a political pickle completely new to her. For the first time, she was running a campaign that meant more to the candidate's wife than to the candidate himself.

In a county like Durham, where Democrats maintain such a stronghold—60.9 percent of the voting population in Durham was Democratic, with a mere 18.9 percent registered Republicans—the Democratic primary *is* the general election. There were no Republican candidates lined up to run for district attorney in the general election. The winner in May would be the winner in November.

The Duke lacrosse case brought with it what the district attorney needed: free press. With the media swarming around Durham and the elite school located at its core, the upcoming election became crucial. It would not only be crucial for the future of the three Duke lacrosse players who had been indicted, but would establish who would pick up the pieces as increasing scrutiny from the national media tore the county apart. Would Nifong receive enough votes to remain atop the case he had commandeered just a few weeks earlier? Or would Black be able to ride on her name recognition from the Peterson case and defeat him? The answer lay within the African-American community.

Of the ten most populous counties in North Carolina, Durham has the highest percentage of African-Americans; 39.5 percent of its total population. This gave the African-American electorate significant power within the community. They knew it, and so did Nifong. He needed their votes. They could—and would—resuscitate his campaign in the last weeks.

"I've never seen a prosecutor use the African-American community in the vote like this," said Greta Van Susteren, host of her own show on Fox News' *On the Record.* "It certainly looks to me that this white prosecutor who wanted this job so badly, curried favor with a huge voting bloc and used the African-Americans there. That's far more egregious than the allegations of white on black in the alleged sexual assault."

Although Nifong had made one smart decision in soliciting Brown's help, his campaign was sinking well before she came aboard. Look no further than his campaign finance reports for proof.

Around mid-February, the contribution well began to run dry for Nifong. He had received an overwhelming percentage—more than 80 percent—of his campaign contributions from local attorneys who wanted to curry favor with the current and likely future DA. Of course, the local attorneys would continue to fund his campaign if they were confident he would indeed win. However, if that confidence were shaken, or nonexistent, no local attorney would want to be tagged as a contributor to the winning DA's opponent.

By February, confidence in Nifong was gone. His campaign contributions had dwindled to nothing, with no change in sight. He had to decide how much he was willing to personally sacrifice. In order to stay afloat in the race, he took out a personal loan of $6,601 and pumped the money into his campaign.

Just four weeks later, on March 24, Nifong took over personal command of the Duke investigation. He hoped the attention he was receiving would bolster his campaign account. It did not. His finances still dangerously low, he was once again forced to take that financial plunge, only this time diving much deeper into his own pocket. In April, Nifong took out his second personal loan to fund his campaign.

This one was for $22,388.

Nifong claimed that his motivation in this case was never political. But the numbers don't lie. Nearly $30,000 worth of personal loans. Seventeen points behind in the polls. Everything Mike Nifong had worked for was at stake when police told them they were investigating a crime that had it all.

"I went and I did early voting," Jackie Brown said in an interview for this book. "I sat down with the ballot in front of me and I did something I have never done before. I didn't vote for the district attorney. I left the district attorney space blank because by then, I didn't know the person. Mike had become someone that I just didn't know."

After struggling to do her job for months, after discovering all of the "little lies" Nifong had told her, it became clear to Brown as she sat down and stared at that ballot. Mike Nifong was the candidate she signed on to help win this primary election. But he was not the one running in this race anymore. If she put a check next to his name, she was voting for someone else. She was electing Cy Gurney for district attorney.

The ballot listed three names; Mike Nifong, Freda Black, and Keith Bishop. But those were just the names. What the people of Durham really had the chance to choose from, Brown said, was an arrogant, unstable, incumbent DA who was dominated by his wife; a white female prosecutor who was aggressive in the courtroom but had numerous critics within the legal community; and a local African-American defense attorney who was inexperienced and had been previously censured by the State Bar in 2001 for "an improper delay in a civil case." It seemed that no choice was a good choice. The three candidates were fortunate that "none of the above" was not an option. None likely would have won on May 2, 2006.

Nonetheless, Nifong had done something right. As much as he tried to inadvertently sabotage his own campaign by ignoring the advice of his campaign manager, mishandling what little campaign funds he did have, and making unethical comments about the lacrosse players to the national media, he was right. This case was worth a million dollars in free advertisement. And he needed every one of these intangible dollars.

His stance on the Duke lacrosse case skyrocketed his popularity in the African-American community, and within weeks, this formerly obscure prosecutor enjoyed the popularity that national media attention can bestow. Sadly, though, even the publicity from a case of such epic proportions proved to be barely enough to get him elected.

Nifong held on to his position of power by the slimmest of margins. He had gained enough momentum to get 883 votes more than Black.

With 45.5 percent of the votes, he did not receive a majority, but made the cut above the state-mandated 40 percent to avoid a runoff election. His desperate attempts to remain in office had paid off. But now the pressure was on. With an alleged victim who was losing credibility by the minute, a defense that was gaining strength by the hour, the days were quickly approaching for this newly elected DA to prove he wasn't just blowing smoke.

"He got so wrapped up in it—on such a tale—that he couldn't get out of it," Crone said. "He backed himself into a corner." Nifong's own campaign manager knew his media ambitions would soon come back to bite him in the ass. Brown said, "He got caught up in this whirlwind of media and he was inexperienced. He didn't know they were going to tear him to pieces and spit him out when they got through with him."

> I'm not proud of this, but sometimes I think back to the day Mike Nifong fired me. It changed the course of Durham County history, and it changed the course of a lot of people's lives. If I had not been fired or forced to resign, however you want to say it, then I wouldn't have run against him. If I hadn't run against him, then he wouldn't have used this case for political reasons. April 28, 2005, to me is what changed everything—Freda Black

Firing Black may have been Nifong's first official act and may, if you accept Black's theory, have set in motion a series of events that led to the Duke lacrosse case becoming his personal political passion play. Only time would tell how far he would be willing to follow that passion. Nifong proved to be prescient in many ways as he worked to win the Democratic nomination. No statement proved more true, though, than his promise to

Brown that the media notoriety he was about to generate would be "worth a million dollars."

Actually, he sold himself short. A year later, his name recognition ranked among the highest of any elected official in America, talk show hosts would discuss his work without ever having to mention his first name (think Madonna, Cher, Nifong), his name would be entered in online dictionaries, and he would become a national laughingstock.

CHAPTER EIGHTEEN

ALL IN

There was nothing polite about the conversations between fathers and sons in the days after the party at 610. Every father interviewed for this book remembers the moment vividly. So do the sons. And all of the conversations began and ended similarly. One by one, each father looked his son in the eyes and asked the key question: "What really happened that night at 610? Don't lie to me."

"My conversation with Dan went just as it did for every other dad," said Everett Flannery, whose son, Dan, was one of three Duke senior captains who rented the home where the team party was held. "I wanted the truth and I wanted him to remember this is not the time to be the sacrificial lamb here. This is not the time to cover up stuff."

Over and over, the players told their parents this wasn't a cover-up.

Dan Flannery, who turned twenty-two years old on March 16, 2006—the day Durham police officers searched 610 for evidence—said his father was angry but not "violently angry" when he explained the party's sequence of events to him, man to man, eye to eye. "One of the first things he said was, 'You're telling me the truth?' " Flannery said. "I told him, 'Yes, I was there the whole night, there was no contact with the girls, nothing happened. Do you really think that: A, someone on my team would be capable of doing this; B, I would let someone do this if I saw it; and C, do you really think any of us would sacrifice our future to defend somebody else on our team of a heinous act?' I think right away he [Dad] was on the same page. No, we didn't do this."

Once those conversations between fathers and sons took place, involved families locked arms in vigorous defense of their sons and their sons' teammates.

They went all in—ironically, those two words served as the motto for the 2005 Duke team that lost to Johns Hopkins in the NCAA national title game.

"I called my sister-in-law, she's twenty-eight and a lawyer in Manhattan," Everett Flannery said, "and she called Dan up and said, 'Dan, listen to this, okay? If you know anything, get yourself a lawyer and go tell the district attorney what you know. If there was a rape, whoever makes the best deal, is going to walk away.' Dan told her, 'I am telling you, nothing happened.'

"From the very first night, we believed our son."

While Duke's reputation is one of privilege, many lacrosse players on the 2006 team weren't born with silver spoons in their mouths. They were sons of firemen, teachers, store owners, nurses, and construction workers. Their families worked to make ends meet, much like the majority of Americans. As the scare of indictments loomed over the forty-six players during Easter weekend 2006, worried families wondered how to pay for legal representation, including the first step after arrest: bail.

"I had pretty much accepted the fact that I was going to get indicted," Dan Flannery said. "So when I went home before Easter, I had a conversation with [Dad] and we agreed that whatever happened, we were going to do what it took to clear my name." At what cost? "Sell our house . . . [use] every bit of money we had," said Rita Flannery, Dan's mother.

Mike Pressler also promised to dig into his bank account. "Coach offered to pay for my bail because I wasn't going to be able to cover it," said senior captain Matt Zash, who thought he would be indicted since his first name was one of three identified by the accuser. A plan was quickly devised by a lacrosse player's parent, Lincoln Payton, and Durham attorney Bob Ekstrand.

Payton, whose son Sam was a freshman on the 2006 team, and Ekstrand, who represented many of the players, knew the importance of being prepared financially when indictments were announced. Bail in this high-profile and explosive case was expected to be set dramatically high, in the two-hundred- to four-hundred-thousand-dollar range. So, Payton, an international banker for most of his professional career, telephoned his fellow parents—many of whom he had never met or talked with previously—on the Saturday night before Easter in an effort to raise money.

"Although the team was painted as being made up solely of white, rich kids, that's actually very far from the truth and there were some families that, no question, would not have been able to come up with even a bond at that very short notice," Payton said in a British accent that reflected his United Kingdom upbringing.

Payton discussed another important consideration with the eight to ten parents he telephoned. The case and its salacious elements had fueled a firestorm, stoking the tension between Durham and Duke, blacks and whites, locals and Dukies. "My wife would come in and listen to me explain to some other dad what we don't want is one of these kids thrown into the holding tank with a bunch of deliberately aggravated, racially charged drunks," Payton said. "And a blind eye turned by the local police force because they consider it good sport. The more she heard it, the more my wife worried for Sam. I was delivering a message and frightening my wife at the same time. It was painful."

Payton, who contributed one hundred thousand dollars to a fund that exceeded nine-hundred thousand dollars—parents promised more if needed—said the response demonstrated an unyielding bond between families. People don't put up their own money for other people's kids if they don't believe. "The fact that it was actually nine or ten people coming together and doing that—and not just one person who had so much money that it's not an issue—actually speaks volumes about the credibility of the kids and the belief of the parents from day one," Payton said.

At the same time Payton made his calls, he also shared in the fear that his son would be indicted. Payton watched television at his office the day when indictments for Reade Seligmann and Collin Finnerty were announced. "Without a doubt, it was the worst day of my life," Payton said. "It was indescribable, the anxiety level of that day. I've seen people talk about it, but there was that mixed emotion—one I think the kids still live with today—which is one of relief and guilt. When it wasn't you, it was, 'Thank God.' But it was also unbelievably outrageous and terrible."

Lacrosse is a family sport. It's not uncommon for families to pile into their cars and drive hours to watch their children. It was the same way for the 2006 Duke families, who were scattered primarily in the Northeast—but as far away as Texas and Canada. With twelve home games on the 2006 schedule, families had planned to spend most of their spring in Durham.

Those arrangements changed when Duke's season was canceled after eight games. Families didn't file into Koskinen Stadium to cheer; instead they sat in their living rooms, forced to cope with the allegations and uncertainty that swirled around their sons and the Blue Devils' lacrosse program.

"My mom was on antidepressants for a while. She had a nervous breakdown right in the middle of this thing," Zash said. "There was a point where I kind of accepted the fact that I was going to get indicted. . . . We were in my lawyer's house at the time and, at that point, my mom just collapsed. She couldn't breathe. It was definitely a very significant experience in our life and something that she'll never forget and has vowed to make sure that [Mike] Nifong has that same feeling one day."

Dan Flannery conveyed his feelings to Duke President Richard Brodhead during the university's Senior Athlete Ring Dinner at Brodhead's home in late spring 2006. Flannery admitted that when he was greeted at the door by Brodhead and his wife, Cynthia, he "shook the shit out of their hands, [I] almost tried to break their hands." Brodhead later thanked Flannery for attending. "He said, 'I have to believe we will be better someday because of this, of the situation,' " Flannery remembered. "I said, 'I don't share the same opinion. I'll believe that when mothers no longer have to take antidepressants.' I think he was shocked when I answered him like that."

Parents of players established an email network that allowed them to share their feelings and keep each other abreast of news. Slowly, families attempted to recover from days, weeks, and months of tension-filled uncertainty. Rob Bordley, David Evans's high school lacrosse coach at Landon School in Bethesda, Maryland, told the *Raleigh News & Observer,* "I think, frankly, this is tougher on parents. Kids tend to be resilient . . . I think it's good therapy to be someplace where they don't have to defend their child."

Mike and Sue Pressler were on the front line, without cover, caught in the middle of a national frenzy. Not only did Mike Pressler deal with the turmoil of his forty-seven players, his own family had come under vicious attack. The Presslers received veiled and overt threats by email, telephone calls, and signs left in their yard and on their front door in the middle of the night. A squad car from the Duke Police Department drove by the Pressler home in the Duke Forest neighborhood every fifteen minutes. The Presslers disconnected two telephone lines in their home for fear the lines were tapped following an unauthorized visit by a technician from the local telephone company.

"It was just growing exponentially out of something that was just so far from what we knew happened," Sue Pressler said. "It was sort of like, 'Who are these people? Where do they come from? Why do they hate us? Why do they want to harm us?' So it sort of meant that every day you were waking up with no idea what is going to happen. You have no idea."

Pressler's two young daughters—Janet (fourteen at the time) and Maggie (eight)—also were caught in the crossfire. While Sue and Mike did their best to shield their children from the controversy around them, they weren't immune to pointed questions and quizzical stares from their peers. Janet, a champion volleyball player at Cardinal Gibbons High School in Raleigh, North Carolina, is very much like her father; strong but quiet, close-lipped and guarded. Janet kept her innermost feelings bottled inside for months following news of the lacrosse party. But there were private and painful days when her emotions exploded to the surface.

"I don't know how often she did, but there were two occasions that I can remember vividly hearing her sobbing uncontrollably," Sue Pressler said as she wiped away her own tears. "I remember the first time I went upstairs, I walked into the room and she's on the floor, she's sobbing uncontrollably. I said, 'Oh my God, did you fall? Are you hurt?' 'No, Momma, I don't know what's wrong.' A teenager, what's the first thing that goes through your mind when you hear that? I'm just a mother, 'What is it this time?' Except that if you have the background of who Janet Pressler is, it is so far out of character for her that she didn't know what it was that threw her into this sort of hysteria."

Yet, Janet also demonstrated her steely resolve—just like her dad—when a party was scheduled for the last day of school. The teacher suggested the children bring snacks to school, and a guy in the back of the classroom blurted, "Yeah, Pressler will bring the dancers." Sue Pressler asked her daughter, "What did you say?" Janet responded, "Five months ago it would have made me cry, but now . . ." Sue said, "Oh, so you see him for who he is?" And Janet answered, "No, Mom, I have always seen him for who he was. I'm just like Daddy. I'm just in a different place and how I handle it and how I see what these people are doing."

Janet also showed her feisty side months later on Halloween when her classmates shared costume ideas. Two seniors had selected the popular theme of the time—one planned to dress as a stripper and the other as a Duke lacrosse player. "Janet came downstairs a little pissed off that morning," Sue Pressler said, this time with a smile. "I said, 'Have a great day, honey, I love you.' And she goes, 'Mom, I might get into a fight today.' And I said, 'With whom?' And she explained the situation to me, and she turned and she was so angry. She said, 'They can be strippers, but they don't get to be Duke lacrosse players.' "

If Janet is reserved, pigtailed Maggie is rambunctious, blessed with the ability to brighten her father's day under most circumstances. Maggie once pedaled her bicycle into Duke's team huddle during a Blue Devils scrimmage. "Janet has always been more grown up—Maggie will probably never grow up," Sue Pressler said. "Now she says, 'I don't want to grow up, because then I can't do cute things anymore. I only have a pound of funny left in me.' And I said, 'Oh, I think you have more than a pound of funny in you. Daddy still has more than a pound of funny in him and look how old he is, and you're just like him.' She giggles and thinks that's the greatest thing ever that she gets to be."

But there was a time when the frenzy intensified at such an incredible pace that Maggie, in the second grade, couldn't brighten her father's day. That prompted the Presslers to send Maggie to her grandmother's (Sue's mother's) home in Illinois for a few weeks in late March. "Maggie had never seen her daddy so sad," Sue Pressler said. "He was battling so hard every day for these kids and the truth. She just couldn't understand why she couldn't brighten his day anymore. She had always believed she could make the sun come out for him, and she couldn't. I didn't want her to start redefining herself and feeling there was something wrong or different between her and her dad, that she could no longer brighten his day. I had to send her away. I couldn't allow her to feel any level of responsibility for whether he was sad or not, or happy. They had a relationship and they had a place where they joked and they had their thing. I didn't want to take that away from them. It was a great decision as things even became more hysterical around here."

But the hysteria and harrowing moments did not divide the Presslers. They rallied around each other and their players, demonstrating a quiet bravery not lost on friends.

"Her cloth is very unique," Debbie Krzyzewski Savarino said of Sue Pressler. "Some angels wove it. She is a strong woman, a very strong woman. The high road was taken by Sue and Mike Pressler. They never said a word, all for the betterment of these boys. They were so afraid because their words could be taken and misconstrued, which always happens. They never said anything. Many people would have thrown somebody under the bus to save themselves. Not these two. It's so amazing they had the strength to do that."

An early observation from Janet Pressler, the quiet one, helped her father cope with the madness that surrounded the family and Duke lacrosse when she asked, "Dad, if you tell the truth, why do you need a good memory?" Mike Pressler, just like his daughter, needed a moment. "You are who you are," he said. "When the shit flies, who are you? That's it. You've got to decide what is right and what is true and you make a stand. You've got to judge now, what are the consequences here? The truth.

"As soon as you deviate from that, then it's over."

When a group bonds as the Duke families did, passions don't die easy. Eleven months after their worlds collapsed in unison, families with returning players from the 2006 team were gathered again in a private meeting called by Duke President Richard Brodhead and Bob Steel, current chairman of the university trustees and leader of the search committee that hired Brodhead three years ago.

A conference room at Duke's Fuqua School of Business was standing room only. It was two hours before the start of Duke's second game of the 2007 season, against visiting Denver on February 25, and the euphoria from the Blue Devils' emotional victory over Dartmouth a day earlier still hung in the air. But if the university leaders thought the meeting would be a relatively quick, reasoned discussion, they thought wrong.

"I think they believed this meeting was going to be fairly short," said Donna Wellington, who attended the meeting with husband Bob and traveled from Texas for the weekend. Their son, Rob, was a sophomore midfielder on the 2006 team.

Instead, the meeting went for nearly ninety minutes. Brodhead and Steel stood in front of the conference room, while parents and family members sat in rows of chairs; others lined the back wall. Mrs. Wellington said Brodhead opened the meeting by expressing his commiseration for the events of the previous spring and calling the 2007 opener a positive step forward. But the tone changed quickly when it was the parents' turn to talk.

"I think at that point they thought [their] comments were going to appease us and I think they were very surprised to be hit with a barrage of questions, very well articulated, very heartfelt, from some still very angry and confused parents about why our boys were just thrown under the bus; why the coach was fired; why the season was cancelled, etcetera," Mrs. Wellington said.

"They were asked, 'Why, to date, they still had not made a positive statement defending the boys' innocence? One father asked them, 'Why they couldn't have just said, 'These are our students, we've talked to them, we have to operate under a presumption of innocence, and if it turns out they are guilty, appropriate punishment will happen, but in the meantime we will stand by them and defend our otherwise very successful program.' "

Their response?

"They hedged, they backtracked; they kept defending all of their actions last spring based on what they knew at the time and reiterating their reasonable (to them) assumption that a DA is usually standing on the facts," Wellington said. "And that really wasn't an answer. Now, they have a totally different set of facts in front of them and still haven't retracted their earlier remarks, such as, 'What they did was bad enough!' They still haven't come forward and said we know now that this was a hoax, a terrible injustice perpetrated on our students. They really weren't able to adequately defend themselves to us because most of us believe they were acting out of pure self-interest at the time, and now they are trying to pretend they had an objective justification for their decisions."

Chuck Sherwood, the first African-American lacrosse player at Duke (1972–75), whose son Devon was a freshman on the 2006 team, said he understood some decisions made by Brodhead and university administrators during the ordeal. But he also stressed that they misjudged the lacrosse team.

"Did it ever occur to them they may have the kind of kid—this team—that if they saw one of their teammates doing something that was inappropriate that the other guys would intercede and stop it?" said Sherwood, a teacher in the Hempstead school district in New York for the past twenty-three years. "Those are the kind of kids that I believed they had on the team."

But many people—at Duke, in Durham, and around the nation—did not believe, forcing parents to embrace their own and each other.

They were all in . . . from the beginning to the bitter end.

CHAPTER NINETEEN

Crumbling Case

Most observers point to the release of early DNA findings showing no match as the first nick in the prosecution's case, the first victory for the defense. But this case would ultimately suffer a slow and lingering death from a thousand cuts. Perhaps the deepest cut came when Dave Evans stepped before the microphones and with the passion, power, and believability political candidates would love to have, delivered a seven-minute statement that told the world he—and his teammates—were innocent.

"I am innocent. Reade Seligmann is innocent. Collin Finnerty is innocent. Every member of the Duke University lacrosse team is innocent," Evans said on May 15, 2006, after becoming the third player charged in the case but the first to speak out. "You have all been told some fantastic lies. And I look forward to watching them unravel in the weeks to come, as they already have in the weeks past, and the truth will come out."

For the first time, every mother in the country saw that this could be her son. For the first time, most men in America saw that there but for the grace of God stood them. There was a face and statement, something this story hadn't had previously. Speaking to more than one hundred reporters while surrounded by his supportive senior Duke teammates, a calm yet confident Evans ferociously proclaimed a miscarriage of justice.

"He hit a home run," said Joseph Cheshire, Evans's attorney. "I've never been any prouder . . . I have two boys. They both played lacrosse, they're both young. I've never been prouder of anybody that I've ever been with than I was with Dave Evans on that day."

Even Duke's Vice President John Burness described Evans' message as "stellar." "It was like, 'Holy cow,' " Burness said of the reaction after Evans put a face on the young men who were being charged in the case.

Licensed to practice law in October 1973, Joseph B. Cheshire V became the fifth Joseph Blount Cheshire to practice law in the courts of North Carolina, dating back to the late 1800s. That experience and lineage helped Cheshire come to an immediate conclusion when he first met David Evans. That conclusion also deepened Cheshire's disdain for Nifong and Mangum.

"I know people who are charged with crimes, and I pretty much know who they are and what they do," Cheshire said. "And after three minutes or so with Dave Evans, looking at him and listening to him talk to me, I knew he was innocent. I knew he was incapable of doing what they say he had done. And then when Reade Seligmann and Collin Finnerty were indicted, I mean it was just a joke to me. In fact, I can almost tear up when I talk about what that son-of-a-bitch and this woman have done to these boys and their families. My boy [Evans] is tough, my boy's strong, my boy has graduated from college. My boy is a man now. These other two boys [Seligmann and Finnerty], they are still boys, and he [Nifong] has just taken the heart out of them and their families."

On Friday, May 12, Evans received a disconcerting phone call from Cheshire's staff. There had been talk of a third indictment—Seligmann and Finnerty had been arrested a month earlier on charges of first-degree forcible rape, first-degree sexual offense, and first-degree kidnapping, a series of crimes for which they could serve thirty years in prison if convicted. But until this moment it had never been a reality. When Evans heard his lawyers wanted to talk, he immediately called them and said, "Don't call me to tell me you'll have news tomorrow. Tell me what's going to happen."

"You're going to be indicted on Monday," they replied.

This was not good news, but the Evans family stood strong and prepared for a fight. The Evanses were not going to be taken quietly because the truth needed to be heard. Dave Evans and his family met with Cheshire at his office on Saturday, May 13. And it was during this meeting that Cheshire hatched an idea that, to many defense lawyers, would have sounded crazy: What if Dave Evans stood on the steps of the police station and made a statement, letting the world see his sincerity and hear his declaration of innocence?

"I said yes in a second," Evans said. "There was a brainstorming session about it. There were ideas of preparing a long statement I would read or to just release a statement, but I just told him all I needed was five bullet points and that's the way I wanted it." Evans relied on his confident manner. "I don't practice reading or stuff like that . . . that's not the way I work."

So it was set. Evans wanted to address the public with the truth when he arrived at the Durham Police Department in two days. Reality began to sink in for him and his family. "I never cried . . . but this was the first time it really hit me that it was going to happen," Evans said. Cheshire spotted him getting emotional at this realization and said, "You can't cry on Monday, you've got to be strong. You think you can do this?"

"Yes, I can do this," Evans answered.

A graduation dinner was planned that Saturday night—Evans and more than four thousand other Duke undergraduate, masters, or doctoral students were scheduled to participate in the school's annual commencement ceremony the following day, Sunday, May 14, which also coincided with Mothers' Day. But before Evans attended the party, he was faced with a simple but important question.

"What was I going to wear on Monday?" Evans remembers asking.

On the way to dinner, Evans stopped at Nordstrom, an upscale department store, to pick out a dress shirt. Evans, with help from his parents and his older sister, looked for a shirt that would "look good on TV when I get indicted for these three counts," Evans said. "My dad was coming up to me saying, 'What do you think about this?' And I'm replying, 'We're picking out a shirt that would look *good* on TV.' Then he says,

'Don't wear stripes.' I'm thinking what the hell is going on? For all my friends it's graduation weekend, which is such a big time for them, and I'm picking out a shirt so I can go talk to millions of people about my innocence."

Evans settled on a simple yet sophisticated light blue button-down. With a haircut mandated by his mother, Evans joined his graduating teammates for dinner at a local Italian restaurant. The Evanses walked in late, but all eyes immediately turned their way. "Everybody knew [of the pending indictment]," Evans said. But Evans used the opportunity to mix levity with seriousness.

"People start doing all these little minispeeches, and I get up in front of my friends and it's like the first practice run," Evans said. "Can I give a speech at this time without tearing up? I stood up, and it was pretty heavy and I was already getting a little bit emotional. And I said, 'Guys, I've got some bad news. It turns out that Nifong really got us, I guess he was right. We all look like a bunch of preppy assholes right now.' Everybody was wearing all these pink shirts, seersucker and stuff, and I said, 'God, he really got us.' It was exactly what everyone needed, a little levity!"

As laughter and tears erupted around him, Evans continued, saying, "I am glad it was me [indicted]. I can handle it, my family can handle it. He doesn't know what he's getting into by bringing my family into this. He picked on the wrong family. If he learned anything about us, he's going to get a left jab from my dad, a right hook from my mom, and Joe's going to kick him," he said, raising his knee as if to nail Nifong in the groin.

That was Evans's practice run. By Monday, he was ready.

Graduation is supposed to be a celebration. Following Saturday night's dinner, Evans went out for a few hours with friends. He had a couple of beers but wasn't in the mood to party. "People were getting drunk, everyone was with their family, and everyone was so happy, and I said, 'I can't be around this right now.' "

As Evans met his graduating teammates on Sunday at Wallace Wade

Stadium, they used white athletic tape to scribble Seligmann's jersey number 45 and Finnerty's number 13 on their mortarboard caps. "Soon they'll get to add number 6," Evans, who had worn that number as a three-year starter, said to his parents in a moment of gallows humor.

After the massive graduation ceremony, students divided up by school to receive their diplomas. On his way to Cameron Indoor Stadium, where Trinity College grads would be honored, Evans noticed the television crews and cameras that were searching out graduating lacrosse players. That's when he realized he had to walk across a stage to receive his diploma. That wasn't going to happen. "My dad went and got it [diploma] for me," Evans said. "I said, 'I don't want to walk across the stage.' I didn't want to give them the satisfaction of a picture."

Following a quick family photograph, the Evanses piled into their car and drove away. The following day was a far different kind of walk for Dave Evans.

Cheshire stood in front of the podium to introduce Evans on Monday, May 15. Addressing the sea of reporters, Cheshire reminded them that Evans was not there to answer questions; instead he would tell the truth. He asked the audience to be mindful of what the Evans family was going through, "They are victims, and they are suffering, and I would appreciate your respect." Cheshire moved aside so his client could speak.

Evans was confident as he stepped up to the podium adorned with over a dozen microphones, but that was not a surprise. The son of Washington, D.C., lawyer David Evans and his lobbyist wife, Rae Evans, who is also chairwoman of the Ladies Professional Golf Association board, Evans was known as a gutsy athlete who used his brains and tenacity to compensate for lesser physical gifts. Evans once played an entire lacrosse game in high school with walking pneumonia without telling anyone—Evans went directly to the hospital after the game. While there was a mixture of pain and disbelief on the faces of Evans's loved ones as he stood at the podium, Dave Evans had an intense certainty in his eyes. Surrounded by family and his senior lacrosse teammates, Evans—his lower lip trembling slightly—spoke from the heart:

> I want to thank you all for letting me speak to you today. My name is Dave Evans, and I'm the captain of the Duke University men's lacrosse team. I have to say that I'm very relieved to be the person who can come out and speak on behalf of my family and my team and let you know how we feel.
>
> First, I want to say that I'm absolutely innocent of all the charges that have been brought against me today, that Reade Seligmann and Collin Finnerty are innocent of all the charges that were brought against them. These allegations are lies, fabricated—fabricated, and they will be proven wrong.
>
> If I can go back to two months ago, when the police first came to my home, I fully cooperated and have continued to try to cooperate with them. When they entered in and started to read the search warrant, my roommates and I helped them find evidence for almost an hour and told them that if they had any questions we would gladly answer them to show that nothing happened that night.
>
> After that, I went down to the police station and gave an uncounseled statement because I knew that I had done nothing wrong and did not feel that I needed an attorney. After going through photos of my teammates and identifying who was there, I then submitted, perfectly willingly, DNA samples to the police. I then turned over my email account, my AIM account, any kind of information that they could have to show that I had not communicated any way that anything happened, because it did not happen.
>
> After that, I asked to take a polygraph, which was refused by the Durham Police Department. Over the past several weeks, I've repeatedly, through my lawyer, tried to attempt—tried to contact the district attorney. All of my attempts have been denied.
>
> I've tried to provide him with exculpatory evidence showing that this could not have happened. Those attempts have been denied. And as a re-

sult of his apparent lack of interest in my story, the true story, and any evidence proving that my story is correct, I asked my lawyer to give me a polygraph.

I took that polygraph, and it was administered by a former FBI top polygrapher with over twenty-eight years of experience. He's done several hundreds of sexual cases, and I passed it absolutely. And I passed that polygraph for the same reason that I will be acquitted of all these charges, because I have done nothing wrong and I am telling the truth. And I have told the truth from day one.

I'd like to say thank you to my friends and family, my coach, and members of the community who have stood by us through everything from the initial weeks to now. Their support has given me the strength to come through this. But the thing that gives me the most strength is knowing that I have the truth behind me, and it will not faze me.

If I can close, I've always taken pride in my name. I take pride in my name today. And I'll gladly stand up to anything that comes up against me. I've never had my character questioned before. Anyone who's met me knows that this didn't happen. And I appreciate your support. As for my teammates, I love you all. I've never—the honor of being voted captain of all of you, the forty-six best guys you could ever meet, has been the greatest honor of my life.

If I can clear things up and say this one more time, I am innocent. Reade Seligmann is innocent. Collin Finnerty is innocent. Every member of the Duke University lacrosse team is innocent. You have all been told some fantastic lies. And I look forward to watching them unravel in the weeks to come, as they already have in the weeks past, and the truth will come out.

Thank you for your time.

Evans's sincere words echoed in the hearts of everyone who heard them. At that moment, mothers and fathers saw their own sons in the face of Dave Evans. They realized this harsh reality could have happened to anyone, and they shared in the pain and frustration that all who were close to him felt. How could an innocent man be subjected to this punishment with such shifting accusations? Evans's public address had sparked a desire in people to seek the truth. It shattered Nifong's finely crafted public opinions.

"It was an enormous moment," Cheshire said. "You talk about a kid standing on the foul line in the NCAA Tournament having to make a free throw. That didn't even come close to what Dave Evans had to do that day. And he went out there and he stood out there and nobody who looked at him at that press conference or looked at him on TV thought he was guilty. Nobody. If you didn't bring an immense racial or left-wing feminist agenda to a case so that you couldn't have an open mind, nobody thought he was guilty. And if he wasn't guilty, then the case wasn't a case."

Moments after his speech, Evans, twenty-three, turned himself in to Durham police and was charged—just like teammates Seligmann and Finnerty—with first-degree forcible rape, first-degree sexual offense, and first-degree kidnapping. He was released later that day after posting four hundred thousand dollars bond. Nifong also released a statement that said he didn't anticipate any further indictments, saying that "none of the evidence that we have developed implicates any member" of the team other than the three charged. But it was Evans who had become the spokesperson for truth and the poster child for the wrongfully accused.

"It could have been the worst day of my life but instead it was the day that prepared me for the rest of my life," Evans said.

What to believe?

"I thought it was hilarious when Brodhead was interviewed and he said the facts kept changing," said William Wolcott, a senior on the 2006 team. "I felt like calling the guy and saying, 'Hey, facts don't change. The truth doesn't change. Lies and versions of events, those things change. But the truth doesn't change.' "

The truth according to Nifong was changing constantly. The district attorney, who publicly condemned the defendants before he completed his investigation, also suggested that the Durham police sidestep department procedures for the administration of photo lineups.

From that lineup, Mangum identified Evans with "90 percent certainty." She told police she would be 100 percent sure if Evans had a mustache—something Evans has never had. Attorneys also claimed they could prove that neither Seligmann nor Finnerty were at the party at the time the rape was alleged to have occurred.

There were other obvious holes that defense lawyers began sharing with the media. Durham attorney Butch Williams, a successful African-American lawyer who had chosen to represent one of the lacrosse captains, became a go-to source for reporters who were starting to become more skeptical.

"If you start to look at the facts as they were becoming known, you had to conclude that this didn't happen," Williams said months later as he explained some of the details that reshaped public opinion. "There was no blood from her anywhere in the house, there were no bruises on the players. Not one of the players had a black eye. Because believe me, they could have grabbed all they want, but this girl was tough. She would have kicked somebody in the nuts. The girl would have protected herself, period. And then the other thing, we had a video of her trying to go back in the building. She was laughing and joking. A girl who was raped going to go back in the back door of the house? She's fleeing, she ain't going back there. That let me know there were things totally inconsistent with a victim of a brutal rape. It didn't happen."

Nifong also found himself defending a stripper who couldn't keep her stories straight. At one point she was raped by five players. At another point, she said she wasn't raped at all. Finally, she settled on the fact that she had been raped and the number of players who had squeezed into the tiny bathroom at 610 was three.

In a June letter to the *Raleigh News & Observer*, Duke law professor Jim Coleman became the first to demand that Nifong remove himself from the case. He laid bare what he considered the most significant procedural flaw of this case—Nifong's instructions to police that they violate their own procedures and keep conducting photo lineups, including a final lineup where *only lacrosse players were included,* until the alleged victim gave prosecutors three names to focus on. The flawed approach, Coleman wrote to the *News & Observer,* "strongly suggests that the purpose of the identification process was to give the alleged victim an opportunity to pick three members of the lacrosse team who could be charged. Any three students would do; there could be no wrong choice."

Coleman ended his letter, "Whatever the truth is, Nifong can no longer personally restore public confidence in the prosecution of this case. Someone with professional detachment and unquestioned integrity must review the case and determine whether the evidence against the three students warrants further prosecution. That would serve the best interest of the alleged victim, the three defendants, and public."

By the time summer 2006 ended, the case looked just like Mangum did when she showed up to dance at 610: trashed.

SARA D. DAVIS

Mike Pressler, then head coach of the Duke lacrosse team. His team had a 153-82 record with 3 ACC championships and 10 NCAA tournament berths. Pressler also had the remarkable record of a 100 percent graduation rate for his players. His world would turn upside down on March 13, 2006.

SARA D. DAVIS

The house rented by the four lacrosse captains became the center of a firestorm in a community already divided by race and privilege. Matt Zash (below, left) was reduced to living in his car; it was safer than living in the house. Zash with David Evans (right), who was one of the three team members charged.

SARA D. DAVIS

SARA D. DAVIS

On March 29, convinced that the university would support them, the lacrosse team practiced. Steadfast in their belief in the system, the entire team cooperated with authorities. Reade Seligmann (right) was also charged.

SARA D. DAVIS

"Take Back the Night"—a previously scheduled rally on March 29—added fuel to the fire. Here graffiti call for the lacrosse (LAX) team to "speak out."

SARA D. DAVIS

T-shirts written by sexual assault victims from the Durham community hang on the campus of Duke. The university's Sexual Violence Awareness Week, March 26–31, coincided with the charges and the rising fury.

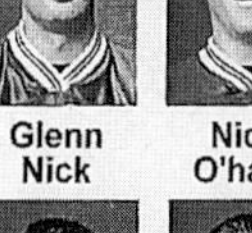

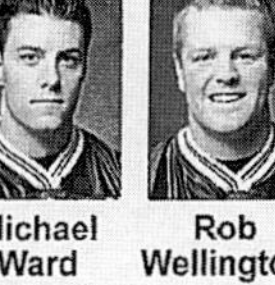

PLEASE COME FORWARD.

"We're not saying that all 46 were involved. But we do know that some of the players inside that house on that evening knew what transpired and we need them to come forward."

- Durham Police Cpl.
David Addison

ABCNews
3/26/2005

Please call
Durham CrimeStoppers
Callers may
remain anonymous.

Breck Archer · Bo Carrington · Casey Carroll

Mike Catallino · Tom Clute · Kevin Coleman · Josh Coveleski · Ned Crotty · Matt Danowski · Ed Douglass · Kyle Dowd

David Evans · Collin Finnerty · Dan Flannery · Gibbs Fogarty · Zack Greer · Erik Henkelman · Jay Jennison · Ben Koesterer

Fred Krom · Peter Lamade · Adam Langley · Chris Loftus · Dan Loftus · Kevin Mayer · Tony McDevitt · Ryan McFadyen

Glenn Nick · Nick O'hara · Dan Oppedisano · Sam Payton · Brad Ross · KJ Sauer · Steve Schoeffel · Rob Schroeder

Reade Seligmann · Dan Theodorisis · Bret Thomspon · Chris Tkac · John Walsh · Michael Ward · Rob Wellington · Matt Wilson

NOTE: There are four more players that were not retrieved from the GoDuke.com website before Duke took down the lacrosse team's roster on Monday morning, March 27th.

A flyer handed out at the "Take Back the Night" rally.

SARA D. DAVIS

Duke University President Richard Brodhead leaves a closed meeting with students on March 29. The previous day he had announced the suspension of the lacrosse season until the legal situation was cleared. On April 5, Mike Pressler would "resign."

SARA D. DAVIS

On May 1, the national chairman of the New Black Panther Party speaks to the media about his group's eight demands.

SARA D. DAVIS

May 15, David Evans (center at microphones) with his attorneys beside him and the lacrosse team seniors behind him, proclaims his innocence to the media before he is charged.

The Pressler family. Their lives were structured around Duke and lacrosse.

JOE CAULFIELD

Jack Emmer (center in suit coat)—with 326 wins he holds the NCAA record—recently retired after over two decades as the coach for the Army lacrosse team. Here he speaks to Pressler's new team at Bryant.

CHAPTER TWENTY

Summer Camp

The party went well into the early morning hours. A bonfire crackled and burned brightly from a pit in the backyard, flicking red embers into the dark sky. The annual get-together at Mike Pressler's home with his senior lacrosse players was, at least on the surface, like any other in past years. It was a celebration of relationships that now extended from the athletic world to the real world.

"You kind of go from the coach-player relationship to more of a coach-friend relationship, which will last a lifetime," William Wolcott said. "Certainly, after your playing days are done, you get a chance to get together with the coaches and enjoy reliving your last four years together. It was a neat day to spend with Coach Pressler. Coach was always great about having us over to his house and making us feel like a part of his family."

But this family was also grieving, its psyche badly shattered if not ruined. It was May 2006, a month since Pressler had been fired from Duke and the Blue Devils' season had been canceled because of the fallout from the alleged assault at 610. A nationally recognized coach was unemployed and eleven seniors saw their collegiate careers end in a meeting room in the Murray Building instead of at Lincoln Financial Field in Philadelphia, site of the NCAA Men's Lacrosse Championship, where top-seeded and undefeated Virginia (17-0) beat Massachusetts 15–7 on May 29.

Duke pounded Virginia, its Atlantic Coast Conference rival, 17–2, in a regular-season meeting on April 16, 2005, en route to the national title game versus Johns Hopkins. Duke and Virginia each returned its core—more than fifty lettermen combined—entering the 2006 campaign. The teams were scheduled to play on April 15 in Charlottesville, Virginia, and could have easily met in the ACC Tournament later that month in Baltimore. While the Cavaliers soared to a national title and tied Duke's NCAA single-season record of seventeen wins, the season had crumbled for Duke. And many seniors were still dealing with their raging emotions, including guilt over how the situation spun wildly out of control during their watch.

Wolcott, for one, was extremely apprehensive when he arrived at the Pressler home for the party. Wolcott and his teammates had had many opportunities to share their feelings with Coach Pressler over the past few weeks. But Wolcott had not talked at length with Pressler's wife, Sue, who also dealt with the maddening turmoil on a personal and a family level. She was a head coach's wife and mother of two young daughters. Their lives were battered daily by this fierce storm but still, in a way, wrapped tightly in Duke Blue.

"It was a terrible thing what happened to their family," Wolcott said. "I actually got a chance to speak with Mrs. Pressler alone [at the party], which I am thankful for. And just to hear her not put the blame solely on us was very comforting. I think we feel a lot of guilt about what happened to coach and his family.

"Certainly there is a feeling among us that we were responsible. To hear her say she didn't blame us was greatly comforting to me, that she blames the university and Nifong. That she didn't put the blame squarely on us was sort of a relief for me. The way that she and Coach Pressler have handled this entire ordeal is incredible. I am forever indebted to them for what they did for me and my friends."

Senior teammate Kyle Dowd also didn't know what kind of reception to expect at the party. Sure, he knew it would be a nice time on one hand simply because of the camaraderie between the seniors and Pressler. The class, as sophomores, had helped Duke rebound from a 5-8 season in 2004, the program's first losing season in fifteen years, to an NCAA-record seventeen victories and a national championship appearance in 2005. The 2006 campaign arrived with lofty expectations that were shared by the seniors and Pressler in their preseason get-together. But Dowd also knew the climate had changed drastically over the past month. Like Wolcott, Dowd was on edge when he walked through the doors with his fellow seniors.

"That party brought back the memory of a get-together before our first game with Coach Pressler and the seniors," Dowd said. "What a different atmosphere it was between those two nights. The one before the first game, it was all about celebration, our class, our relationship with Coach P., and where that season would lead us. The one at the end of the year, the senior get-together, it was quite a different atmosphere, and the events that transpired in between those two nights, none of us could have foreseen. It was a tough night.

"For me personally, that was the first time I actually broke down and got upset. This whole thing broke . . . we were all telling stories about Coach Pressler. For me, I lost it. You love talking to the guy but it's tough every time you talk to him. He understands what this whole thing meant to him. For us, what am I going to say? We're beginning our careers right now. I still get to play [professionally]. We still have our jobs. For him, he was at Duke for sixteen years and that's a big commitment. You know, I've been alive for twenty-two so I can't even imagine that kind of commitment. And then it was all gone."

Sue Pressler also didn't waver in her commitment to Duke's 2006 senior class. A party had been planned and, by God, a party was held. "The seniors were graduating and we will never get to coach them again," Sue Pressler said. "It [the party] was something they looked forward to every year, every senior class enjoyed that party, so there was no way we could not do it for them. For years, it was legendary. You get to hang out with Coach and get to share all the CPIs—Coach Pressler-isms."

Sue Pressler stressed that she and her husband would not allow the situation to ruin their outlook and relationship with players, specifically the 2006 seniors. "I think one of the things that both Mike and I are committed to is not emerging from this as bitter, angry people," she said. "We've seen it. I've said on many occasions in friends and other people,

I've seen bitter, angry people and they are not fun to be around, and they cannot have a fun life. It's a choice."

Wolcott said the Presslers' choice not to emerge bitter and angry has helped him cope with guilt that still lingers to this day. "Ultimately, we feel incredibly guilty about what happened to Coach Pressler," Wolcott said. "Coach knows that. We've expressed that to him. We expressed that to him at the senior party we had with him. But I think he always encouraged us not to feel guilty and not feel sorry for him. He was going to be fine. One of the things I will never forget, I think he always had a special bond with our class. He said he took some comfort in going out with our class, leaving Duke the same time as the Class of 2006."

Mike Pressler continued to show up at his Duke office for nearly six weeks after his forced resignation on April 5. He followed his daily routine, even if he was no longer a school employee. And what did he do? "Finish my command," Pressler said. He didn't dodge one person, including former superiors, and answered every telephone call. "And then the players, the underclassmen, started coming by my office," Pressler said. "And this is when it really hit me. 'Coach, what do I do? Should I transfer? Should I stay?' "

Kevin Cassese, one of the most decorated players in Duke lacrosse history, was in his first season as an assistant coach under Pressler in 2006. While at Duke (2000–2003), Cassese led the Blue Devils to three NCAA Tournament berths and a pair of ACC championships. He was a two-time team captain and three-time All-ACC and All-America selection. When Pressler was fired, Cassese's first inclination was to leave and head home to Port Jefferson Station, New York, sixty miles east of New York City. But Pressler wouldn't allow it, telling Cassese he was needed more than ever at Duke.

"Coach told me this is more your program than it is mine," said Cassese, who celebrated his twenty-fifth birthday on April 5, 2006, the day Pressler was forced to resign. "For me, that said everything I needed to know about Mike Pressler right there. He's out the door and he's still coaching me—he's more worried about other people than himself. I asked him flat-out why, why would I want to stay? And he said because there's still forty-seven guys that need you. I am thinking, 'Okay, so if I leave now, I am turning my back on all the players that are currently here and I am turning my back on the guys that I graduated with, my classmates, all the alums that came before me. It took me a while to come to that realization, but I eventually did and said I know what I have to do. I have to stay here. It's my job to stay here and try and get us through this."

Cassese was named the Blue Devils' interim head coach from June 5, 2006, until John Danowski was hired on July 21, 2006, to replace Pressler. Pressler also fulfilled his promise to "finish my command" at Duke: He convinced three of seven incoming recruits to honor their commitment to the Blue Devils; he helped returning players deal with their questions and concerns; and he refunded the registration fees of three hundred youth players who signed up for his camp at Duke—many with personal notes of gratitude for their expression of support. Pressler's camp, both highly successful and lucrative, had grown from thirty-six players during its first session in 1991 to one that attracted some of the best young talent from around the country.

"I worked his lacrosse camps every summer," said Mike Hawley, one of Pressler's best friends, who retired in March 2006 after twenty-one years as the athletic equipment manager for Duke. "I was in charge of security in the dorm. There were a lot of camps going on at the same time, women's lacrosse, volleyball. We had a big meeting with all the campers in the football stadium and Mike would introduce me and my staff as the TURKS. We were in charge of security. We would be there from eleven in the morning to two in the morning. It was fun. In fact, when I was [recently] hiking the Appalachian Trail, I was wearing my Duke hat and ended up meeting with former campers who attended Mike's lacrosse camp."

It was in late May when another cold, hard fact floored Pressler, the national Division I Coach of the Year in 2005.

"My career was over," he said. "That's what I was concerned about. I was thinking what else can I do? I thought my career was gone. There were interviews—or lack of interviews—with some other colleges, even high schools. The lack of interest solidified it for me. I was looking into sales, looking into other careers outside of coaching. I was thinking about a bunch of other things, trying to be proactive and avoid saying, 'Woe is me,' but rather, 'What's next?' I knew one thing. We had to get out—there was no way I could exist in Durham. I just couldn't be around here."

Pressler, who had turned forty-six years old on February 27, had another concern that reached deep into his soul and squeezed. "I was scared to death of how the lacrosse community viewed me. I had no idea—I hadn't been out of the house," he said.

To his surprise—and pleasure—the lacrosse family began to reach out to Pressler, a noted speaker on the summer camp circuit. Pressler knew the importance of summer camps and the relationships that are fostered through these gatherings, having traveled that circuit for the past twenty-four years. During Pressler's coaching stops at VMI, Army, and Ohio Wesleyan, he asked head coaches from around the country to speak to his teams. "I asked to practice and play at their events, and I got snubbed everywhere," Pressler said, smiling. "I told myself if I ever get a chance to be in that spot, I am going to help out every one of those guys. For years, you name it. Everybody that came through could play at Duke. Every speaking engagement I did. It came back to fulfilling that promise I made to myself."

In the summer of 2006, one of Pressler's early invitations was as the guest speaker at a three-hundred-player camp out West [California] in Danville, located in the San Francisco Bay Area and noted for its exclusive country clubs. Pressler—who had committed to the camp before the alleged assault in March—said a camp official voiced concern whether he was still a good choice, but others decided to keep the former Duke coach on their speakers' list. Pressler fulfilled his commitment—and a few months later received an email from the camp asking him back in 2007.

Pressler's message to campers centered on the importance of sportsmanship, individual skills, and team skills, as well as life lessons off the field. He talked about how lacrosse was similar to basketball—without the ten-foot goals—and stressed transition from offense to defense, defense to offense. Pressler, who coached defense for many years before he switched to offense in 2005 at Duke, taught that he wanted his players to create in open spaces and play physical on defense. He also wanted them to understand the importance of decision-making. Though he didn't get into the details of the party at 610, everyone understood his message: Every decision you make can change your life.

While summer camps continued to reach out to Pressler, none left a more vivid impression on him than when he was the guest speaker in Gettysburg, Pennsylvania. Following his speech, he received a standing ovation. Then, spontaneously, the four hundred campers lined up in single file to shake Pressler's hand. Pressler noticed that one camper had intentionally stayed behind until the final handshake. The high-school-aged boy was five-feet-eleven, but thin. He didn't have any facial hair. He appeared nervous and avoided eye contact.

The player finally approached Pressler and asked, "Coach, do you have a minute?"

Pressler naturally answered yes, extending his hand. Pressler later admitted the young player had a "lot of guts. Again, toughness comes in all different sizes, different shapes." The two talked lacrosse and Pressler offered him encouragement and a smile.

The young man then thanked Pressler for the speech, for the lesson, and for the private moment of encouragement. He sheepishly introduced himself. His last name was familiar—Nifong.

He was Mike Nifong's nephew.

CHAPTER TWENTY-ONE

General Election

When Mike Nifong won the Democratic primary on May 2, he celebrated as if he had won the office of prosecutor in Durham County for the next four years. In Durham County, it had been more than three decades since the Republican party had even fielded a candidate in the general election, even longer since one had been elected. When Brad Crone, a North Carolina political strategist, was asked when the last Republican had been elected as district attorney in Durham County, his response was telling: "Probably not since Reconstruction."

With a political track record like this, it was no wonder Nifong assumed his worries were over in May. At that time, there were no Republican candidates running for district attorney. By defeating fellow Democrat Freda Black, it seemed he had eliminated his only worthy adversary. If history was any guide, he should enjoy the same lack of competition as had the Democratic candidates who came before him.

But Mike Nifong was all about changing history.

Behind closed doors in the Durham County courthouse, Nifong was coming to a realization all his own: His case was falling apart. Only a few months earlier, this same case seemed to be his ticket to election as district attorney. Suddenly things didn't seem so sure.

Although the Durham electorate were not voicing their discontent with their current DA with all-night vigils and protests, the sentiment was present. As Nifong's intentions became more and more transparent and the evidence in this case began to shift in favor of the defense, people realized they needed to remove this man from his position of power. They could not give Nifong a free pass.

A movement was begun, a committee formed, and the search was on to find someone, anyone, to run against Mike Nifong. Their search led them to an established Durham lawyer and member of the Board of County Commissioners, Lewis Cheek.

Cheek had successfully run in three prior elections and seemed to have enough name recognition to give Nifong a battle. "It started as a matter of one person, then another, then a bunch more people started asking me if I would consider running against him," said Cheek. This was a hefty proposal and one that required some serious consideration before Cheek agreed. He was already a member of the Board of Commissioners in addition to running a law firm that was largely focused on him and the business he brought to his fellow associates.

There was another dynamic to this proposal that Cheek needed to consider. He knew the man these people were asking him to run against. "I have known Mike for a long time," he said, "and frankly, I had always known him to be a friend of mine." Cheek had even previously extended a helping hand to Nifong. "I have run in three campaigns successfully, and I know a little bit about politics in Durham and running a campaign. So, I offered to give him some suggestions and help him if I could. I even sent him a campaign contribution for the primary."

After Nifong took control of the lacrosse investigation, Cheek again tried to offer some advice when the mounting criticism began. However, each of Cheek's efforts to help his friend were "suggestions that were not well received," he said. Nifong's actions made it clear he was not concerned with who he offended, or what friendships he destroyed.

On June 15, Cheek received another call from "those folks" who had asked him to consider running against Nifong; they had another request. They told Cheek, "We have been in touch with the Board of Elections and we can get your name on the ballot. It wouldn't be the standard kind of write-in candidacy, because your name would actually be on the ballot if we can get a petition signed by about sixty-four hundred registered voters."

The deadline for this petition was midday, June 30.

While Cheek was still considering if he would actually be able to fill the role of district attorney if elected, he gave the go-ahead to attempt this petition campaign. To get sixty-four hundred signed petitions returned in a fifteen-day span seemed like an impossible feat. The media and others were openly skeptical that a task this large could be completed in such a short time. But these concerned Durham voters did not falter. One of those, in particular, was already quite invested in this election. Her name was Jackie Brown.

May 2 marked the last day Brown worked as Nifong's primary election campaign manager. She realized too late that the man was unfit to remain as DA of her hometown, so she decided to do something, as she said, "to get him unelected." Brown accepted the lead role in this growing anti-Nifong movement. She made that phone call to the Board of Elections. She was the one who found out that in order to get Cheek's name on the official ballot as an unaffiliated candidate, they needed to get a petition signed by 4 percent of the county's registered voters; 6,303 voters exactly.

Brown and the other Cheek volunteers didn't waste another moment. After obtaining a list of the twenty-five thousand registered voters in Durham, they began to print letters and stuff envelopes. Chalk it up to Brown's experience in politics, or just plain common sense, but they stuffed something else in those envelopes that made all the difference in the success of their campaign. Self-addressed reply envelopes.

It was unanimously decided that the only way to ensure people would actually return these petitions in ten days' time would be to make it as easy for the respondent as possible. "It cost us a bunch of extra money," Brown said, but the results would pay off exponentially. "We were opening them up and at first, you would just see the husband's and the wife's names. Then they started opening some and they had copied another sheet and those names had been filled up too. All of a sudden we have 2,000. The next thing, we had 4,000." The returned petitions were coming in droves. So much so that "the post office was putting them in those big bins," Brown said.

At noon, on Friday, June 30, the final list of signatures was turned in to the Board of Elections; it exceeded 9,800 names. After Brown and the others realized they would well surpass the 6,400 required petitions, they stopped checking if the signers were even registered voters. Brown said, "We probably got close to 12,000 or 13,000 because we had more come in after the deadline."

Brown and the other Cheek volunteers made this seemingly impossible task very possible. Although they, and the thousands who had signed the petition, were blatantly dissatisfied with Nifong and his handling of the lacrosse case, Cheek still couldn't make up his mind. Regardless of his decision to run, one more name would be printed on the November ballot for the position of district attorney.

The furor that had been brewing since the primary election was finally given a voice. The Durham electorate would, in fact, be granted the choice they so desperately longed for.

By November, Nifong's name had become synonymous with the Duke lacrosse case. People had begun to catch on to who he really was, and those who were closely related to him began to jump ship.

The rippling effect of Nifong's behavior would extend into waters he never would have thought to charter. For example, his past actions in the Democratic primary, and subsequent actions in the general election, contributed to the world of academia. His behavior provided a perfect case study for one Vanderbilt professor, Christian Grose, whose research entitled "Cues, Endorsements, and Heresthetic in a High-profile Election: Racial Polarization in Durham, North Carolina," focused on the racial voting patterns in both elections as a result of "Nifong's strategic use of this racially charged rape case."

Nifong's actions would continue to send shockwaves throughout

Duke's campus in the following fall semester. His mishandling of the lacrosse case was now hard to ignore, and it would soon awaken the dormant shallows of student-voter activism.

"We got involved pretty much right off the bat starting with school," Christiane Regelbrugge, a junior at Duke, said in an interview for this book. Regelbrugge and two fellow juniors, Emily Wygod and Brooke Jandl, decided to spearhead the effort to encourage other Duke students to register to vote in the upcoming Durham County general election. All three founders were involved in various other organizations on campus, and due to their previous activism, they felt they would be able to muster the large volunteer effort necessary to make this campaign a success.

"It was a voter registration effort to make sure that Duke students, who are citizens of Durham, vote and make sure their voice is heard within the community," said Regelbrugge. The name they chose for this registration effort would make their ultimate goal very evident.

"Duke Students for an Ethical Durham" was born.

With school beginning in late August, and the October 13 voter registration deadline less than two months away, they couldn't waste any time. DSED, as it became known, and its volunteers set up tables throughout campus, spoke at meetings for other campus organizations, and opened up lines of communication with the fraternities and sororities at Duke, sending one specific message: Register and vote. Their campaign even received national media attention.

"The media have swarmed this case from the get-go, and when we first got back to school there was kind of a lull, there wasn't anything new going on [in the lacrosse case]" said Regelbrugge. "The first week of school, Emily and I appeared on the Greta Van Susteren show, and we were thrilled to have the publicity of making an appearance."

With the attention from this TV appearance as well as the many articles written, DSED tried to reach out to all Duke students, undergraduate and graduate. Their goal was to register one thousand new voters. However, getting nonregistered students to register was not the challenge. Instead, it was getting those students who were already registered in their hometowns to change their registration to Durham County. Not only was the paperwork necessary to switch their registration cumbersome, but many Duke students preferred to vote in the elections in their hometown. "A lot of people have some ties to local politics in their hometown," explained Regelbrugge. "They want to vote for a family friend who is running for office, that sort of thing. So a lot of students were wary of transferring their voter registration."

Further, for those Duke undergrads who had their sights set on a specific graduate school or law school, a change in their residency could affect their chance for admission or, more important, created a difference in tuition. "That was obviously frustrating," said Regelbrugge, "but you see both sides of the argument." Luckily, though, the current DA's actions in the lacrosse case seemed to give many Duke students enough reason to go to all that trouble.

Although Regelbrugge described the campaign as a "big unified effort" across campus, DSED did face some opposition. DSED volunteers were turned away when they tried to register voters at a Duke home football game.

Who stopped them? Duke officials.

"There were several students who were getting ready to go in and try to register voters on their way in and they were stopped because the university didn't want—solicitation is not the right word—but that sort of thing, in the football stadium," Reggelbrugge said. To all involved, it looked as if Duke was trying to keep its students from becoming a political force in the DA's race.

Despite the opposition from their own university's administration, the efforts from DSED and its multitude of volunteers paid off. On October 12, they had a "final push" to increase their numbers. "We, along with several other groups on campus, had a big BBQ and it was great. There was tons of food, lots of people registered, and Lewis Cheek spoke. Steve Monks [another candidate for DA] also made an appearance," said Regelbrugge months later.

By the registration deadline the following day, Students for an Ethical

Durham had successfully registered approximately twelve hundred new student voters. DSED had managed to register nearly 20 percent of Duke's entire student body. "We really met, if not surpassed, our goal of voters registered," said Regelbrugge proudly.

If there was anything Mike Nifong was proving, it was that he certainly could stir passions.

The efforts of Regelbrugge, her fellow founders, and the other DSED volunteers did not end when the last voter registration application was turned in to the Board of Elections on October 13. "After the registration forms were all in, our efforts went toward really making sure students voted," she said. Although DSED did not set out to endorse any one specific candidate in the general election, "At this time, we really thought Lewis Cheek had the best chance to beat the DA," said Regelbrugge. Volunteers manned the polls each day early voting took place, in addition to Election Day, holding signs and passing out stickers to support their choice for district attorney: Lewis Cheek.

From the very start of their campaign, many within the community assumed that Students for an Ethical Durham was a less-than-veiled attempt to unseat Mike Nifong. Regelbrugge denied that claim, stating that the campaign was not intended to tell students who to vote for, but just to make sure they "exercised their constitutional right of voting."

However, there was no denying that Nifong's actions had struck a chord within the Duke student body. Notwithstanding each student's personal opinions on the lacrosse case, this case made it strikingly clear how the public officials in Durham, and the decisions they made, could affect them in their four-year academic career at Duke.

"You had a lot of people who felt very passionate about this," said Regelbrugge. "Students were frustrated that Duke's name and their classmates' names were dragged through the mud for what they felt like was a very unfair reason. Duke students are doing really amazing things. In terms of the Durham community, there is always more you can do, of course. But I don't know a single student here who has not, in some point in their academic career, volunteered in the community."

For one DSED founder, in particular, encouraging her peers to roll out of bed on November 7 and go to the polls was not something she took lightly. For Brooke Jandl, the future district attorney in Durham would steer the course for someone she knew very well: her boyfriend, Reade Seligmann.

Although students around Duke's campus were aware of Jandl and Seligmann's relationship, Regelbrugge and Wygod remained the active voices for their campaign within the media. Their relationship was something that needed to remain under wraps to ensure DSED's perception remained as objective as it sought to be.

"The people who got involved in this group were not just the lacrosse team's best friend," Regelbrugge said. "This could have happened to any student, it could have happened to anyone in Durham, and that's what's so scary. Yes, it took this event to open our eyes to some of the corruption among government officials. It may have looked that way, but this wasn't just about the lacrosse team."

The momentum was building, and it seemed likely that Nifong could be removed—until July. That's when Cheek decided he couldn't accept the job of district attorney even if he won. Cheek didn't ask that his name be removed from the ballot, however. "I felt like they, the voting public, were being offered the ability to make a choice," Cheek said. "If there were more votes cast for me than for Mike Nifong, he would be unseated as district attorney."

Although the end result of the valiant petition effort was not the gung-ho candidate they had hoped for, the ten-thousand plus signatures sent a clear message to the current district attorney. His unreasonable actions would no longer go without consequences.

Cheek and the others involved in the anti-Nifong movement tried to publicize and spread this sentiment. They tried to encourage voters not just to voice their concern, but to do something about it on Election Day.

It was a difficult message to convey: Vote for me and I won't take the job. Skepticism about the fledgling movement grew. If Cheek did receive more votes than Nifong, the choice for the next district attorney would be left to Governor Mike Easley, the same governor who had appointed Nifong.

Many worried voters expressed their concern to Cheek directly. "I had some people say, 'Well my gosh, the governor was the one who appointed Mike Nifong in the first place,' " Cheek said. " 'He might re-appoint him.' That was hilarious as far as I was concerned. I mean, for Christ's sake, the person who probably has suffered the most through all of this has been Mike Easley. He is looked upon as the idiot who appointed Mike Nifong in the first place."

This skepticism made one thing clear: It seemed the Durham electorate was afraid of the unknown. Voting for Cheek was like choosing the mystery door and waiting to see what lay behind it. The people of Durham County were sick of surprises. Although they may have been dissatisfied with his recent actions, at least they knew exactly what they got when they voted for Nifong.

The anti-Nifong crowd weren't the only ones to believe they had an opportunity to beat the badgered DA. Some Republicans, who had known little success in the liberal county of Durham, thought they had a chance, too. Maybe this was their chance to elect a Republican to the powerful job of district attorney. But they needed a real Republican to run. Steve Monks, chairman of the Durham Republican party, decided he would offer his name for consideration.

Monks's petition efforts did not enjoy the same success as Cheek's had. He would have to run as a traditional write-in candidate. This meant that if voters wanted to vote for Monks, they would have to physically write his name on the ballot. He would be a Republican candidate, running in a county that is majority Democratic, and his name needed to be physically written on each ballot. As Cheek said, "I didn't see any way on this God's earth that he could win. Casting a vote for him was like throwing it in the trashcan."

Still, nearly six thousand Durham voters did just that. Maybe those few Republicans who did live in Durham were simply excited they could finally vote for a fellow Republican, or maybe some voters were just too afraid to vote for a man they knew would not accept the position. But the 5,927 votes Monks received were pivotal in the outcome of this race. For Mike Nifong, Democrat, the greatest gift he could have been given was provided when the chairman of the Republican party decided to run in this election.

Blame it on Monks for siphoning off just enough votes to allow Nifong to squeak out another political victory. Blame it on Cheek for not giving the people an actual candidate to vote for. Supporters for both campaigns had no problem accusing the other of standing in the way of their victory. But, in the aftermath of the nasty accusations, one thing remained the same: Mike Nifong was still district attorney of Durham.

Once again Durham voters had to choose the lesser of the evils. This time, the names on the ballot stood for a guy who didn't want the job, a guy who wanted it too much, and a guy who had no chance.

On the night of November 7, Nifong sat in a big room on the second floor of the old courthouse in the Board of County Commissioners chambers, watching the polling results come in. He would not be alone. All the candidates, the members of their campaign, and citizens go to this same big room to wait for the results to post.

"It's a big room where there is a big screen on the wall," recalled Jackie Brown. She was there to support the Cheek campaign. About seventy-five people—not including the media personnel, who seemed to outnumber the citizens in attendance—waited patiently to see the final numbers.

The measly number of people who were there that night did not compare to the overwhelming crowd that had come to support Nifong in May. Brown said, "It certainly wasn't like it was in the primary. Mike and the few people who were with him sat on one side of the room, and the Lewis Cheek supporters sat on the other side of the room. Monks didn't come, but there were a few Monks people there."

Sometime after 8:00 p.m., the "big screen" came to life. As the results from each precinct were posted, it did not take long for Brown to realize the outcome would not be as she had hoped. "Because I have been doing this for so long, I knew with the precincts that had come in, that Mike was probably going to win."

Less than thirty minutes later, it was confirmed. Although Nifong once again fell shy of a majority, receiving 49.5 percent of the vote, he had done it. For the second time in the past year, a man who had never won an election eeked out a victory.

"There wasn't a lot of shouting and hollering and clapping," Brown said. "Mike was smiling, but he wasn't rejoicing like he had done in May. I don't know if at that point he had realized that between Monks and Cheek that the voters in Durham actually said, 'We don't want you.' I am sure at some point he realized he did win the election, but he really didn't win it. The citizens of Durham sent him a strong message that night."

Nifong may have felt like the "million dollars" in publicity he said the case would bring him. But despite the smug expression on his face, his victory was largely hollow. To win this position, Mike Nifong would one day pay the ultimate price.

CHAPTER TWENTY-TWO

"No Penetration"

Rare is the live national broadcast in which the word "vagina" is uttered seven times and the word "penis" fourteen times without the cameras' cutting away or the FCC filing a complaint. But on December 22, 2006, Joe Cheshire and the rest of the lacrosse defense team held a press conference that managed to do just that. "I've been thinking about applying to the Guinness Book of World Records for the person that said 'vagina' and 'penis' more on live TV than any other person in one setting," Cheshire joked after delivering a press conference that anyone interested in the lacrosse case will never forget. "I think I've got Eddie Murphy beat and pretty sure I beat Richard Pryor, too."

As shocking as some might have found Cheshire's language, the reason for this press conference was even more so. It all started back in October, when the complete findings from the private analysis firm DNA Security—approximately eighteen hundred pages worth of data—were finally handed over to the defense attorneys and some very interesting information came to light.

No one on the defense team was a DNA specialist. Cheshire had made arrangements with Rob Cary and Chris Manning—lawyers at the prominent Washington, D.C., law firm of Williams & Connolly—to help with analyzing the massive stack of reports. Before Cary and Manning sent the documents off for further study, Cheshire's partner and cocounsel for Dave Evans, Brad Bannon, began to scrutinize the information. He had a hunch that there was more there than met the eye.

An English major from the University of South Carolina with no science background, Bannon was determined to make sense of the data that the district attorney's office had provided. At Rob Cary's suggestion, Bannon went to Amazon.com, bought a six-hundred-plus-page college textbook on DNA, and started to read. A week later, having read the book from cover to cover, Bannon returned to the DNA Security findings and made a startling discovery.

Bannon pulled Cheshire into the law firm's conference room and offered a blunt assessment of the data collected from Crystal Mangum. "This woman is swimming in other men's DNA and not only was she swimming in other men's DNA, there's no DNA of any lacrosse player anywhere on her," Bannon said, his sly smile breaking wide.

The young lawyer then drafted a memo to Williams & Connolly and flew to Washington to meet with Cary, Manning, and their expert, Hal Deadman, who once ran the DNA lab for the Federal Bureau of Investigation. Everything Bannon thought he had found proved true. Deadman confirmed Bannon's analysis that the accuser did not have a single piece of DNA on her that was consistent with the profiles of any of the lacrosse players, while she did have the DNA of at least four other unidentified men in her genital region or on her underwear.

Suddenly, the initial medical reports that she had evidence of swelling in the vaginal walls made sense—she had indeed been penetrated by multiple men within just a few days before her examination, but not one of them had been present at the party where she insisted the rape had occurred.

The defense team was vindicated—here was a treasure trove of information that not only bolstered their own claims of innocence, but also further called into question the truthfulness of the accuser. Worse, none of this information had been presented to them, even though the prosecution had been fully aware of it since the spring.

"I believed all along we would win this case," Cheshire said. "But when Brad was able to break down the data that the prosecutors were counting on us never understanding, I realized that what we were looking at was the worst miscarriage of justice in the history of North Carolina."

Bannon's findings altered the focus of the defense team dramatically: Why had they not been informed of these findings, and was the prosecutor's office aware of them as well? Documents submitted to the court on December 13, 2006, show that "on April 8, 9, and 10, 2006, DNA Security analyzed the DNA profiles extracted from the cheek scrapings, oral swabs, vaginal swabs, rectal swabs, and panties from the rape kit items taken from the accuser at Duke Hospital in the early morning hours of March 14. While DNA Security's final report would not reflect the findings from that analysis, underlying documents provided to the Defendants on October 27, 2006, reflect that *DNA from multiple male sources was discovered on the rectal swabs and panties from the rape kit; it was all compared to the known reference samples from the lacrosse players; and none of it matched any of the players.*"

There was no DNA match from any of the players to any trauma, or evidence of sexual activity on the accuser's body. And though both DNA Security and Nifong were aware of this fact, these findings were not made known until October. The only result mentioned in the May report was the failure to match with Evans, Finnerty, or Seligmann.

The documents also showed that on May 8, 9, and 10, DNA Security examined the DNA sample taken from the boyfriend of the accuser and, as it became clear, while he "would not be excluded as the single source of the male DNA profile taken from the sperm fraction of the rape kit vaginal swab," he could be "excluded as the source of the male DNA also found on the other vaginal swabs, panties, rectal swab, and pubic hair comb." Not only was the boyfriend not the only recent sex partner (despite the accuser's initial claims that she had not had sex for more than a week before her alleged attack), as Bannon pointed out, the stains from the panties had Y chromosomes from at least four different men, so in fact, "It could be more because there could be males that share the same marker."

And none of the patterns of markers matched the DNA samples from any of the lacrosse players. There was absolutely no evidence that even one of the forty-six tested lacrosse players had ever been engaged in any kind of sexual contact with the woman.

In a motion filed by the lacrosse team's lawyers on December 13, Bannon's findings were boiled down to the most powerful statement:

> The Defendants have, upon examining those thousands of pages, discovered that DNA Security identified DNA from multiple males in the accuser's anus, in her pubic region, and on her panties. Enough of that DNA existed for DNA Security to conclude that none of it matched the Defendants, their teammates on the 2006 Duke University men's lacrosse team, or anyone else who submitted a DNA sample in the investigation.
>
> This is strong evidence of innocence in a case in which the accuser denied engaging in any sexual activity in the days before the alleged assault, told police that she last had consensual sexual intercourse a week before the assault, and claimed that her attackers did not used condoms and ejaculated. In short, these discoveries by DNA Security show that male DNA was discovered on *multiple* rape kit items, which did *not* match *any* Defendant in this case or their lacrosse teammates.

As damning as that evidence was, Bannon recited facts in the motion that appeared to provide ample evidence that the prosecution had blatantly attempted to hide this data that would be of value to the defense. "By April 20, 2006, DNA Security analysts had discovered DNA from multiple male sources on the rectal swabs, pubic hair combing, and panties from the rape kit; had compared it to the lacrosse players' DNA; and had concluded that none of it matched the lacrosse players, including the Defendants," the motion said. "They had also apparently discovered possible contamination in the testing of at least one item in this case. However, none of those findings would be included in DNA Security's final report."

Further, between April 25 and April 27, DNA Security tested the false fingernails and, like the SBI lab, "They failed to recover sufficient DNA to identify a profile on any of those items. However, none of those activities or findings would be included in DNA Security's final report." After further testing by DNA Security, the lab eventually determined that

Dave Evans may have been one of several males whose DNA was in a mixture on the false fingernails taken out of Evans's bathroom trash can at 610 North Buchanan. The lab could not call an absolute match to Evans and excluded everyone else on the lacrosse team, as well as the accuser's boyfriend and drivers. A handwritten note reflected that the DNA mixture was also consistent with that of fourteen people in the database used by the lab to do statistical analysis, who had nothing to do with the case. In other words, in the fingernail DNA mixture, there were a few common DNA markers that were consistent with Dave Evans, but they could not be assigned to any one individual with absolute certainty.

While the report published the findings about the boyfriend's DNA on the vaginal swab and Evans's DNA possibly being in the fingernail mixture with that of several other unidentified males, there was no report from the prosecutors or the lab that they had discovered DNA from at least four other unidentified males on the rape kit items that did not match any of the lacrosse players, the accuser's boyfriend, or her drivers. According to the December 15, 2006, court testimony of DNA Security's Brian Meehan, "It is true that we did not release the full profiles of all the players in this case. And I did that after discussions with Mike Nifong, because of concerns about getting those profiles out into the public media. . . . [W]e were trying to do what we thought was the right things to do was minimize the exposure of the rest of the players. It would have meant that we produced profiles and names of all the people."

It was this kind of convoluted reasoning that the defense team was seeking to cut through. Though Bannon had pored over the DNA documents and knew them better than anyone, he had not planned on being the one tapped by this all-star defense team to conduct the cross-examination of Meehan, possibly the most important witness in the case. But just before the hearing was set to begin, Cheshire turned to his young associate.

"This is going to be your witness," Cheshire said to the suddenly wide-eyed Bannon. "I remember saying to Joe, 'I am not prepared to do this. This is an expert in DNA, do you know what I mean? I have no notice. I don't even know what I am going to say when he turns it over to me.' We were sitting at the table. Joe said, 'Listen to me. The difference between a good lawyer and a great lawyer is moments like this. And you are a great lawyer. I've always told you that you are a great lawyer, and you never believed it about yourself, but I know it. So you just need to do this."

"I said, 'Okay.' And I just did it. It was weird because I have never been a fan of sports at all, and I've never been involved in any sporting teams. And I felt, for the only time in my life, like what it must feel like to be like a player in something and having a coach look at you and say, 'This is what you can do, and this is how you can do it.' That was kind of interesting, too, because this case was about sports. As I got up to start asking questions, I just kind of ran around the field for a little while and had fun."

Bannon's "fun" was more than just an amusing diversion, though. As he prodded Meehan with his casual but calculated questions, a larger and even more incriminating picture of the behavior of the prosecution began to develop.

Later in his testimony, after Bannon pointed out that the limited release was in violation of the company's protocol, Meehan repeated his earlier explanation: "It's not just because the district attorney told me to. And, you know, I don't know a better way to say this . . . it may not hold any weight in your legal arena, but we were legitimately concerned about a report that could become explosive if it had overly detailed all those profiles from all those players in it, okay. Now, so we agreed with Mr. Nifong that we would report just the stuff that matched . . . so the report was limited in its scope. . . . But we do indicate on the report that there is additional information."

As Bannon handed off the questioning to another defense lawyer, James Cooney, the thread was continued. One final time, Meehan was asked about the incomplete report as Cooney confirmed: "And that was an intentional limitation arrived at between you and representatives of the State of North Carolina not to report on the results of all examinations and tests that you did in this case?"

To this Meehan simply answered, "Yes."

A handwritten note in one of the margins of the report from Meehan's office also revealed that there was a DNA specimen taken from the accuser's body consistent with Meehan's own profile, raising questions about whether contamination took place in the lab. "Our systems are so sensitive it's just one or two cells, sometimes not even a whole cell," Meehan explained. Given Meehan's admission that some of his own DNA was possibly on the rape kit items despite the lab's precautions against contamination, suddenly the existence of some of Dave Evans's DNA on items taken from his bathroom trashcan made perfect sense. It also made the complete lack of DNA from any of the lacrosse players even more significant.

But despite the astounding sensitivity of the machines, Meehan insisted, "It is possible for a person to be raped and no semen left there. . . . Just because a person doesn't leave DNA at the scene, it doesn't mean he was not there. Simple analogy, and it may be an over simplification: A person can rob a bank and never leave a fingerprint. It doesn't mean they didn't rob the bank."

Nifong adopted the same defense. Despite his previous confidence in the DNA tests, he told the *News & Observer* on April 12, 2006, that a lack of DNA was no problem, since it was a fairly new innovation anyway. Before it came along as a reliable source of information, he said, "We had to deal with sexual assault cases the old-fashioned way. Witnesses got on the stand and told what happened to them." Interestingly, though, neither he nor any of his staff had ever interviewed their primary witness, the accuser, about the details of the night in question until December 21, more than nine months after the alleged attack. And the accuser's words proved to be almost as damning to Nifong's case as the evidence he'd tried to hide.

The alleged victim's story had already changed multiple times—as Charlotte Allen of the *Weekly Standard* pointed out: "During her December 21 interview with prosecutors, the accuser offered either the seventh or twelfth (depending on how you count) significantly different version of the story she had been telling medical personnel, police officers, and news reporters."

But this change was the most dramatic. According to Nifong's brief written explanation on December 22, "The victim in this case indicated that, while she initially believed that she had been vaginally penetrated by a male sex organ . . . she cannot at this time testify with certainty" that such an act actually took place.

This twist was huge for the case—North Carolina law requires penetration for a rape conviction. Without this accusation, the charge could not go forward. Thus, on December 22, at 11:37 A.M., Nifong's office made public its decision that the rape charges would be dropped against the three accused players.

It was this announcement that brought about Cheshire's memorable press conference, which was marked by a note of vindication mixed with disgust and anger: The other two counts of kidnapping and sexual offense would stand, and sexual offense carries the same penalty as rape under North Carolina law—approximately twenty to twenty-five years in prison.

The defense team knew that their reaction to this news needed to make an impact in order to stress to the media and the public exactly how dramatic the latest change to the accuser's story really was, and how serious the two remaining charges were.

"Almost the only consistent thing the accuser has said throughout the many varied different statements she has made was that a penis was used in the assault that she describes and that it was used in her vagina," Cheshire said as he launched the press conference, the rest of the defense team, including Bannon, at his side. "In March—on March 16, she told the investigator, Mr. Himan in his notes, he relates that Brett and Matt—and you will remember, she referred to the three people that assaulted her as Brett, Matt, and Adam—that Brett and Matt put their penis in her anus and her vagina. And that Adam put his penis in her mouth.

"In her handwritten statement, her statement, handwritten on April 6, she said that 'Matt had sex with me in my vagina and then placed his penis in my anus for about three minutes. Brett had sex with me in my vagina for about five minutes and then put his penis in my anus for about two minutes. And Adam ejaculated in my mouth and I spit it on the floor.'

"At the time she made her identifications, of the young men, she said, on tape, which you can get referenced on the motion to suppress, about one of these young men, quote, 'He put his penis in my anus and in my vagina.'

"About one of the other young men, she said, 'He was the one standing in front of me and made me commit oral sex.'

"Almost the only consistent thing that the accuser has said, throughout the many varied different statements that she has made, was that a penis was used in the assault that she describes and that it was used in her vagina.

"Last week, it was clearly demonstrated that significant exculpatory evidence had been purposefully withheld from the defense in this particular case. It should not be lost on you all, who have covered this case, that that significant exculpatory evidence proved that there was no sexual contact between these young men and this woman.

"Apparently, for the first time, yesterday, the first time, representatives of the district attorney's office talked to the accuser. This certainly begs the question, ladies and gentlemen, which I hope you all will ask, why, after all of these months, and all of what these young men have been through, did the district attorney's office first talk to this accuser [now], which leads to the dismissal of one of these charges? Why are they investigating the case now, after they've brought it for months? . . .

"When the DNA results came back from the state DNA lab which found no DNA of these young men in or on the accuser, the prosecutor in this case supposed that they must have been using condoms, although the accuser had said they were not using condoms. . . .

"That, again, is a troubling, transparent coincidence. But let me also point out to you that if it's now going to be the shifting sands again, the shifting factual theory to meet whatever we understand the truth is by the prosecution, that if this woman had been penetrated with a finger, a penis, a mouth, or any other body part, there would have been DNA left in and on her of these young men and there was none left in and on her. . . .

"In his dismissal [of the rape charge], the prosecutor says, since there is no scientific or other evidence independent of the victim's testimony that would corroborate specifically penetration by a penis, the state is unable to meet its burden. . . .

"This prosecutor by dismissing this one charge and saying what he has said to you that his entire case rises and falls on the statement of the accuser, that there is no other evidence, and, yet, just yesterday, he gets, yet again, a different story from her which disputes and is against the other stories that she has told, which all dispute and run against each other.

"So what we have now, ladies and gentlemen, is a prosecutor who has said his case rises and falls on the statement of the victim, the accuser, excuse me, and is going forward with the case when he knows he has multiple different contradictory statements from that person.

"Is that seeing that justice is done?" Cheshire asked rhetorically, "Or is that simply trying to fit facts into a prosecution to prosecute it at all costs?"

"I didn't think about softening it," Cheshire said about his speech that day. "Those were the words that had the impact. . . . You have thirty or forty minutes to get together what you are going to say. I was going to make a point. If people didn't want to listen to it, they could turn their TV off."

He laughingly recalled the reaction he received from his office upon his return. "We came upstairs after that press conference—that had been quite a wild day, been a wild couple of weeks, really—so the younger people were in the office watching a replay of the press conference and they decided to create a drinking game," Cheshire smiled. "And every time I said the word 'penis' or 'vagina' somebody had to take a drink. Before long, they had a marketing plan and everything thought out.

"We wanted that day to leave an impact, for everyone to know how dramatic a turn the case had taken, how obviously deceptive the prosecution had been, and how sad this whole story had become," the diminutive lawyer said, sitting in his award-laden office.

"I think we accomplished all that."

CHAPTER TWENTY-THREE

"You Can't Make Me"

Through the summer and into the fall, as the case was rapidly crumbling around the prosecution, the lacrosse players and their families waited for what they increasingly believed would be the end of the legal case. They waited, too, for something that proved far more elusive than justice: an apology from the Group of 88 and other faculty and staff members who had rushed to judgment in March and April with their demonstrations, poisonous words, and the now-infamous "We're Listening" ad. Surely, the families felt, with all of the opinions that had shifted and the overwhelming evidence that had come out in their favor, surely now the team deserved some kind of explanation for the behavior of the faculty and some sign of regret for the manner in which they had publicly maligned players.

Nothing would come from the liberal Duke faculty, who had fueled the fire with their ad by painting this as a racial clash, with a predominantly white team asserting social and political dominance over a member of an ethnic minority; as an instance of barbaric men preying on an honest, innocent woman just trying to live her life; and as an economic struggle of the haves bullying the have-nots—the very conflicts that lie at the heart of many leftist professors' educational and cultural philosophies. For many of the faculty, this situation was a chance to be heard as experts, an opportunity to promote their own agenda, to bollster their own belief system, and to justify their own fields of study.

According to Stephen Miller, a Duke senior and student columnist with the *Chronicle*, many professors seemed to be in a contest of their own. "It seemed like one of those situations where they were asking each other,

'Who can go the farthest? Who can say the most outrageous things? Who can attack the establishment the most?' It was almost a weird sort of competition amongst these people," said Miller, who would be interviewed more than a dozen times about the situation on national television. "It was just so clear it was never about the victim, it was never about the players. They came in advance with their social agendas, they have had them for years, this was the perfect moment to really let things fly."

For the players, however, the stakes were a bit higher—it was their reputation, their education, and possibly even the rest of their lives. And still, no apology.

"We have always said, we just want an apology," said captain Matt Zash. "But, now, [after] how long it's lingered, you can see that there is this underlying hate these professors have for us, just being white men, and elitist in their terms. We wanted apologies from the school, we wanted apologies from the president, apologies from the athletic director, and now that time has passed it is apparent that is not going to happen and that these people are not remorseful for what they have done."

As public opinion began to turn on a prosecutor who had hitched himself to an accuser's ever-changing story, it also began to turn against the professors who had been so quick to condemn. What kind of faculty is in such a rush to pummel its own students that it not only throws them to the wolves, but actually joins the wolves? The Group of 88 had always maintained that they were, indeed, student-focused with their ad and protests. They insisted that they were speaking out on behalf of the women, minorities, and economically disadvantaged students in their midst—groups they claimed had no voice on campus and, apparently, the only groups they felt deserved to be heard at all.

Journalist Charlotte Allen reflected on the sentiments of the faculty in a *Weekly Standard* article in January 2007. She discussed the inherent tension on the Duke campus between the athletic program and the academic philosophies, and composed an astute synopsis, noting the excitement that some theorists seemed to draw from the case: "Although outsiders know Duke mostly as an expensive preppie enclave that fields Division I athletic teams, the university's humanities and social sciences departments—literature, anthropology, and especially women's studies and African-American studies—foster exactly the opposite kind of culture. Those departments (and especially Duke's robustly "postmodern" English department, put in place by postmodernist celebrity Stanley Fish before his departure in 1998) are famous throughout academia as repositories of all that is trendy and hyperpoliticized in today's ivy halls: angry feminism, ethnic victimology, dense, jargon-laden analyses of capitalism and 'patriarchy,' and 'new historicism'—a kind of upgraded Marxism that analyzes art and literature in terms of efforts by powerful social elites to brainwash everybody else. . . .

"There was a fascinating irony in this. Postmodern theorists pride themselves in discerning what they call 'metanarratives.' They argue that such concepts as, say, Christianity or patriotism or the American legal system are no more than socially constructed tall tales that the postmodernists can then 'deconstruct' to unmask the real purpose behind them, which is (say the postmodernists) to prop up societal structures of—yes, you guessed it—race, gender, class, and white male privilege. Nonetheless, in the Duke lacrosse case the theorists manufactured a metanarrative of their own, based upon the fact that Durham, North Carolina, is in the South, and the alleged assailants happened to be white males from families wealthy enough to afford Duke's tuition, while their alleged victim was an impoverished black woman who, as she told the *Raleigh News & Observer* in a credulous profile of her published on March 25, was stripping only to support her two children and to pay her tuition as a student at North Carolina Central University, a historically black state college in Durham that is considerably less prestigious than Duke. All the symbolic elements of a juicy race/gender/class/white-male-privilege yarn were present. The theorists went to town."

There were, of course, some faculty members who recognized the damage that the Group of 88 had caused, but those professors were chastised when they voiced their concern or tried to offer a voice of reason in the midst of the initial chaos. An article published in the *Chronicle of Higher*

Education on February 16, 2007, included comments from Steven Baldwin, a professor in the Chemistry Department at Duke. Baldwin had been the first professor to question whether the "We're Listening" ad was appropriate. In Baldwin's words, the faculty who signed the document "publicly savaged the character and reputations of specific men's lacrosse players" and the professors "should be tarred and feathered, ridden out of town on a rail, and removed from the academy." The *Chronicle* article goes on: "His letter drew plenty of heat. Mr. Baldwin was chastised for his use of the phrase 'tarred and feathered' because of what some see as its racial connotations. He points out that the origins of the phrase are not racist. He thinks the Group of 88's ad was ill advised. 'My personal view is that their social agenda was at the forefront of their thinking,' he says. 'I think there was a collision between political correctness and due process, and I think political correctness won.' "

Though it took months for anyone to join Baldwin and stand up publicly against the Group of 88, that moment finally came in January 2007, when professors from the Department of Economics issued a letter signed by seventeen faculty members. Released to the campus paper, the document opens by acknowledging that "to date, the only collective signed statement by faculty members concerning the events of last March was an advertisement in the Duke University *Chronicle* subsequent to protests and a forum on March 29, 2006. We are aware too that the advertisement was cited as prejudicial to the defendants in the defense motion to change the venue of the trial involving the three Duke lacrosse team members."

The economics professors then listed several points that had changed the dynamic in recent months, including the fact that "it appears that there were a number of irregular acts committed by members of the Durham law enforcement agencies and District Attorney's Office." They concluded by saying that they "welcome all members of the lacrosse team, and all student athletes, as we do all our students as fellow members of the Duke community, to the classes we teach and the activities we sponsor."

This letter was viewed as a hopeful sign by many—evidence that the faculty were not, in fact, as obstinately set in their blanket condemnation of the as-yet-untried lacrosse players as previous actions seemed to indicate. The response, however, was hardly positive and the Economics letter was not the gesture of healing that it seemed intended to be. According to the piece in the *Chronicle of Higher Education,* many of the faculty prejudices against not only the lacrosse players, but all student athletes, became quite apparent: "Mr. Surin, [a] literature professor, fired off an email message to Thomas Nechyba, chairman of the economics department, complaining about the letter. Many people were bothered by the implication that the Group of 88 were not welcoming to all students, Mr. Surin says.

"When asked whether he 'welcomes' all students to his classes," the *Chronicle of Higher Education* reported, "Mr. Surin dismisses the word itself. 'I admit students to my classes. I do not welcome them,' he says. 'I am not at the door shaking people's hands. They just come in and take their seats.' "

Besides, he told the newspaper, athletes would never take his classes. " 'I do not give quizzes,' he says. 'I give very hard reading.' "

Anyone hoping the Economics Department letter was a sign the rift between the Group of 88 and those outraged by their original ad was healing were thrown a curve two weeks later when the remaining members of the group released a second letter. It was called a "clarifying letter," but it clarified little.

In this document, a list of "concerned faculty" issued what they termed "An Open Letter to the Duke Community" in which they reiterated the same claims of racial- and sex-based hostility that they had made in the original "We're Listening" ad. Unfortunately, the only thing "open" about the letter was the authorship and support.

The message itself showed a remarkable degree of closed-mindedness: "The [original] ad has been read as a comment on the alleged rape, the team party, or the specific students accused. Worse, it has been read as rendering a judgment in the case," the letter stated. "We understand the ad instead as a call to action on important, longstanding issues on and around our campus, an attempt to channel the attention generated by the incident to addressing these."

To some, the letter suggested the Group of 88 might consider adding a new degree program: Revisionist History.

The faculty continued justifying their previous action, and in what many critics felt were the most telling lines, the letter concluded: "There have been public calls to the authors to retract the ad or apologize for it, as well as calls for action against them and attacks on their character. We reject all of these. We think the ad's authors were right to give voice to the students quoted, whose suffering is real. . . . We stand by the claim that issues of race and sexual violence on campus are real, and we join the ad's call to all of us at Duke to do something about this. We hope that the Duke community will emerge from this tragedy as a better place for all of us to live, study, and work." The letter was followed by the names of eighty-seven faculty members, including sixty-three of the original Group of 88 (many of the others no longer worked at Duke) and twenty-six new signers.

When the second ad was released, Miller, the student columnist, had no problem laying bare the prejudices of those liberal professors. "It is kind of like in chemistry when you have a presence of a certain chemical and you can put in an indicator and it will turn purple if it is actually there," he said, offering an example straight from his classroom experience. "You have always had this dark underbelly to the university. The only difference is that now everybody sees it—it's been exposed to the whole nation. And the student body as well. The students didn't realize before how insane some of these professors were. [Group of 88 member] Houston Baker showed during this time period that he is, in my opinion, actually an unhealthy person. And here he is teaching kids year in and year out. God knows what went on in those classes. But now people realize it.

"You open up the paper and there is an email from Houston Baker talking about the scourge of white privilege released upon people—he didn't even know if this alleged crime has happened yet and he was talking as though he had witnessed a crime," Miller said. "And when certain members of the faculty heard this accusation, it was like a eureka moment for them. This is perfect. You have got these kids, they said to themselves, they are rich—they didn't know that, but they said it—they are rich, they are white. Perfect. Let's unleash."

Miller, in one of his newspaper columns, openly chastised Houston Baker, quoting a December 31 email Baker sent to lacrosse player Kyle Dowd's mother: "LIES! You are just a provacateur [*sic*] on a happy New Years Eve trying to get credit for a scummy bunch of white males! You know you are in search of sympaathy [*sic*] for young white guys who beat up a gay man in Georgetown, get drunk in Durham, and lived like 'a bunch of farm animals' near campus . . . umhappy [*sic*] new year to you . . . and forgive me if your [*sic*] really are, quite sadly, mother of a 'farm animal.' "

Many felt that the first ad was irresponsible and mean-spirited but the second was inexcusable. How could the faculty still refuse to admit that they had rushed to judgment and worsened the situation for the accused group of students? At other major universities around the country, many tenured faculty were questioning the wisdom of their Duke colleagues' behavior. The situation actually provided fodder for several national pundits to begin lampooning the Duke faculty. Fox News talk show host Bill O'Reilly wrote an email to every member of the Group of 88 asking why they refused to apologize for their original ad. When none responded, O'Reilly sent a camera crew to Durham to confront several of the faculty and ask them point-blank why they maintained their stance.

The piece aired on January 23, 2007, and allowed the sardonic O'Reilly to use the video clips to laugh out loud at the Duke faculty. Associate Professor of Cultural Anthropology Lee Baker said, "This was a very, very troubling time for all of us. We did not rush to judgment. We presumed innocence the whole time. I mean, I did." Ronen Plesser, associate professor of physics and mathematics, told O'Reilly's crew, "I received your call. And I was hoping that you would interpret my lack of response as 'No, I'm not interested in an interview.' I'm not interested in being interviewed on camera. Thank you." Plesser, who was caught off guard by the camera crew, answered a couple of questions from the doorway of his home looking disheveled and with the sounds of his oriental wind chimes in the background. O'Reilly chuckled at the sight.

O'Reilly summarized the clips, and the anger of many Americans, when he said, "Well, the fact is that none of the eighty-eight teachers who signed the original ad will apologize or even explain themselves—not one. The university itself has now invited the accused players back on campus, but these professors continue their irresponsible behavior. If I were those students, I wouldn't go back."

Republican pundit Ann Coulter had even more fun at the expense of the "loony left" faculty at Duke. "Duke English Professor Cathy N. Davidson recently wrote an opinion piece defending her signing of the 'listening' letter, noting that it was 'not addressed to the police investigation,' but rather 'focused on racial and gender attitudes all too evident' after the alleged rape," Coulter wrote in her column. "She explained that the letter had merely 'decried prejudice and inequality in the society at large.' This would be like defending a letter written during the Dreyfus affair on the grounds that the letter did not explicitly accuse Alfred Dreyfus of treason against France, but simply took the occasion of his arrest to decry the treasonable attitudes of the Jews in society at large. Professor Davidson's column—written when it was clear to everyone except Nancy Grace that three innocent men were facing thirty years in prison for a rape they did not commit—notes that she remains 'dismayed by the glaring social disparities implicit in what we know happened on March 13' and says the incident 'underscores the appalling power dynamics of the situation.' Okay this one they made up, but the case still illustrates a larger truth!"

"If you look at it, their whole argument is, 'We only put that ad out there to start a dialogue about these issues'," said lacrosse player Kyle Dowd months later. "The only problem is, you are willing to start dialogue but now you refuse to speak to the media, you refuse to speak to us, you refuse to speak to other professors. So you've actually decreased dialogue about these topics, which is in complete contradiction to your original goal. No matter which way you look at it, they've failed."

• • •

While most members of the Group of 88 have refused media interviews—constructing their own blue wall of silence, if you will—there was one professor who signed both documents who was willing to speak to the authors of this book. Susan Thorne, associate professor and associate chair of the Department of History, said her decision to attach her name to the "We're Listening" ad was quite simple: "It started with a small group of faculty saying, 'Our students are literally saying, "What do you all have to say about this?" I guess we have to say something.' And that format seemed at the time a measured way of acknowledging the extreme distress and dismay at the thought that those allegations could be true, acknowledging the possibility that they were true without calling for anything to be done or said about the specific case . . . I think history rendered this believable. Otherwise a hoax wouldn't have worked. But certainly enough came out in a court of law to suggest that what evidence has been alluded to has not existed. . . .

"I had three lacrosse players in my class that semester, and they came to talk to me to reassure me of their innocence and I really did feel for them," Thorne continued. "I tried to be compassionate regardless of whether they were guilty or innocent. What I told them was that I would definitely suspend judgment on their guilt or innocence, but I also had to view their accuser as being truthful until proven deceptive. So it continually felt like a schizophrenic position.

"I wish we had used the word 'alleged' in the ad. At the time, I thought that ad came as close to anything I could have constructed that I could live with at the end of either scenario—at the end of my students having committed such an offense or my students having been victimized by such a lie . . . I deeply regret, deeply regret contributing to tremendous harm that was done to them. I can understand any hostility they feel for me. I did feel torn loyalties and I tried to take care of all of my students to the best of my abilities, but their needs seemed conflicted.

"I shared with the ones that came to talk to me all the sentiments behind that ad and was so impressed by their compassion and openness and shame for having been a part of anything associated with racism. And I was really, really proud of their not spinning this atrocity in racist directions. We talked outside of class about understanding the context, which produced a public so willing to believe the worst of them and not demonizing their critics, and they didn't. At least in conversation with me, they were mainly sad. And that's how I feel now is mainly sad."

Thorne also saw fit to sign the "Open letter" because of her stance that the original ad did address some legitimate concerns and, in fact, "seemed the most careful and moderated document I could attach myself to."

On the same day that the Economics Department published their letter, lacrosse player Kyle Dowd rocked the campus when he filed suit against the university for what he claimed was prejudicial and illegal behavior by Assistant Professor of Political Science Kim Curtis, one of the original Group of 88 and later signer of the "Open Letter." The lawsuit became the first of what many believe will be dozens of civil lawsuits filed against the university and its faculty by members of the lacrosse team.

Dowd said he and lacrosse teammate Kevin Mayer were both enrolled in Curtis's Politics and Literature class in the spring 2006. "According to her online profile at the time," the lawsuit said, Kim Curtis "specializes in political theory with particular concentration in contemporary continental work and feminist theory" and had authored numerous articles on women's liberation and feminist history.

It was during her class that, as the suit alleges, "Before the 'scandal' broke, both of the players were earning passing grades on their assignments in that course. After an accuser made allegations of rape and/or sexual assault against three other members of the team, Defendant Curtis assigned both of the lacrosse players in her 'Politics and Literature' class (and *only* the lacrosse players) failing grades on their final assignment in the class. Plaintiff Kyle Dowd was given an 'F' as his final grade in the class."

Dowd contends that his treatment was in violation of the understood contract between the university and the student who paid tuition to that institution, and that both the professor and the university were remiss in resolving the situation. Before the failing grade from Curtis, the suit maintains, Dowd had maintained "a GPA of approximately 3.4 on a 4.0 scale, and had received a grade of less than 'C' on a paper only one time prior in any class."

"My first two papers in that class, I will be the first to admit, they weren't my best papers that I've written in college," Dowd said. "But the one that was graded before this whole thing broke, I got a C-plus on. I know the two I wrote after—I am 100 percent certain—were better papers than my first one. Yet I received a worse grade. You can't tell me that it's a coincidence. And then we [Mayer and Dowd] both received an F on our final paper. To me, that can't just be coincidence."

Dowd also said he received an F grade for class participation, saying Curtis told him he had missed too many classes. Yet Dowd maintains he informed Curtis "every time I was missing class I was missing due to a meeting with my lawyer or some other type of meeting pertaining to the [lacrosse] situation. And she told me not to worry about it, it's not a problem. . . . By no means did I think I was going to fail that class."

Dowd's lawyers wrote in their complaint that "initially Duke refused to entertain any arguments by Mr. Dowd and his parents that the grade was incorrect. The Dowds, anguished in their belief that Kyle would not graduate, pleaded with Professor Curtis and Duke to admit their error. Duke rebuffed their requests, but eventually agreed to instead recognize certain credits that Kyle had earlier earned at Johns Hopkins University, thereby allowing him to graduate. In the months after Kyle Dowd graduated, Duke has since stated that the 'F' grade originally given to Kyle Dowd resulted from a 'calculation error,' and has changed Mr. Dowd's final grade to a 'D,' a grade that still has no basis in reality."

Duke asked a court to dismiss the claim, saying there was no legal precedent for suing a university for academic malfeasance. As this book goes to print, the case remains unresolved. "I think the most important thing for me is getting the grade changed, because the changing of the grade, that says everything," Dowd said. "That proves their wrong doing. . . . I want to get it changed to P—passing. Nobody is ever going to agree on what the grade should have been."

The view *from* the ivory tower might show one thing, but the view *of* the ivory tower by the players, their families, alumni, and the public at large was rapidly deteriorating. In fact, a poll taken for Duke in its attempt to understand the damage this case had done to the university's reputation showed one outstanding statistic: 82 percent of alumni queried in the 2007 poll said they were troubled by the actions by the Group of 88.

Despite those numbers, despite the national ridicule, Duke President Richard Brodhead has steadfastly refused to condemn the actions of those professors.

"In the time I've been at Duke, our faculty do and say all kinds of things," Duke Vice President John Burness said, defending Brodhead, who would not be interviewed for this book. "The university doesn't comment on that. I was quoted in the [Duke] *Chronicle* saying something to the effect of, 'Our job is to provide a venue for free speech, and let the debate go. We hope it's enlightened, but at the end of the day you have these debates and people learn from them.' We don't go condemning faculty members for what they're saying when they do that."

Though Burness wouldn't condemn the faculty's actions, he was not so kind to the lacrosse team, repeatedly implying—nearly a year after the party—that the team was "out of control" and its actions were of great concern to the administration.

The bizarre and inexplicable behavior by the faculty continued into spring 2007, when a new rape charge was filed after another off-campus party. This case, which alleged that a female Duke freshman was raped on February 11 in a house on Gattis Street in Durham—and was another case of interracial violence—resulted in no angry letters from faculty, no collective statements, no pot-banging demonstrations.

But if the Group of 88 was only concerned about racial and sexual tensions, as they contended after their involvement with the lacrosse team scandal, why was this case so very different? Why did this situation not warrant the same response? Unfortunately, this time, the roles were reversed in a way that did not speak to the political agenda of many of the activist faculty members: The alleged victim was white and her attacker was black, and the party was hosted by several members of Phi Beta Sigma—an African-American fraternity—and more than three hundred students had been invited through their Duke Facebook accounts.

This time, the faculty silence was deafening

"I think the thing that might be most disheartening to me," Mike Pressler said a year after the party at 610, "is that in all this time the only people that have stood up and apologized for the way they handled themselves were the players. The kids are the only ones to say, 'We made a mistake and we're sorry for it.' The adults in this picture—the faculty, the administration—they haven't apologized for anything. That to me is among the saddest facts in this whole mess.

"The 'adults'—and I put that in quotes—who are supposed to be teaching the young people have shown they have the most to learn."

CHAPTER TWENTY-FOUR

Cruelest of Ironies

In the spring of 2007, it seemed ironic that as the case against the Duke lacrosse players was falling apart, the person whose life now hung in the balance was the man who started it all—Mike Nifong.

In March 2006, Nifong acted as if he was invincible. He paraded for the media, he operated on the assumption that the accuser—despite her employment, medical, and criminal histories—was credible, and some of those white lacrosse players had to be guilty. Nifong never stopped charging forward. Fellow attorneys cautioned him that his actions bordered on—or crossed the line of—unethical conduct in the legal world. But Nifong ignored their warnings.

The North Carolina State Bar finally stepped in, filing serious ethics charges against the district attorney twice within a four-week period between December 2006 and January 2007. The bar's first complaint alleged that Nifong had violated rules on pretrial publicity; its second complaint claiming he had knowingly withheld evidence from the defense and lied to both the court and bar investigators. Nifong—who withdrew from the lacrosse case in January 2007—could be disbarred if convicted by the disciplinary board.

The initial bar complaint regarding pretrial publicity showed that Nifong had become an "A-list" interviewee with a who's who of America's media. As he began his interview barrage, Nifong received a letter from lacrosse defense lawyer Joe Cheshire warning him that he was nearing the edge of disaster. Bar rules prohibit the kind of show Nifong was starring in—but they also allow the defense to engage the media in an effort to level the playing field. The only winners in that situation, defense lawyers argued, were the media, who would never run out of copy or video. Cheshire's letter to Nifong, dated March 30, 2006, three days after Nifong started his public statements about the case, which warned that the DA had crossed ethical boundaries, ultimately found its way into the media, as well. The *Raleigh News & Observer* detailed Cheshire's letter in a story on January 15, 2007:

> Your reported comments have greatly prejudiced any court proceedings that may arise. I do not understand why you will reportedly speak to the media in such certain, condemning terms before all the evidence is in, but you will not have the courtesy to meet or even speak with a representative of someone you have publicly condemned, despite your knowledge of the presumption of innocence and your position as an officer of the court bound by the Rules of Professional Conduct related to pre-trial publicity.

The *News & Observer* reported that Cheshire wrote in his letter that on March 29, he had his paralegal, Moira Bitzenhofer, call Nifong's office to set up a meeting so the defense lawyer could talk to the prosecutor either in person or on the phone. Nifong, through his assistant, Sheila Eason, declined to talk with Cheshire. The newspaper said Cheshire wrote a strongly worded response and faxed it to Nifong at 3:42 P.M. on March 30. "You and I have known each other for a long time, and I do not mind telling you I was amazed at that response," Cheshire wrote. "In thirty-three years, I have never seen such a request denied by a prosecutor, nor in such a manner. Your responsive comments, reported to Ms. Bitzenhofer by Ms. Eason verbatim, seemed to suggest I should call the Durham Police Department and have my client charged with a crime before you would have a conversation with me on a topic you have demonstrated no reluctance to discuss with myriad local and national news reporters over the last several days."

More than ten months later, Cheshire, in his downtown Raleigh office with this book's author, explained the strategy of his letter to Nifong:

"I said, 'You are creating a situation in which you are forcing us to go out and defend our clients,' " Cheshire said. " 'We do not want to do that. You are creating that situation.' He did create that situation. He's a fool. And we tried to warn him. Some people have said to me, 'Don't you feel a little sorry for Mike Nifong?' I don't feel sorry for the man in the slightest. And one of the primary reasons I don't feel sorry for him is because we warned him. We tried to warn him. We gave him every chance, every time, every way, every step of the way, we gave him an out. Always. We were gracious and gentlemanly and we gave him an out. Every time he just stuck his middle finger up at us."

He obviously stuck it up at others, too. And the gestures didn't go unnoticed.

Raleigh, North Carolina, television station WRAL News reported the State Bar Association actually opened its case against Nifong on March 30, 2006—the same day Nifong received Cheshire's letter. The bar also found on October 19 after an investigation that there was reasonable cause to refer the case to the bar's disciplinary commission for trial. While the bar's file on Nifong was filled with his raucous quotations, the legal community and others later learned that Nifong's deception went far beyond what he was telling the media.

"It has been one of the biggest examples of prosecutorial misconduct that the general public [has] seen, certainly one of the greatest that the public has been enamored with," Cheshire said.

With his career on the line, Nifong rolled the dice on a story told by a stripper; they came up snake eyes . . . with blond highlights.

The bar's first public complaint against Nifong was stunning not just for its unusualness—few can remember a more significant rebuke of a prosecutor by that state bar—but also for its depth. It laid out numerous examples of the DA's press statements that were "prejudicial to the administration of justice" and also "engaged in conduct involving dishonesty, fraud, deceit, or misrepresentation." The seventeen-page complaint accused Nifong of breaking four rules of professional conduct when speaking to reporters about the high-profile case. The complaint listed fifty examples of public statements Nifong made to the media over a ten-month span that could prejudice the case.

In a humorous twist, the camera-loving Nifong had little to say on the day the ethics bomb was dropped. "I'm not really into the irony of talking to reporters about allegations that I talked to reporters," Nifong said in published reports.

Irony dripped from the Durham County Judicial Building on 201 East Main Street in downtown Durham.

A prosecutor who chastised players for needing legal representation suddenly needed a lawyer himself. In early January 2007, Nifong hired David Freedman, a Winston-Salem attorney who is noted in North Carolina for defending lawyers battling state bar complaints. Freedman, as it happened, also criticized Nifong's early handling of the lacrosse case during a national television interview in April 2006. Freedman told the *News & Observer* he regretted comments he made on MSNBC's *The Abrams Report.*

"My opinion was just based on media reports," Freedman told the newspaper. "As an experienced trial lawyer, I should know better than to base my comments just on what I read." Nifong's silence on the ethics complaint didn't matter. It read loud and clear.

Among the major allegations made in the bar complaints:

- On more than one occasion, Nifong suggested condoms may have been used in the attack—this after he had read the report, which stated the victim said no condoms were used. Nifong knew the statements were false, but he still suggested circumstances that excused the exculpatory evidence.
- The DA insinuated that results of certain tests performed as a part of the investigation proved their guilt. No such evidence existed.
- Nifong openly proclaimed the players' guilt, poisoning a potential jury pool.
- Nifong should not have castigated the lacrosse players for their al-

leged refusal to cooperate with or make statements to law enforcement authorities. Nifong painted a picture that the players hid behind a wall of silence, which, it was noted, was false. They voluntarily helped investigators with the search warrant, offering personal statements and DNA.

- Nifong also "defamed the character, credibility, and reputation" of the accused. This, along with his expression of opinions and views of the nature of the alleged crimes, had a substantial likelihood of heightening public condemnation of the accused. The bar cited sixteen comments that attacked the reputation of the accused white men and their "ganglike rape" of a black woman.

It wasn't Nifong's best day.

Veteran Raleigh lawyer Burley Mitchell, a former chief justice of the State Supreme Court, told the *News & Observer* that the bar's first complaint was truly extraordinary. "From the time I was Wake County's elected attorney until I was chief justice, I can't recall the bar filing a complaint against a district attorney for pretrial publicity," Mitchell told the newspaper. Lisa Williams, a former Durham prosecutor turned defense attorney who had known Nifong for more than a dozen years, said the accusations created a conflict of interest for Nifong. "I feel like this is the first shoe," Williams told the *News & Observer*. "And the second shoe is coming."

It landed with an authoritative thud.

Faced with the first round of ethics charges, Nifong quietly requested to be removed from the case on January 12, 2007, when he faxed a letter to the state attorney general and asked for a special prosecutor to take over the case. Under North Carolina law, only a district attorney can formally request a special prosecutor. "His withdrawing from the case has nothing to do with how he feels about the merit of the case," Freedman told the Associated Press. "He's disappointed he has to get out of the case. He likes to see things from beginning to end."

Though he stepped aside, Nifong stressed he believed in the case and wanted the accuser—not the accused—to receive a fair trial. In the minds of his critics, fairness arrived less than two weeks later, when the state bar lodged new and more serious ethics charges against Nifong. On January 24, 2007, the bar accused Nifong of withholding evidence from the defense and lying to both the court and bar investigators. "If these allegations are true and if they don't justify disbarment, then I'm not sure what does," Joseph Kennedy, a law professor at the University of North Carolina, told the Associated Press. "It's hard for me to imagine a more serious set of allegations against a prosecutor."

The new charges were tied to Nifong's decision to use a private lab for DNA testing as his office investigated allegations against three lacrosse players—David Evans, Collin Finnerty, and Reade Seligmann. In March 2006, the State Bureau of Investigation examined Mangum's underwear and swabs taken from her body following the party at 610. The SBI couldn't find semen, blood, or saliva. The following month, Nifong received a judge's permission to use a private laboratory—DNA Security—for more sophisticated testing. DNA Security found DNA from at least four unidentified men but no genetic material from any lacrosse player.

Once DNA Security had collected data from its multiple tests, lab director Brian Meehan approached Nifong with the results. Nifong and Meehan agreed that the final report would not include all of the results. Instead, it would be limited to the "positive results," which meant the report would not mention anything about the other male DNA found; only that there was no match to any of the lacrosse players. The bar complaint pointed out that "this agreement between Nifong and Dr. Meehan meant that the potentially exculpatory DNA evidence and test results would not be included in the report and, therefore, would not be provided to the Duke Defendants or the other player suspects."

According to the complaint, Nifong had just met with Meehan and was aware the results were omitted when he provided the reports to defense attorneys. When defense lawyers for Finnerty served discovery requests on Nifong on May 17, 2006, they specifically requested that any expert witness "prepare, and furnish to the defendant, a report of the results of any and all examinations or tests conducted by the expert." Nifong did not do so. This failure to provide the complete report of the DNA tests and examinations, including the potentially exculpatory DNA test, was a violation state law.

The complaint also stated that when defense attorneys in June 2006 specifically requested a report or written statement of the meeting between Nifong and Meehan to discuss DNA results, Nifong said at the court hearing that no information beyond what was in the report was discussed. "That's pretty much correct, your honor," Nifong said, according to the complaint. "We received the reports, which he has received, and we talked about how we would likely use that, and that's what we did."

"Lying is really at the top of the list in terms of things lawyers just can't do," Kennedy told the *News & Observer.* "The whole thing is premised on integrity. And lying about something as important as evidence suggesting innocence in a serious case, it just doesn't get any worse than that."

The complaint said Nifong lied to the court, either on paper or in direct comments to a judge, on five occasions from May to September 2006. Nifong also withheld evidence in a September discovery hearing. Defense lawyers wanted to seek the results of any test finding and any additional DNA on the alleged victim even if it did not match any of the players. The complaint noted that Nifong referred to the defendants' request for the complete file and underlying data as a "witch-hunt list."

When defense attorneys realized that DNA evidence was being withheld, they filed "a Motion to Compel Discovery: Expert DNA Analysis." Nifong claimed during an October 27, 2006, hearing, "The first I heard of this particular situation was when I was served with these reports." But Nifong's cover was blown. He relented and provided defense lawyers with 1,844 pages of material. After the hearing, Nifong told the media, "We are trying to, just as Dr. Meehan said, trying to avoid dragging any names through the mud but at the time his report made it clear that all information was available if they wanted it and they have every word of it."

But it was obvious that Nifong wasn't trying to protect anyone's reputation other than his own.

Nifong's questionable actions didn't go unnoticed by the media, which directed their venom at Nifong and coined a neologism that used his name. "Now we can 'Nifong' someone when we want to trump up criminal charges based on flimsy evidence allegedly for political purposes," columnist Kathleen Parker of the *Orlando Sentinel* wrote.

"In short, when we want to screw up someone's life."

Nifong may have inexplicably "Nifonged" himself. At least from the sounds of his early boasts, Nifong surely figured the lacrosse case would take him triumphantly into a cushy retirement and define his thirty-year law career. But his acts of gross negligence could ultimately cost him both.

And that would be one of the cruelest ironies of all.

CHAPTER TWENTY-FIVE

Duke Lacrosse 2007

The music began to pump through the speakers at Koskinen Stadium around twelve-forty in the afternoon. The symbolism may have been lost at that particular moment—it was more than ninety minutes before the start of the Dartmouth-Duke men's lacrosse game—but the opening song fit perfectly as the Blue Devils continued their warmups on the field.

The song was an oldie but goodie called "Pick Up the Pieces," recorded by a group called Average White Band in 1974. A primarily instrumental track and former number-one pop hit, the dance tune was a one-chord jam built on swinging lines alternating between horns and guitars, punctuated by the lone but persuasive lyric "Pick Up the Pieces." It seemed to be the perfect prelude to a day that many felt was the most emotional and bittersweet in Duke lacrosse history. The program was indeed about to pick up the pieces.

After its abbreviated 2006 season, there was a question whether the Blue Devils could rise again and chase an NCAA title in 2007. In many ways, the season opener on February 24 between visiting Dartmouth and Duke was aimed at giving the Blue Devils' new coach, John Danowski, and the program a step toward normalcy.

"There has been nothing normal about this program for the last year," said Chris Kennedy, Duke's senior associate athletic director and twenty-nine-year employee of the university who watched the opener from the Blue Devils' sideline and wept when the team took the field. "I don't think people understand the extent of the emotional and psychological damage to these kids in all kinds of ways. Guilt, survivor's guilt, remorse, anger, righteous indignation, and everything else. I think there's a sense among some people that now they are playing lacrosse again, everything is fine and all that stuff just goes away. That's not true. That's not going to be true for a long time. If they win the national championship and go undefeated, that's not going to erase things. You know these kids aren't insensitive, stupid louts. They are not capable of just putting that all behind them, all this turmoil and all this pain. It's going to be there."

Sixth-ranked Duke overcame its nerves and a shaky opening half to beat unranked but pesky Dartmouth 17–11, giving way to a bellowing sigh of relief that was surely felt across Duke's campus. The last time the Blue Devils had been able to play or practice together without it being an event was the team's 11–7 home loss to Cornell on March 21, 2006.

"First, it's a relief for this to be over," said an emotionally drained Danowski, sitting on a chair and leaning forward with his elbows resting on a table, following the Dartmouth game. "I could feel it in my body. I could feel it in the muscles in my legs. Certainly the amount of emotion that has been carried forward by everyone, it has been tremendous."

Duke was determined to splash the program with a new coat of paint for the opener against Dartmouth. The buzz surrounding the game was closer to a Duke–North Carolina basketball game than the lacrosse season opener for the Blue Devils. But the feelings went far deeper: It was another challenge for a team that was looking forward to a time when it could just play games and not dwell on the past. "We know what it's like when something is taken away from you," senior defenseman Nick O'Hara said. "Anytime you get out there, we're excited. I guess it's kind of a relief, emotionally speaking. It's good to finally get on the field and to play with all these guys. It feels a little like the weight is off your shoulders, we can get going now."

Fans began lining up to enter Koskinen Stadium more than two hours before the two teams were set to take the field. By the time the gates opened at twelve-twenty-five, the number of media, support staff, family, friends, alumni, and fans easily exceeded the announced crowd of 425 that had attended the Blue Devils' season opener against Butler in 2006. Although

Duke doesn't charge admission or sell tickets for lacrosse games, the crowd quickly grew to 6,485, just a few hundred short of Duke's home record, on a brilliantly sunny but chilly North Carolina winter afternoon.

More than sixty reporters covered the game, which was nationally televised on sports cable network ESPNU. For most Duke games, no more than a handful of local beat writers normally follow the Blue Devils. The remote television trucks that camped on campus during the early weeks of the scandal in 2006 also returned, but this time to detail a celebration. Duke president Richard Brodhead, whose handling of the case was heavily criticized, attended the game. He was flanked by administrators such as Joe Alleva, the school's athletic director, whose role in the controversy was silently and angrily scrutinized by his own coaches.

From tailgaters in the parking lots to the students filling the stands, it seemed as if everyone was wearing a Duke lacrosse T-shirt. There were also those who wore shirts with a line crossed through the name of District Attorney Mike Nifong, who secured the indictments but recused himself after being charged with ethics violations for his handling of the case. Fans also wore buttons with slogans like "Innocent Until Proven Innocent" and "Fantastic Lies." Others wore "Save Duke Lacrosse" shirts and held "Free the Duke Three" stickers.

Duke tried to make the game a special event, even bringing in an inflatable tunnel and smoke machines for the players to make a grand entrance to the field from their locker room. The school's pep band also played for the first time at a Blue Devils' lacrosse game, and the players were even sporting new, deep-blue uniforms. The Duke bookstore set up a booth inside the stadium, and the team's paraphernalia was in high demand. Children, many wearing lacrosse gear, waved blue-and-white pompoms that were handed out like free candy. "It was a great atmosphere, better than I expected," senior defenseman Tony McDevitt said. "I am sure there were a lot of people out there in the stands who didn't even know what was going on in the field. But it was great. Anytime you get support, it's great. And it was definitely emotional. It's just that next step—we took one more. We all know just what happened."

Reminders of that past turmoil were certainly visible. Before the game the Blue Devils wore black warmup jerseys bearing either a 6, 13, or 45—the numbers of charged players David Evans, Collin Finnerty, and Reade Seligmann. Senior attackman Peter Lamade developed the idea for the pregame tribute and the rest of the Blue Devils supported it. The jerseys of underclassmen Seligmann and Finnerty were hung in the locker room. In January Duke said Seligmann and Finnerty were invited to return to school and were eligible to rejoin the team, but neither had accepted. Evans graduated in May. The trio did not attend the opener.

A sticker reading "MP"—the initials of former coach Mike Pressler—was placed on helmets. The Blue Devils ordered sweatbands and other stickers adorned with the three players' numbers and another to honor former Blue Devil Jimmy Regan, who was killed in early February while serving as a U.S. Army Ranger in Iraq. Following a moment of silence before the game to honor Regan, many in attendance probably didn't notice the irony, or divine intervention depending on one's religious faith—Duke's opening goal was scored by junior midfielder Brad Ross, whose jersey number, 10, was the same number worn by Regan during his four-year career (1999–2002) with the Blue Devils.

Game security was unlike that for any other in Duke's history. Kennedy, Associate Athletic Director Mitch Moser (Facilities and Operations), and members of the school's Student Affairs Division and Duke police met two weeks before the opener to discuss game-day security. The group didn't know what to expect. Would the protestors and pot-bangers return? What about the New Black Panther Party, which marched on campus in the spring of 2006 and verbally threatened lacrosse players? Would there be physical confrontations between people with opposing views? Kennedy said the group didn't think anything was going to happen but "we couldn't act that way."

A second sixty-minute meeting was held on Wednesday before the game to review policy that had yet to dry on university letterhead. The first step was to lock down Koskinen Stadium Friday night before the game: a first. The second step was unprecedented but far more dramatic.

A bomb dog sniffed for explosives inside the stadium on Saturday morning at eleven o'clock. "We really didn't think there would be a bomb, but we thought somebody might phone in a bomb threat to try to disrupt the game," Kennedy said. "So if we could send the dogs in there and lock the stadium down we would know if that happened not to have to react to it. . . . Those people who were so convinced and so self-righteous and so holier-than-thou last spring outside the house with their little pots and pans, I am convinced that some of them are disappointed that it didn't happen. Would they come back? Or there's the whole camp that believes, 'Well, maybe that didn't happen but they are no angels.' Would those people show up and demonstrate that they still don't like the lacrosse team and think the lacrosse team [members] are hooligans or whatever? We didn't think so but we had to prepare for it."

While fans were prohibited from bringing signs into the stadium, Duke had installed signs on the fence lining the field with the Latin phrase *Succisa virescit*—the motto for the Delbarton School in Morristown, New Jersey, where Seligmann and three current Blue Devils went to high school. Adopted by the Duke lacrosse program in the preseason, it means: "When cut down, it grows back stronger." Parents of current Duke players, alumni, and the more than thirty former players in attendance also were pleased to see the Blue Devils return to the playing field, viewing it as a milestone. The victory was embraced at a school that prides itself on athletic success. While many said they have witnessed changing perceptions of Duke lacrosse over the past year, others also felt the return was "bittersweet" because of those who were not in attendance due to alleged crimes.

"It's unfortunate in terms of these charges and allegations, as opposed to the fact that the program has been put in the elite status by Coach Pressler over the last sixteen years and was on the way to the national championship," said Chuck Sherwood, a former goalie and coach at Duke (1972–77) and the father of sophomore reserve goalie Devon Sherwood. Chuck made the drive from his Long Island, New York, home with wife, Dawn, for the game. "It would have been better had this [atmosphere] been because of the national championship they won last year as opposed to the circumstances. You know, in a lot of ways, I am sort of happy light has been shed on the Duke lacrosse program. It's just unfortunate why light has been shed on it." Dr. Thom Mayer, father of junior defenseman Kevin Mayer, told ESPN that "when I walked onto the plane wearing my Duke lacrosse jacket, the entire plane applauded. And I wore the Duke jacket when it wasn't as popular. I think Duke has become everyone's second-favorite team."

Six-hundred-and-eighty-four miles away in Smithfield, Rhode Island, there was another season opener that mattered little to fans nationally. There wasn't a television crew broadcasting the game across the country or print media representing the nation's most respected magazines and newspapers. It was a game of consequence only to the 610 fans who braved a wickedly cold New England afternoon and to those fans back at Duke who searched for Bryant University updates by telephone or text message.

Mike Pressler landed a job as the head coach at Division II Bryant, where his Bulldogs fell to Adelphi University 6–5. With day-old snow surrounding the bright green Astroturf field and a steady wind blowing across Bulldog Stadium, Bryant was unable to mount a consistent offensive attack and give Pressler a win in his coaching return. Adelphi scored four unanswered goals in the second half to take a commanding 6–2 lead heading into the fourth quarter. The Bulldogs rallied with three goals in the final four minutes by Brad Burton, Kevin Hogland, and Matt McAllister, but it wasn't enough. "We have some work to do," Pressler said. "Our defense played exceptionally well. We need to work harder to finish our scoring opportunities."

While there was no public acknowledgment of the Adelphi-Bryant game at Koskinen Stadium, McDevitt admitted that Pressler was on his mind. "I probably will hear from him tonight, and we will talk," McDevitt said. "I feel bad that he lost, but he will get those guys on track and I am sure he's happy for us. Absolutely."

• • •

Duke's triumphant return wasn't lost on the throng of students, many of whom began to gather and tailgate with beer and other drinks in a bottom parking lot behind the stadium at least two hours before the start of the game. Concern about how the lacrosse team would be received by students and the curious proved unfounded. School officials had sent an email earlier in the week requesting that students be on their best behavior. There were also no protesters, though they had been a common sight on campus and in Durham in the days after the accusations became public. Garrett Wood, a junior biomedical and mechanical engineering major, told ESPN, "I think today will do a lot just getting back on the field to kind of put some of the stuff behind us. Obviously the case is not over, but maybe . . . if we can put that behind us and can come out and play a game, I think it'll help a lot."

It also helped that Duke gave fans plenty to cheer about, though Dartmouth didn't lie down. The anticipation grew inside the Blue Devil's locker room as players shouted and danced to techno music that blared from a portable sound system set up in one corner. Screaming, "Let's go boys," and, "It has been a while," as they lined up in two single-file lines inside the blue inflatable tunnel that led from their locker room, players sprinted through generated smoke onto the field to a standing ovation, jumped around, and mobbed each other in a bouncing huddle at midfield.

Following Ross's goal to open a game that began nearly twenty minutes late due to programming challenges on ESPNU, the Big Green scored three unanswered goals. But the Blue Devils were able to catch their breath and settle down, making a run of their own to end the first quarter and tie it. In the second half, the offensive tandem of Zack Greer and National Player of the Year candidate Matt Danowski, the head coach's son, put on a show. The duo finished with a combined nine goals and six assists.

"It [emotion] kind of got the best of me in the first quarter," Danowski said. "I think I kind of got carried away by it. I think I was just so wound up, finally back out there again, trying to make plays, the crowd was here. I kind of had to take myself out of that and settle down." Senior midfielder Ed Douglas said the Blue Devils attempted to prepare themselves for any and all distractions, saying, "There were certainly many, from the media, from the great crowd we had. Running out of the tunnel with smoke—all sorts of distractions. I thought the guys focused very well. You could sense there was excitement in the locker room before we ran out. I think that showed itself in some of the mistakes we made but also in the spirit of play we had." Coach Danowski wasn't surprised by his team's start after arriving in the locker room to give his pregame speech. "The guys were having a great time," he said. "The music was on, the guys were singing. It was great. But nevertheless it was emotion, and emotion takes its toll. What happened in the first quarter was about what I expected. I thought we may get a little overzealous, I thought we may foul a little bit. But I also thought Dartmouth was a very good team."

The game's emotion was also felt by those who were unable to attend. William Wolcott, a senior defenseman on the 2006 squad who lives in New York City with former teammates Kyle Dowd and Bret Thompson, watched the televised game with thirty other alumni in a Big Apple sports bar that was decorated with balloons in Duke's blue-and-white school colors. "It was bittersweet to say the least," Wolcott said. "I was excited to see those guys back out there, running around and playing lacrosse, doing what they love. But at the same time it was a little weird to not be out there and not to see Coach Pressler stalking up and down the sidelines. It brought back a lot of good memories; we had a lot of fun playing lacrosse for Coach Pressler at Duke. It was just good to see the positive energy and all of the support there for those guys. The fans, students, press, everyone was so supportive. It was a good day for Duke lacrosse."

It was a good day, and the start John Danowski wanted. Duke entered ranked fourth by *Lacrosse* magazine and eighth in the preseason Nike/Inside Lacrosse men's Division I media poll. Defending national champion and Atlantic Coast Conference rival Virginia was first in both polls. Danowski also believed the day delivered an underlying message. Many fans remained behind to wait for players, who received congratulatory hugs as they emerged from their stadium locker room and walked across the field with equipment in hand back toward the William David Murray Building. Returning players remembered that it was in that bottom-floor meeting room where the 2006 team was informed by Pressler that he had resigned effective immediately and the remainder of the season was canceled.

Surrounded by red oak trees that had yet to spring back to life as a harsh winter neared its end, the Bulldogs were ringing in a new era for Bryant lacrosse under Pressler. The day before the season opener as the Bulldogs emerged from their makeshift locker room, two of Pressler's former players and captains stepped up to tell the coach's newest players what to expect.

Dan Flannery and Matt Zash were impeccably dressed in suits, crisp shirts, polished black loafers, and Duke ties, a sign of loyalty to Pressler and their lasting pride in being Duke lacrosse players. The thirty-seven Bryant players, sitting on benches and couches, were awestruck as Flannery and Zash stood to speak. Not one player twitched or blinked, afraid they might miss a word from their guest speakers.

Pressler made the introductions, telling his team that the appearance of Flannery and Zash was a sign of support, not only for him, but for Bryant lacrosse. Zash, called the "most dominant midfielder I have ever had, end line to end line" by Pressler, opened by describing how his former coach wanted him to talk about the lessons he had learned at Duke. Zash said he had learned a lot of good things and a lot of bad things, especially about "what one night can do to your reputation." Zash also wanted to focus on what he called Pressler's finite-numbers speech.

"There is a finite number in everything," Zash said. "You have a finite number of practices in your career. You have a finite number of days at this school. And, more appropriately, you have a finite number of times to strap on the equipment and these jerseys and do battle with somebody else. And that's one of those things that I might have taken for granted. I thought I was going to have six or seven more games to play and I didn't really get to fulfill that in my last game."

Flannery, whom Pressler called "the cleanest attackman I have ever coached," admitted he was initially unsure what to say after being invited by Pressler. Flannery talked about how the Duke lacrosse "rape hoax" had helped him become stronger.

"You know, in life you are dealt cards in every situation," he said. "And sometimes you are dealt good cards and sometimes you are dealt shitty cards. And, in this case, we were dealt a really shitty hand. Well, you know what, just like anything else in life—what do you do when you get dealt bad cards? You work harder, you get tougher, you get meaner, you get nastier. And that's what we did. We had to come together as one if we were going to beat this. How did we do that? Well, accountability. We accepted responsibility for our actions, we apologized, we stood up for each other, we told the truth—always tell the truth. We did the right thing, especially in times of inconvenience, and we never ever gave up on each other. That's how we got through it. We created this forever bond of loyalty that was unwavering, and it remains unwavering today. . . . You won't be a successful lacrosse team if you guys don't come together as one, as selfless individuals who sacrifice the individual for the collective. . . . Tomorrow, I have all the faith in the world in you guys. You go out there, you play as hard as you can, as tough as you can."

Flannery knew whereof he spoke, for it was his telephone call to Allure Escort Services and the party at the home he shared with Zash and Evans that had set off the perfect storm.

CHAPTER TWENTY-SIX

Exonerated

The door shut behind North Carolina Attorney General Roy Cooper as he entered a bottom-floor conference room in the RBC Center on the campus of North Carolina State. Cooper, who had taken over the criminal case against the three lacrosse players in January 2007, told a gathering of national and local media that his investigation showed there was "insufficient evidence to proceed on any of these charges. Today we are filing notices of dismissal for all charges."

The statement was sweet. But the word that David Evans, Reade Seligmann, and Collin Finnerty waited patiently to hear was still to come. As the players, their parents, and attorneys sat in a nearby hotel suite, they all knew in advance that the charges were to be dropped. But what they wanted, more than anything else, was for Cooper to "say the 'I' word," Evans said.

Just three sentences later, they got their wish. "Based on the significant inconsistencies between the evidence and the various accounts given by the accusing witness, we believe theses three individuals are INNOCENT of these charges."

There it was. The 'I' word. The players and their families exploded, emotions pouring out around the room. Legal analysts would spend the next day explaining to television viewers how absolutely rare it was for one prosecutor to dismiss charges brought by another, and then publicly announce that the onetime defendants were innocent.

The sensational lacrosse case, which had been troubled almost from its start thirteen months earlier, ended (at least in the criminal court) on Wednesday, April 11, 2007, amid a flurry of news conferences, apologies, and continued debate. Cooper, who brought long-awaited freedom for the trio that lived under the threat of decades in prison, also harshly criticized Mike Nifong's handling of the case, calling him ". . . a rogue prosecutor" and saying the charges resulted from a "tragic rush to accuse and a failure to verify serious allegations." Cooper concluded by calling for a law that would allow the North Carolina Supreme Court to remove a district attorney from a case where justice demands it.

On a wet and dreary day, Cooper's announcement helped brighten the mood of Evans, Seligmann, and Finnerty, who were greeted by applause, whoops, and hollers as they strolled out onto a platform with their families in the Oak Forest Ballroom of Raleigh's downtown Sheraton Hotel two hours later. Dressed in coats and ties, the three sat among a half-dozen lawyers who had represented them. Behind them sat their parents and siblings. In the crowd of more than a hundred people were Sue Pressler and Duke's men's and women's lacrosse teams.

Absent in this time of support and celebration, however, was Duke's hierarchy. Chris Kennedy, associate athletic director and lacrosse proponent, was the lone Blue Devils' administrative representative. Meanwhile, Duke President Richard Brodhead issued a statement later in the day that applauded Cooper's decision but did not offer an apology to the players for the university's stance during the case. Duke, Brodhead said, ". . . won't be afraid to go back and learn what we can from this difficult experience." Robert Steel, the chair of Duke's board of trustees, also released a carefully worded statement, "Much as we wish that these three young men, their teammates, and their families and indeed the whole community of people who love Duke could have been spared the agony of the past year, we believe that it was essential for the university to defer to the criminal justice system. As imperfect and flawed as it may be, it is the process that brings us today to this resolution."

"It's been 395 days since this nightmare began, and there's finally closure," Evans said. "We're just as innocent now as we were back then."

"For everyone who chose to speak out against us before any of the facts were known, I truly hope that you are never put in a position where you have to experience the same pain and heartache that you've caused our families," Seligmann said. "While your hurtful words and outrageous lies will forever be linked to this tragedy, everyone will always remember that we told the truth."

Evans graduated from Duke in May. Seligmann and Finnerty said they wanted to play lacrosse again and resume their studies. Both were invited to return to Duke after being suspended early in the investigation but neither has accepted.

Joe Cheshire, Evans' attorney, bitterly accused the media of portraying the athletes as criminals, and said: "We're angry, very angry. But we're very relieved." Cheshire confirmed to the authors of this book that he telephoned Brodhead early in the case, leaving a recorded message to the president that reminded him of the presumption of innocence.

"I said, 'You really ought to walk out of the front door of your building and walk down to the law school and walk in there and get somebody to remind you what the presumption of innocence is, because you have a pretty good law school over there,' " Cheshire said. "It's just extraordinary to me. I am sure he's a nice man and he's under a lot of pressure, but they really did throw those boys under the bus."

Cheshire added that Duke's stance added to the controversy.

"They just let the world assume these boys were guilty," he said. "And the way they dealt with Coach Pressler, they just took him and just gutted him, as if all of this was his fault. I know the general sometimes gets the blame when things go wrong, but gracious, canceling the season and all that overreaction was amazing and really fed the fire."

Following the hour-long news conference, Evans, twenty-four, Seligmann, twenty-one, and Finnerty, twenty, shared emotional embraces with their former teammates behind a screen.

A few minutes later—and hundreds of miles away—Mike Pressler held his first meeting with the press since the scandal had begun. At a news conference on the campus of Bryant University, Pressler joined the chorus of those praising Cooper, criticizing Nifong, and pleading for "something good to come from all this pain."

Pressler was actually in Durham for a memorial service for Duke men's golf coach Rod Myers, who passed away of cancer on March 30. At the invitation of Duke coach John Danowski, Pressler spoke to his former team. "I've had a speech rehearsed about a thousand times to give those guys," Pressler said. "It was emotional in the beginning but we had some laughs and hung out and caught up. I don't know if the *players* got anything out of it, but *I* certainly did."

Pressler made clear what he got out of a case that cost him his job and life at Duke. "Well, I think early on I was pretty angry and bitter when I didn't have a job," he said. "But a lot of that changed to excitement when I came to Smithfield (home of Bryant) and was given this opportunity. We try not to live in the past. We're moving forward. Duke has a new coach and a new way of doing things and they're doing well. Bryant has a new coach and we're doing well, too."

Pressler said he was most proud that Evans, Seligmann, and Finnerty and their 2006 Duke teammates remained committed to each other and never wavered during a horrific situation. "Not many can claim to have stuck together when the truth wasn't popular," he said. "But they, like me and my family, always believed that those two words—the truth—would one day win out."

As bad a day as April 11, 2007, was for Mike Nifong, it was nearly as bad for John Burness.

Over the preceding thirteen months, Duke's vice president had pulled reporters aside, including authors of this book, to disparage the reputation of Duke lacrosse players. As the case fell apart, Duke lacrosse families had become increasingly aware that were being undone from within. Some of the worst actions taken against them, in their minds, were from Duke administrators like Burness, who became famous for "off-the-record, not for attribution," slamming of the players.

Rae Evans, David Evans' mother and a lobbyist, understands the press. She said Burness, ". . . never had the guts to put his name on anything. All the off-the-record quotes, steering reporters in the direction he wanted, leaking information to the press, it was all intended to make this a story about out-of-control kids rather than a story about an out-of-control situation."

A professional in behind-the-scene maneuvers, Burness continued his slash-and-burn assault on the players and former coach Mike Pressler in an on-the-record interview with *Newsday* that ran just before Cooper's announcement.

In the interview published on April 9, 2007, Burness openly ridiculed the players and Pressler. Burness's comments were so venomous that Duke quickly released a statement that distanced itself from its embattled vice president. Burness, in turn, offered an apology of his own, saying his comments ". . . are not consistent with the viewpoint or sentiment of the leadership of Duke University."

In the *Newsday* article, Burness said a major component in the Duke assessment of the case was coaching. "One of the things we certainly have to come to understand in this case is that the coaches in general in each of our sports are responsible for the behavior of their teams," he told the newspaper. Current Duke head coach John Danowski, Burness said ". . . is night and day (from Pressler). As our president said, 'This guy's a mensch. This guy gets it.' " Burness also said he believed other hurdles existed for the university, specifically civil suits, saying casually, "that comes with the turf."

Burness's poor timing was obvious when he admitted there was a segment of the population that had asked him if Duke would apologize to the players if their legal problems disappeared. Burness responded tersely, "For what?"

In different ways, both Nifong and Burness staked their reputations on their belief that the players were capable of mayhem. Both felt the bright heat of ridicule as Cooper ended the case.

• • •

The production crew from *60 Minutes* was up early on April 12, 2007, arriving at the Durham home of Mike and Sue Pressler at seven in the morning. The home, which the Presslers had just sold, as the family planned to join Mike in Rhode Island, sits more than one mile from 610 Buchanan, where a five-minute striptease thirteen months earlier had reshaped so many lives.

On this day, television cables snaked through the house, which was turned into a makeshift studio for CBS news correspondent Lesley Stahl. Stahl had been granted the first full-scale interviews with Evans, Seligmann, and Finnerty.

Sue Pressler, despite the circumstances, was the perfect host as the crew rearranged furniture and set up lights and cameras. Despite an emotional journey, punctuated by Cooper's announcement less than twenty-four hours earlier, Sue Pressler was upbeat and, as always, added her unique spin. "We built this addition so we could do just this," she joked as the five-person crew made sound and camera checks in preparation for the first interview with Evans.

Evans and his family—parents Rae and David and his sister—arrived around 8:30 A.M.; interviews with Seligmann and Finnerty were scheduled for later in the day. The interview, which lasted more than an hour, went smoothly. Evans, wearing a blue dress shirt, was deliberate, thoughtful, and composed. He admitted in the interview, "I am smiling but I am not happy." One of the most powerful moments came when Evans talked about how Cooper, who used the word "innocent" to describe the three players, can't change the facts. "Innocent might be a part of that, but that's just an adjective," Evans said. "When I die, they'll say, 'One of the three Duke lacrosse rape suspects died today. He led a life and did this, but he was one of the three Duke lacrosse rape suspects.' "

Rae Evans, sitting on a kitchen stool in front of the television monitor, shook her head back and forth and looked away for a moment. Her husband, David, stared intently as his son's powerful words could be heard throughout the house. Evans' message also seemed to affect the veteran

Stahl, who praised Evans and his family's resolve on and off camera. After a passionate embrace from Sue Pressler, the Evans family piled into two cars.

Cooper's words could still be heard as David Evans backed down the driveway and turned the corner for his drive back to Washington, D.C.

"A lot of people owe a lot of apologies to a lot of people," Cooper said.

CHAPTER TWENTY-SEVEN

Moving On

From the very beginning of this case, Mike Pressler had told those around him that they had to commit themselves daily to "moving forward," pressing together as a team, supporting one another. Once the charges were dropped, Pressler said over and over, they could begin "moving on."

To some, it sounded like coach-speak. In truth, it was a great life lesson.

The Players

Duke's eleven-member lacrosse class of 2006—with the exception of Ed Douglas, who returned to play for the Blue Devils in 2007—has stepped into the real world.

William Wolcott, Kyle Dowd, and Bret Thompson are roommates in New York City and each works on Wall Street. Erik Henkelman and Kevin Coleman also landed on Wall Street. Dan Flannery and David Evans, one of the three indicted players, are scheduled to join their classmates in New York City's financial district sometime in 2007. Jobs they hoped to take when they graduated were put on hold as they fought the legal case. The Big Apple is also home to Glenn Nick, who works for a law firm, while K. J. Sauer works for a finance firm in London.

Matt Zash, who wants to follow in Mike Pressler's coaching footsteps, returned to his hometown of Massapequa, New York, where he teaches and takes classes for a master's degree. Zash and Dowd also play lacrosse professionally in the sports seasonal leagues. Douglas, a fifth-year senior midfielder, could have graduated with a degree in biomedical engineering in 2006, but he opted to return to the Blue Devils for a final season. He was one of the 2007 team captains.

The 2006 seniors, forever linked, refused to allow the lacrosse scandal to overshadow friendships developed and accomplishments achieved at Duke.

"In its [the case's] infant stages when I got home, I joined a gym and I refused to wear anything else but my Duke stuff," Flannery said. "I got stared at, and I got ridiculed by all the trainers and all these coffee-klutch mothers who were outraged that I would wear such stuff. But you know what? That's who I am. I am not ashamed of this. When I look back on my life and when I have kids, hopefully one of the things that I will use to define myself, my personality, and my life was I was a Duke lacrosse player. And I was a captain."

The University

As a private university, Duke is blessed that it can hide from the public most of the statistical damage this case has done. Vice President John Burness, in an interview for this book, attempted to put an amazing spin on the few details that have become public.

Burness said that in the fundraising year that ended four months after the party at 610, Duke reported receiving $342 million in overall donations, including those to the athletic department. "It was the highest amount we had ever had," he said. "That gave us some confidence that the alums were still seeing this place as a really good place they wanted to invest in and they believed was a good place. We're not seeing any evidence that this has been a problem, not in a tangible way."

Burness declined to share numbers for donations since that time.

"Now admissions is fascinating," he continued. "We had to go deeper into our waitlist last year than anticipated, about 125. But if you know anything about admissions at places like this, the last 400 kids admitted and the first 400 kids on the waitlist, you and I couldn't tell a difference. So there was no diminution in the quality as a result of having to go there.

"This year," he said of the applicants who will enroll in 2007, "we have record applications in every single group. We have more African-American applications than we've ever had before. We have more international applications, we have more Latino applications. We have more Asian applications."

Do you have fewer applications from Caucasians, he was asked.

"Yeah, but that's been a trend line for years. One school of thought is that maybe this is the year that a lot of kids who figured that if ever I was going to apply to Duke, do it this year because it may be easier to get in. I have no idea, but this is all out there, blah, blah, blah."

Then Burness made a startling disclosure: Duke entertained 20 percent fewer high school juniors during the summer of 2006 than it had the previous year. Asked to explain that number, Burness put his spin cap back on.

"We don't know why it was down 20 percent . . . we're rethinking it because we thought it was probably lacrosse," he said.

Then with a straight face, he added: "We are now of the view that that may have been a reflection of the gas crisis at the time."

A parent preparing to spend $45,000 a year on a Duke education won't visit because gas is $3.00 rather than $2.25? Burness was asked. "That's what we're thinking."

In a moment of candor, Burness did acknowledge that it will take the university "two to five years" to recover from the barrage of negative publicity.

What Duke will lose during that time, he wouldn't hazard a guess.

The District Attorney

As Mike Nifong continued the struggle to hold on to his job and fight the ethics charges brought against him, he suffered a serious blow when the governor who had appointed him took the unusual step of openly apologizing for his decision.

In January 2006, Governor Mike Easley was speaking to law students at NYU, and when the discussion turned to Nifong and his decision to run for the office, Easley's response was direct: "I almost unappointed him when he decided to run." He would trail off halfway through his next comment, but this thought was clear also. "I rate that as probably the poorest appointment that I've . . ."

You can fill in the blanks.

Several members of Congress, including U.S. Senator and presidential candidate Barack Obama, joined a chorus of leaders asking for a federal inquiry into Nifong's work in the case. United States Representative Walter B. Jones, a Farmville, North Carolina, Republican, also asked the United States attorney general to determine whether Nifong was guilty of prosecutorial misconduct.

The Lawyers

Rae Evans said her phone has been "ringing off the hook" in the last months of the criminal case as civil trial lawyers called offering their "help." They each asked for the opportunity to represent Dave Evans, Reade Seligmann, or Collin Finnerty as they began the process of suing Duke, the district attorney's office, the Durham Police Department, and even some of the more outrageous members of the university faculty.

By some estimates, the civil judgments or settlements that ultimately will come from this case could stretch past $30 million. "The depth of the wrong done to these young men—and to many others like Coach Pressler—is startling," said one of the lawyers who has an interest in pursuing the civil cases and has contacted one of the players' families. "Duke is obviously the deep pocket and I'm told they definitely don't want President Brodhead to have to sit for a deposition and admit his prejudgment of the boys. You can bet that Mr. Nifong and the police don't want to sit for depositions either.

"My guess is that none of these civil suits will ever go to trial," said the attorney, who asked not to be named. "I think everyone wants to see this case in the rearview mirror. But I promise you that won't come cheap."

Nothing about this case was cheap.

Estimates were the three indicted players spent more than $100,000 a month each in legal fees, spawning a nonprofit corporation that was set up to help the players defray legal expenses. The Association for Truth and Fairness, incorporated in Delaware on April 19, 2006, raised $835,000 over its first eleven months. The organization's goal is to raise $5 million to pay the lacrosse team's bills and more.

Among the criminal lawyers, Kirk Osborn, a prominent Chapel Hill lawyer, was an early outspoken defender of the players. He represented Reade Seligmann, knowing that the players had already been convicted in the court of public opinion, and that it would take a stroke of legal genius to mount a convincing defense to combat Nifong.

Osborn did just that. As one of the key players on the legal team, Osborn's offer to the court of phone records and security camera images showing that Seligmann was more than a mile away from 610 at the time of the alleged rape became a major media moment.

Unfortunately, Osborn would not get to see the outcome of the case. On March 24, 2006, Osborn passed away from a massive heart attack he had suffered two days earlier. He was sixty-four. The loss was felt by many. "In a statement, the Seligmann family said they were heartbroken by Osborn's death," the *News & Observer* reported. " 'Kirk stood up for Reade at great personal cost,' the statement said. 'He passionately believed that the truth would emerge.' "

Osborn is survived by his wife, Tania, and his two daughters.

Duke and Durham

The uneasy relationship between Duke and Durham was scrutinized during the lacrosse case. Its recovery from the scandal also will be watched.

"I have no doubt in my mind this community is going to get through it," Durham Mayor Bill Bell told WRAL.com. "Hopefully, we will be better for it, and hopefully there've been lessons learned." While Duke leaders didn't believe the case would define the university, Durham attorney Butch Williams thought the case helped the prestigious university improve a personality trait. "Duke has come down from its tremendous high horse, so to speak, and become a better community partner," Williams said.

The Media

If there was any group for which "moving on" involved little retrospection it was the media. As soon as the story cooled in Durham, national reporters packed their satellite dishes and laptops and headed down the interstate, ending up in Florida where they talked endlessly about a congressman who instant-messaged himself out of office, a diaper-driving astronaut who traveled the country plotting to kill a romantic rival, and a former Playboy bunny who overdosed in a casino hotel room.

Not much thought, it seemed, was given to the tornadolike swath cut through Durham. A couple of forums on the subject of the media's handling of this story—and a brief piece in the trade publication *Editor & Publisher*—were about as deep as the analysis of the media's culpability in the tragedy went.

"I would like to think we in the media learned something," Ruth Sheehan, columnist for the *News & Observer* in Raleigh, said in reflection. "I'm never sure if we learn our lessons, but I do hope that there's some good from all of this."

Greta Van Susteren, who hosts *On the Record* for Fox News Channel, hoped the shameful coverage of the Duke case would bring about a change in journalistic practices. "The media had the opportunity to expose a prosecutor who was very irresponsible with his power," she said. "Maybe now others will put on the brakes when they see people who are accused that maybe they might be innocent."

The Strippers

After filing high-profile charges and appearing in one very influential newspaper interview, Crystal Gail Mangum went into hiding. The only recent reports of her are that she gave birth to her third child, a premature baby girl, on January 3, 2007, and that she may have failed to cooperate with special prosecutors who took over the case when DA Mike Nifong recused himself. Crystal's father told the *Durham Herald-Sun* she's eager to "put it all behind her." (She was not pregnant the night of the party, but was when public outrage was at its peak.)

Kim Roberts's fifteen minutes of fame have passed, as well. After she told the Associated Press, "Why shouldn't I profit from it? I would like to feed my daughter," her motives for telling her story became obvious and the press shied away from her. The only mention of Kim in the final months of the case was that she also refused to speak with investigators. She told them she would do so only if subpoenaed. Once she realized people wouldn't pay for a story from a discredited witness, she stopped talking.

Future Victims

As a group, one of the great losers in the debacle, almost everyone agreed, were future victims of rape. The high profile of the case, along with the outrageous claims of the accuser, "will absolutely have a chilling effect on future victims and the believability they'll be accorded by juries," Wendy Murphy, a Boston-based rape victims' advocate, said as prosecutors prepared to drop the charges. "Lawyers are notorious for using cases like this to plant seeds in the minds of jurors, and though I still believe something happened that night, I know how this will be twisted."

Ruth Sheehan, herself a rape victim two decades ago, voiced a similar concern. "I worry that true rape victims, especially in this area, will worry about coming forward," she said. "I can see where real victims would feel intimidated and afraid to enter into this sort of fray. It would make this tragedy all that much greater."

The Presslers

It was Monday morning, June 5, 2006. Mike Pressler quietly walked Duke's West Campus to collect his thoughts and say good-bye to a university and lacrosse program that had been his life since 1991. An announcement was planned for that day at the Murray Building: The program, which had been suspended two months earlier following accusations of rape, was reinstated, and a national search for a head coach was underway. So Pressler continued his walk into an uncertain future.

Sue Pressler was part of that journey, too.

"If Mike had acknowledged the door was closed and he put it behind him, I needed to do the same," Sue Pressler said. "We needed to be in the same place. It was like, 'We are no longer here. There was no hope anymore. We are not Duke anymore.' And I thought, 'My God, I am going to do the same thing.' I had to run an errand, and I decided to go over there and just drive around."

As Sue slowly turned into the back parking lot at Koskinen Stadium, pleasant memories—and tears—overwhelmed her. There in her mind was daughter Janet, three or four years old, dressed in a red jacket, flirting with Duke lacrosse players. Behind the scoreboard was the Halftime House (stadium fieldhouse), where the Pressler family, including newborn Maggie, had its portrait snapped for the team's media guide before the 1999 season. Nearby was the spot where Sue pulled her "giant" conversion van near the field for games—long before the $2.3 million stadium renovation in 2004 that added new locker rooms, public restrooms (these replaced the "Pressler Memorial Bathrooms" used by players near the van), and a concession stand.

As she neared the Murray Building, however, reality returned like a cold slap to the face. Television trucks were set up to report the Blue Devils would return to the field in 2007. Sue, a former swim captain at the University of Michigan and collegiate swim coach at Ohio Wesleyan, didn't flinch. She quickly wiped away her tears. Steadfast in her Catholic faith and determined to see a silver lining in the darkest of clouds, Sue found her twenty-minute drive around the West Campus that afternoon therapeutic. That's when—like her husband—she detached herself from a program that had meant so much to the Pressler family. The lacrosse field and program had grown from a narrow patch of land among the various intramural and practice fields into a lush, state-of-the-art playing surface and national power under Mike Pressler.

"The program was built because Mike Pressler was willing to work his butt off to do it, and there was nothing beneath him that he wouldn't do himself to meet that end," Sue Pressler, Mike's unabashed biggest fan, said. "I am sure there are things that he'll be doing at Bryant that he hasn't done at Duke in years . . . the truth is there's great memories at Duke that we're going to take with us, and there are—what would I call them?—horrors. I am not going to call them horrible memories. I am going to call them horrors."

When Mike Pressler left for his new job at Bryant University in Smithfield, Rhode Island, in August 2006, it was Sue who remained behind in Durham with daughters Janet and Maggie. Sue cooked, cleaned, helped with homework, and directed traffic at the busy Pressler house. It took nearly a year for their dream home in the Duke Forest neighborhood to sell. Deep, personal friendship help bridge the distance between Rhode Island and North Carolina.

"We're not saying, 'Oh, poor us, our whole lives have been ruined' because none of that is true," Sue Pressler said. "It's just a matter of, we've had to deal with these incoming bogies and when will they stop? And to what damage has been caused to our children? Are they are still just children. The vision that I want is to be able to see my family—anyone in my family—just be happy. Not carefree. But happy."

One door closed during Sue's drive around the West Campus that June afternoon. Another door opened when Mike was hired at Bryant University. "Not only were we going somewhere, we're going someplace really cool—and it's going to be great," Sue Pressler said. "What I want in terms of vindication and retribution is for my husband to work for people of integrity, people who will stand with him, and people who believe in the truth."

Although Mike Pressler returned to his Durham home just once after being hired at Bryant—for Christmas—he penned letters to his daughters once a week. A smiling Mike wasn't sure if Janet and Maggie read them, but they did: Janet in the privacy of her bedroom and Maggie with help from Mom.

Mike's early updates included descriptions of his new home—he rented the top floor of a two-story house owned by a young couple with three children. Mike went from a house with traditional formal areas and a family room that featured a built-in flat-screen entertainment center to one with silver wall heaters in each room, plastic table and chairs, and cardboard boxes that doubled as nightstands and end tables. There wasn't a link to Pressler's past on his walls. He either packed or gave away—with the exception of one T-shirt—his Duke memorabilia. A beautiful, wooden cuckoo clock with a Bryant Bulldog on the stoop crafted by the parents of a former Duke player sat in the "living room." A camouflaged hunting jacket was on the floor. Up the street, an iron chainsaw soldered on a pole served as a street sign that led into the quaint, quiet neighborhood.

"Mike would be really happy even if it were just a corner in a locker room," Sue said, grinning.

The Presslers won't live in a locker room. They purchased a home near Bryant and planned to move in May 2007. Ironically, the Presslers have vacationed in Rhode Island for the last twenty years, spending their summers on Block Island, a slice of paradise that features seventeen miles of beach and more than 350 freshwater ponds. "Of all the places we've been to, it was our favorite spot in the world," Mike said.

Durham was a large and important part of the Pressler world for sixteen years. Janet and Maggie were born at the Duke University Medical Center. And the family's final months in Durham are best described through the eyes of innocence and developing maturity. It was Maggie, only days after the alleged assault at 610, who tearfully asked her father why the boys had to throw a party. And it was Janet who, in her final high school class project at Cardinal Gibbons, penned an emotional, heartfelt letter to Duke president Richard Brodhead.

While Mike Pressler fulfilled a promised to his Duke lacrosse players who were battered by the perfect storm—"One day, gentlemen, we will get a chance to tell our story," he said—Janet also fulfilled a promise to herself by writing a letter to Brodhead nearly one year later.

And Janet asked the university president to make a promise, too.

March 24, 2007

Dear Dr. Brodhead,

My name is Janet Pressler and I am the daughter of Mike Pressler the former Duke men's lacrosse coach. My parents moved to Durham in 1990, when my father began his coaching career at Duke University. I was born a year later. I am 15 years old and presently a sophomore at Cardinal Gibbons High School in Raleigh. I am a student athlete—a player on the Varsity Women's Volleyball team—and our team has won the state championship 8 of the past 9 years. We are a nationally ranked team with players attending Duke, Georgetown, Notre Dame, UCLA, Wake Forest, NC State, and many other prestigious institutions.

The past year has been a tumultuous one for my family and me. Over one year ago, on the way home from volleyball practice one March afternoon, my mother told me that a young woman, an exotic dancer at a Duke party over the weekend, was accusing members of my father's team of rape. Though initially shocked by the allegations, I knew in my heart that the boys were innocent—they have been members of my family for years and this could not be true.

Once the media began running the story, with emphasis on the District Attorney Mike Nifong's inflammatory comments, my life began to change—dramatically. There were changes in school; people didn't know what to say to me. I found that people who were my friends began to ignore me or quote inaccurate or presumptuous comments from the media. One morning, I heard local radio announcers proclaim the guilt of the players based on the assumptions of their race and economic status, "They must be guilty, rich white boys who've been allowed to do whatever they've wanted." I became enraged and broke the radio. Embarrassed and frustrated with my feelings, I became depressed and withdrawn, not knowing what was in store for me and my family.

On April 5th it was announced that my father resigned as the Duke men's lacrosse head coach. The job he has loved my whole life. Our extended family of players, who have been a part of our lives for over 15 years, were taken away from him. I began to worry. What was going to happen to our family? What were we going to do? What about my friends? Volleyball? I worried about my little sister, who had no idea what was going on—just that we were all sad and worried. The media had made our street their new home. We could no longer go outside to walk our dog or to play with our friends in the neighborhood. When taking out the garbage one day, I found that my father had thrown out hateful letters and signs that had been placed in our mailbox and on our front lawn. To protect my little sister, my parents decided that she would be safer living with my grandmother in Illinois for a time.

When the case became one of race, which inflames so many people, our lives became worse. Out of fear for our safety at home, I went to live with a teammate in Cary. Though I lived in relative safety, I couldn't help but wonder what was happening to our home, our neighborhood, our lives. Threats to our family were sent to my mother via email. To have our family threatened using such hateful and malicious language is something that I will never forget. Who was protecting us?

My parents, both successful athletes and coaches, have taught me to face adversity with integrity, dignity, and determination, so I converted my fear and rage to this while playing in a national volleyball tournament—thankfully it was successful as I was named MVP.

My belief in the boys, all of them, has never wavered, and I feel vindicated now since both the community and the press has begun to report how my father and the players were wrongly accused (and convicted in the court of public opinion) of horrific things. I believed their innocence and I never faltered. My father recruited and coached men of character and integrity. I believed in my dad and his choices. Unfortunately you, Dr. Brodhead, did not believe in your players or your coach. Your public statement that my father's resignation was "highly appropriate" clearly demonstrated your lack of faith in him, while casting a shadow of guilt over him in the media.

Did you, the district attorney, the members of the media, the community of Durham, and the nation jump to conclusions about guilt and innocence? Were poor decisions made about the fate of my father and the players made before critical evidence was examined closely? Could you have waited to ask for a resignation from my father until more verifiable data and an internal investigation regarding player behavior were available? It is easy for me to answer yes to these questions, but I wonder if you recognize why that is?

Today, over a year later, my situation is clear. My father is coaching in Rhode Island and I will move there following the end of the school year. I am saddened by the prospect of leaving my friends at Cardinal Gibbons High School. I will no longer have the opportunities to play volleyball for a team like the one at Gibbons or the successful club league of which I am a member.

I would have liked this letter to be one in which I described your heroism in your loyalty, leadership, and decisions during the events of last March, but it didn't turn out that way. The lives of my family and the lives of hundreds of others involved in Duke lacrosse were irrevocably changed because of decisions made by you and your staff. In the end, our sacrifice made no positive difference. No apology or promise can restore the lives we led last year.

I do ask that you make a three-part promise to yourself. The next time you face a challenge at Duke or in any future endeavor, you will act only when you are sure you have sufficient, legitimate information. Make a commitment to ask yourself one question about each challenging decision you make: Is this real action that makes a difference, or the illusion of action to satisfy others? Finally, promise that you will always consider the far- and wide-reaching effects of your decisions upon the lives of others.

Sincerely,
Janet Pressler

A TIMELINE OF EVENTS

3/13/06–3/14/06

- **2:00 P.M.:** Jason Bissey reports seeing at least five men standing in the back yard of 610 North Buchanan Boulevard, drinking and playing "washers."
- **2:00–5:00 P.M.:** Dan Flannery calls Allure Escort Service to request two strippers for a party at their house that night.
- **11:00 P.M.:** The time two girls were scheduled to arrive at a party at 610 to dance for two hours—price: $800.
- **11:05–11:15 P.M.:** The first dancer, Kim, arrives in her black Honda Accord.
- **11:45–11:50 P.M.:** The second dancer, Crystal, is dropped off by Bryan Taylor, who drives a dark sedan.
- **11:50 P.M.–12:00 A.M.:** The girls are seen by Bissey talking outside. They walk inside the house and into the bathroom where Kim changes into dancing clothes.
- **12:00 A.M.–12:04 A.M.:** Dance (time-stamped pictures: 12:00:12, 12:00:21, 12:00:29, 12:00:40, 12:02:16, 12:02:46, 12:03:57—girls shown leaving room).
- **12:05–12:15 A.M.:** Words are exchanged and the two girls lock themselves in the bathroom for a period of time.
- **12:14 A.M.:** Reade Seligmann telephones On Time Taxi and asks for a taxi to pick him up at the nearby corner of Watts Street and Urban Avenue.
- **12:19 A.M.:** Moez Mostafa, owner of On Time Taxi, says he picked up Seligmann and another person on that street corner and drove them directly to Wachovia Bank.
- **12:24 A.M.:** The bank's security camera shows Seligmann withdrawing money from the ATM.
- **12:15–12:25 A.M.:** Kim and Crystal leave the house and Kim gets into

her car. Crystal heads around back in an attempt to re-enter the house and "retrieve her shoe," but the door is locked.

- **12:30:12** A.M.: First picture of Crystal on back stoop (subsequent pictures time-stamped at 12:30:24, 12:30:34).
- **12:30:47** A.M.: Accuser exits smiling, with purse and Dave Evans's shaving kit in hand.
- **12:37:58** A.M.: First picture of accuser lying on her side after she falls (subsequent pictures at 12:38:07 and 12:38:18).
- **12:41:32** A.M.: Accuser is being helped into Kim's car.
- **12:50** A.M.: Kim calls player a "little-dick white boy who probably couldn't get it on his own and had to pay for it." Player counters with, "Tell your grandfather I said thanks for my cotton shirt."
- **12:53:17** A.M.: 911 call by Kim—complains that men in front of 610 screamed racial epithets as she and a friend walked/drove by.
- **12:55:25** A.M.: First police vehicle with Sergeant John Shelton, arrives at 610 Buchanan.
- **12:56:43** A.M.: Second police vehicle arrives at 610 Buchanan. Police found evidence of a party, but house was quiet and no one answered door. Bissey is on his back porch and tells police that the party just broke up.
- **1:22:29** A.M.: Police receive call from Kroger grocery store security guard saying Kim asked her to call because she was worried about the other girl in her car, who is drunk and unconscious.
- **1:32:22** A.M.: First police vehicle, with Sergeant Shelton, arrives at Kroger.
- **1:34–1:38** A.M.: Sergeant Shelton removes Crystal from Kim's car—after several attempts.
- **1:37:27** A.M.: Second police vehicle, with Officer William Barfield, arrives at Kroger.
- **1:49:12** A.M.: Officer Barfield transports a semiconscious Crystal to Durham Access Center. Officer Joseph M. Stewart follows Officer Barfield to assist him if needed.
- **1:55:41** A.M.: Officer Barfield involuntarily commits Crystal at Durham

Center Access. During initial screening process, nurse asks if Crystal was raped. Crystal says yes.

- **1:58** A.M.: Lacrosse player Ryan McFadyen sends email talking about plans for a party that would involve killing dancers—parodying *American Psycho.*
- **2:31:44** A.M.: Officer Barfield transports Crystal to Duke University Medical Center (DUMC).
- **2:40:28** A.M.: Officer Barfield and Crystal arrive at emergency room.
- **2:44:35** A.M.: Sergeant Shelton arrives at DUMC to meet Officer Barfield.
- **2:45:47** A.M.: Accuser is checked into DUMC. Sexual Abuse (SANE) nurse is summoned.
- **2:45–2:55** A.M.: According to his report, Sergeant Shelton questions Crystal about night and she tells him she was not raped. Sergeant Shelton calls police station to tell watch commander Crystal recanted rape allegation. An officer informs Sergeant Shelton that Crystal told SANE nurse she was raped. Sergeant Shelton returns to Crystal's hospital room and asks her if she was raped. She starts crying and refuses to talk to him.
- **2:50:22** A.M.: Accuser submits to three- to four-hour rape kit by a SANE nurse in training.
- **3:13:55** A.M.: Officer dispatched to drive by 610 to determine who lived at the house and confirm that residents were Duke students.
- **7:30** A.M.: Official report submitted to Duke Police Department and reviewed by Duke police director Robert Dean.
- **1:37** P.M.: While at the hospital, Crystal changed her story several times. An officer's report states that Crystal said she was raped by five guys and that Nikki had stolen her money and cell phone. Crystal Mangum is discharged from DUMC.
- **1:40** P.M.: Investigator B. S. Jones awakens to find a voicemail from Crystal. He calls her back and tells her that Sergeant Gottlieb will be handling her case from this point on and gives her contact information. (Sergeant Gottlieb says he that he did not receive the case until the next day.)

3/15/06

- Sergeant Gary Smith from Duke PD directs Durham PD to photos of players on GoDuke.com.
- Duke lacrosse team's annual bowling tournament at Durham Lanes.
- Lacrosse coach Mike Pressler finds out about rape allegations from Duke's dean of students, Sue Wasiolek, and interrogates cocaptains about events of March 13 party. They say nothing happened.

3/16/06

- **11:47 A.M.:** Sergeant Gottlieb and Detective Benjamin Himan meet with Crystal to discuss events of March 13 party. Search warrant issued for 610 Buchanan Boulevard.
- **7:05–7:23 P.M.:** First photo identification lineup. Crystal was told that she would be viewing only Duke lacrosse players who attended the party and was asked if she remembered seeing them at the party and in what capacity. She selected at least five different individuals, one of whom was Reade Seligmann (whom she identified with 70 percent certainty).
- **9:00 P.M.–3:00 A.M.:** 610 residents and Duke lacrosse cocaptains Dave Evans, Dan Flannery, and Matt Zash voluntarily give statements, DNA samples, and email and instant messenger passwords. Durham PD denies captains' request to take lie detector tests.

3/18/06

- First article in *News & Observer*—does not mention that Duke students were involved.
- Duke lacrosse beats University of North Carolina, 11–8.

3/20/06

- President Brodhead first learns of the incident from student newspaper—does not mention Duke students were involved.

- **10:10** A.M.: Detective Himan meets with Kim Roberts. Kim refers to the allegation as a "crock." She also tells Detective Himan that the only time Crystal was alone was a period of less than five minutes.
- Nifong issues a subpoena to Duke Hospital for copies of the records.

3/21/06

- Sergeant Gottleib is quoted in the *Chronicle* saying that the alleged rape occurred at a party and that Duke students, as well as nonstudents, were present. No suspects have been identified, but the residents of the house have been cooperative in locating any possible suspects.
- Subpoena is served on Duke Hospital.
- Duke lacrosse loses to Cornell, 11–7.
- **6:10** P.M.: Detective Himan meets with Crystal Mangum and Jarriel Johnson. Crystal inquired about getting her property back. Himan asked her questions trying to follow up and get a better description of the suspects. Crystal was unable to remember anything further about the suspects (Himan's notes).
- Second photo identification lineup.

3/22/06

- **3:00** P.M.: Scheduled time for interrogation of all forty-seven players–postponed.
- **2:15–4:00** P.M.: Kim Pittman's (Robert's) handwritten statement is dated.
- Sergeant Gottlieb and Investigator Clayton serve a warrant for a probation violation to Kim.

3/23/06

- **3:11** P.M.: Subpoena for nontestimonial evidence from forty-six players faxed to Wes Covington's office.
- **4:00** P.M.: Scheduled time for forty-six players to report to Durham crime lab—media present.

3/24/06

- Press reports that members of the Duke lacrosse team are being investigated for alleged rape at 610.
- Lacrosse cocaptains—Evans, Flannery, Zash, and Thompson—and coach Pressler meet with administrators Joe Alleva, Tallman Trask, and Chris Kennedy regarding the allegations. Administrators say they believe players are innocent.
- Nifong publicly announces he is taking control of "Duke lacrosse rape case."

3/25/06

- *News & Observer* publishes a story based on an interview with Crystal—only time Crystal talked to reporters.
- Duke President Richard Brodhead meets with his senior advisors to determine fate of lacrosse team.
- Georgetown and Mount St. Mary's games forfeited.
- Parent meeting with Duke administrators.
- Captains move out of 610.
- Candlelight vigil held by protestors outside 610.

3/26/06

- "Wake-up Call" held by protesters (pot-bangers) outside 610.

3/27/06

- Sexual Assault Awareness week begins.
- **10:40** A.M.: Sergeant Gottlieb and Detective Himan meet with District Attorney Nifong. They show him the email (obtained by a confidential source) written by lacrosse player Ryan McFadyen on the night of the party. They also brief him on case to date.
- Brodhead meets with captains.
- **5:01** P.M.: Search Ryan McFadyen's dorm room—Edens 2C.
- Sheila G. Eason, legal assistant to DA Nifong, contacts Lieutenant Best

of Duke PD requesting "any and all details documented in writing concerning the incident involving the alleged gang rape by the Duke lacrosse team members of Crystal Mangum."

- First time Nifong addresses the press about case:
    - "The contempt that was shown for the victim, based on her race was totally abhorrent. It adds another layer of reprehensibleness, to a crime that is already reprehensible" (ABC 11).
    - "My guess is that some of this stonewall of silence that we have seen may tend to crumble once charges start to come out" (ABC 11).

3/28/06

- Durham police release 911 tapes.
- Brodhead announces suspension of lacrosse team until case has a "clearer resolution of the legal situation" involving team members.
- In an interview with the *News & Observer,* Nifong refers to the lacrosse players as "hooligans" and urges potential witnesses to come forward.
- Nifong: "Team members are standing together and refusing to talk with investigators." He warned he may bring aiding-and-abetting charges against some of the players (NBC 17).
- Nifong: "I am convinced that there was a rape, yes, sir" (*The Abrams Report,* MSNBC).
- North Carolina State Bureau of Investigation finds no evidence of semen, blood, or saliva in accuser's rape kit.

3/29/06

- *New York Times* front-page story on case: "Rape Allegation Against Athletes Is Roiling at Duke."
- Media release portions of 911 tapes.
- Faculty meets with Brodhead at John Hope Franklin Center at Duke. Some faculty members pressure Brodhead to cancel the season, suspend the entire team, fire coach Pressler, and disband lacrosse program.
- **2:05 P.M.:** Sergeant Gottlieb and Detective Himan meet with Nifong.

- **7:00 P.M.:** Take Back the Night—Rally, March & Speak Out on Duke's East Campus.
- Nifong says publicly that even if DNA results do not match team members, no one is necessarily exonerated.

3/30/06

- Nifong meets with State Bureau of Investigation.

3/31/06

- **12:23 P.M.:** Nifong meets with Detective Himan and Sergeant Gottlieb about photographic lineup. The structure of the lineup is suggested by Nifong.
- Brodhead meets with Durham Mayor William V. Bell, Carol Aamons, ministers, and African-American leaders about situation.
- Larry Moneta, vice president of student affairs, and other Duke officials issue warning to students, the lacrosse team in particular, about drive-by shooting threats.

4/3/06

- Himan collects statement from Jason Bissey, neighbor to 610.
- Nifong stops granting interviews.

4/4/06

- **11:35 A.M.:** Photo ID with accuser and Sergeant Gottlieb. Crystal identifies at least sixteen players. She identifies only two players whom she had also identified in March—Brad Ross and Reade Seligmann. Both have alibis.
- DNA Security, a private DNA lab, is contacted to retest DNA.

4/5/06

- Ryan McFadyen's email surfaces publicly and attempted murder charges are added to the case. Brodhead announces McFadyen is suspended pending the outcome of the rape investigation.

- *New York Times* reports player Collin Finnerty's previous assault charge.
- Duke cancels lacrosse season and forces Coach Pressler to resign after sixteen-year tenure.
- Brodhead announces five committees to "address issues."
- Himan picks up subpoenaed records at Duke Hospital.
- Himan serves subpoena for the records from Durham Center Access.
- Judge Stephens orders DNA to be analyzed by DNA Security.

4/6/06

- Ad signed by eighty-eight faculty members, "What Does A Social Disaster Sound Like?" appears in Duke's *Chronicle.*
- 6:37–7:50 P.M.: Handwritten statement of Jarriel Lanier Johnson is dated.
- 6:58–7:27 P.M.: Handwritten statement of Crystal Mangum is dated—contradicts both of her earlier versions of events and Kim Roberts's statement.

4/8/06

- Defense attorney Bill Thomas says photos taken by a person at the party prove the rape didn't happen—reported April 9.
- Flyer distributed by police that refers to Crystal as "victim," not alleged victim, and says, "CrimeStoppers will pay cash for any information which leads to an arrest in this case."

4/10/06

- North Carolina Bureau of Investigation's DNA Report released to defense.
- Defense attorneys publicly announce that DNA tests find no match between the players tested and accuser. Nifong says he still believes a rape occurred.
- Nifong has first of three meetings with Dr. Brian Meehan, lab director and founder of DNA Security; Detective Himan and Sergeant Gottlieb are also present.

4/11/06

- Nifong attends public forum at NCCU; tells crowd that the investigation "is not going away," and that more DNA tests could be given.
- Nifong, Detective Himan, Lieutenant Rip Berger, and Sergeant Gottlieb meet with Crystal. First and only time Nifong meets with her before seeking indictments.

4/12/06

- **5:00 P.M.:** Nifong attends public forum in Durham County Courthouse with Freda Black and Keith Bishop.

4/16/06

- Jesse Jackson promises to pay for the rest of Crystal's tuition, regardless of the outcome of this case.

4/17/06

- Collin Finnerty and Reade Seligmann are indicted and charged with first-degree forcible rape, first-degree sexual offense, and kidnapping. Bail is set for each player at four hundred thousand dollars.

4/18/06

- **4:45 P.M.:** Search warrants for Edens 2C room 301 and room 203—Seligmann and Finnerty's rooms—are issued.

4/20/06

- Kim Roberts tells Associated Press she did not see rape.

4/21/06

- Talk show host Tom Leykis learns that accuser's name is Crystal Mangum and announces it on his radio show.

4/25/06

- 1:10 P.M.: Cab driver Moez Mostafa is interviewed and provides a written statement saying that he picked up Seligmann and a friend the night of the March 13 party.
- Granville County authorities confirm the accuser told police ten years ago she was raped by three men when she was fourteen. None of the men were charged.
- Nifong says second set of DNA testing results won't be available until May 15.

4/28/06

- Brodhead sends message to Duke community addressing concerns about a New Black Panther Party demonstration on campus.

5/1/06

- *Report of the Lacrosse Ad Hoc Review Committee,* aka the Coleman Report, is released.
- *An Examination of Student Judicial Process and Practices* is released.
- New Black Panther Party demonstrates on Duke's campus.

5/2/06

- Nifong receives 45.15 percent of votes to win the Democratic primary for district attorney.

5/4/06

- *The Duke Administration's Response to Lacrosse Allegations,* aka the Bowen-Chambers report, is released.

5/10/06

- Mostafa is arrested on a 2003 warrant for misdemeanor larceny. Investigators Clayton and Himan participate in this arrest.

5/12/06

- DNA Security produces report for Nifong saying no DNA from lacrosse players was found in or on accuser, or on her clothes and underwear.
- Nifong and Meehan agree not to report that tests found DNA from unidentified men on and in her.

5/15/06

- Grand jury indicts third player, David Evans.

5/27/06

- Duke women's lacrosse team wears wristbands during Final Four competition with the words "No Excuses No Regrets" as a sign of support for the men's program.

6/5/06

- Men's lacrosse program is reinstated under strict rules and close monitoring.

6/30/06

- Ryan McFadyen's reinstatement is publicized through various media sources.
- Mr. and Mrs. Finnerty make appearance on NBC's *The Today Show.*

7/11/06

- Collin Finnerty is convicted of assault in Washington, D.C., for throwing fake punches.

7/17/06

- Gottlieb's interview notes, completely from memory and written months later, are finally handed over to defense.

8/18/06

- Judge W. Osmond Smith III is appointed to preside over the case.

9/4/06

- Duke lacrosse team returns to practice for the first time since rape scandal.

9/22/06

- In a hearing, Nifong claims he has turned over all DNA evidence and test results to the defense.

10/13/06

- Kim Roberts is interviewed on ABC's *Good Morning America.*

10/15/06

- *60 Minutes* airs segment on case. Ed Bradley interviews Kim Roberts, as well as Evans, Finnerty, and Seligmann.

10/27/06

- In a hearing, Nifong admits he brought charges against all three players without hearing the accuser's account of the incident.

10/31/06

- Devon Sherwood, the lacrosse team's only African-American player, is interviewed on ABC's *Good Morning America.*

11/3/06

- DNA discovery is not turned over as instructed by judge on October 27, 2006. DA election is four days away.

11/7/06

- Nifong elected Durham county DA with less than majority vote (Nifong 26,116 votes—49.1 percent; Cheek 20,875 votes—39 percent; Monks 6,193 votes—11.6 percent).

12/13/06

- Defense attorneys file motion in which they allege DNA testing found genetic material from several males in the accuser's body and in her underwear, but none from a Duke lacrosse player.

12/15/06

- In a hearing, Meehan testifies that he and Nifong agreed last spring not to report DNA results favorable to the defendants. (Therefore, as early as April 10—a week before Finnerty and Seligmann were indicted—Nifong knew that the rape kit contained the DNA of at least four males, and the lab concluded that all forty-six members of the lacrosse team were ruled out as possible matches to any of the five sources with a 100 percent degree of scientific certainty.)
- It is reported that Crystal is pregnant and the judge orders a paternity test.

12/21/06

- **1:30 P.M.:** Investigator Linwood E. Wilson interviews Crystal Mangum.

12/22/06

- Prosecutors drop rape charge against all three defendants.
    - Dismissal Notice of Reinstatement, page 2: "In an interview with DA Inv. Linwood Wilson on December 21, 2006, the victim in this case indicated that, while she initially believed that she had been vaginally penetrated by a male sex organ (penis), she can not at this time testify with certainty that a penis was the body part that penetrated her vagina. Since penetration of the vagina by a penis is one of the elements of this offense that the State must prove beyond a reasonable doubt, and since there is no scientific or other evidence independent of the victim's testimony that would corroborate specifically penetration by a penis, the

State is unable to meet its burden of proof with respect to this offense."

12/23/06

- Brodhead responds to Nifong dropping rape charges and asks him to relieve himself of the case.

12/28/06

- State bar files complaint against Nifong, accusing him of violating ethics rules during numerous interviews shortly after allegations become public.

12/29/06

- Nifong tells press, "I'm not really into the irony of talking to reporters about allegations that I talked to reporters."

1/2/07

- Nifong is sworn in as DA of Durham County.

1/3/07

- Brodhead invites Reade Seligmann and Collin Finnerty to return to campus. "We have decided that the right and fair thing to do is to welcome back Reade Seligmann and Collin Finnerty to resume their studies at Duke for the spring semester," he said.

1/4/07

- Kyle Dowd files suit against Professor Kim Curtis.

1/10/07

- Seventeen members of Duke's Economics Department publish letter to the *Chronicle* apologizing for other Duke faculty members' prejudice and welcome lacrosse students into their classes.

1/11/07

- News reports say that Crystal gave birth to a premature baby girl the week before.
- Defense files motion to suppress the alleged "identification" of the defendants by the accuser.
- Defense motions reveal that Crystal changed story again during the December 21 interview about when the alleged rape occurred, how it happened, and who attacked her.

1/12/07

- Nifong sends a letter to state Attorney General Roy Cooper asking his office to take over prosecution of the case.

1/14/07

- *60 Minutes* airs second segment on case; indicted players' parents are interviewed, as well as Dr. Meehan.
- Roy Cooper announces he is taking control of the Duke lacrosse case investigation.

1/16/07

- Concerned Faculty (eighty-seven members) post a letter called "An Open Letter to the Duke Community" in which they defend their controversial ad published in April. They say the ad did not assume the players' guilt and was not published as a reaction to the charges.

1/24/07

- State bar amends complaint against Nifong to include more serious charges, accusing him of lying at least five times—he withheld DNA evidence and then lied to the judge about doing so.

1/27/07

- First practice for 2007 Duke lacrosse team—without Mike Pressler.

2/5/07

- Hearing postponed.

2/24/07

- Duke versus Dartmouth—first game of Duke lacrosse season.
- Bryant versus Adelphi—Coach Pressler's first game coaching the Bryant University Bulldogs.

4/11/07

- All charges dropped.

THE CAST OF CHARACTERS

- **David Addison**—Corporal, Durham Police Department. DPD CrimeStoppers liaison and the person responsible for creating their "wanted" ads.
- **Joe Alleva**—Athletic director at Duke.
- **Houston Baker**—English professor at Duke. Group of 88 member, wrote letter to Duke's provost.
- **Steven Baldwin**—Chemistry professor at Duke. One of first Arts and Sciences faculty members to criticize the Group of 88's rush to judgment in the lacrosse case.
- **Brad Bannon**—Attorney in Joe Cheshire's law firm. Key to understanding of DNA results.
- **William Barfield**—Officer, Durham Police Department. He and Sergeant John Shelton were the DPD officers who dealt with the accuser on the night of the alleged rape.
- **Keith Bishop**—Local African-American defense lawyer in Durham. One of two candidates opposing Mike Nifong in the Democratic primary.
- **Jason Bissey**—Neighbor to 610. Witnessed and reported events that occurred outside the house on night of alleged rape he could see from his back porch.
- **Freda Black**—Former assistant prosecutor for Durham District Attorney James Hardin. Nifong's most formidable opponent in the Democratic primary.
- **Richard Brodhead**—President of Duke University.
- **Jackie Brown**—Well-known campaign manager in Durham. Began working with Nifong's campaign, then resigned her role to assist with the Lewis Cheek campaign.
- **John Burness**—Senior vice president for public affairs at Duke.
- **Tom Butters**—Former athletic director at Duke.
- **Kevin Cassese**—Assistant coach for men's lacrosse team at Duke.

- **William Chafe**—History professor and former dean of Arts and Sciences at Duke. Wrote an article in the *Chronicle* comparing the alleged rape to the murder of Emmett Till.
- **Art Chase**—Sports information director at Duke.
- **Lewis Cheek**—Durham County Commissioners member and local lawyer. Ran in general election against Nifong, although he would not have accepted the position if elected.
- **Joseph B. Cheshire**—Durham lawyer representing indicted senior lacrosse captain Dave Evans.
- **Richard Clayton**—Investigator, Durham Police Department. Assisted with Sergeant Gottlieb's investigation of the lacrosse team case.
- **James Coleman**—Law professor at Duke. His committee's report of the lacrosse team's behavior and disciplinary actions from Pressler were favorable.
- **Wes Covington**—Local Durham lawyer. Dean Sue Wasiolek suggested the players hire Covington as counsel.
- **Brad Crone**—North Carolina political strategist, founder of Campaign Connections. Served as Freda Black's campaign manager in the Democratic primary.
- **Keat Crown**—1998–2000 men's lacrosse player at Duke.
- **Kim Curtis**—Assistant professor of political science at Duke. Now being sued by former student, lacrosse player Kyle Dowd.
- **John Danowski**—Head coach for men's lacrosse at Duke. Appointed to replace Mike Pressler. Previous head coach for Hofstra's men's lacrosse team, and father of 2007 senior captain Matt Danowski.
- **Cathy N. Davidson**—English professor at Duke. Group of 88 member, wrote an opinion piece in defense of her signing "We're Listening" ad.
- **Robert Dean**—Chief, Duke Police Department.
- **Kyle Dowd**—2006 senior Duke lacrosse player. Now suing Duke and his professor Kim Curtis.
- **Mike Easley**—Governor of North Carolina. Appointed Mike Nifong as interim district attorney in April 2005.

- **Robert Ekstrand**—Lawyer representing multiple lacrosse players.
- **David Evans**—2006 senior Duke lacrosse captain, one of three residents at 610. Third player to be indicted.
- **Collin Finnerty**—2006 sophomore lacrosse player. One of first two players to be indicted.
- **Dan Flannery**—2006 senior Duke lacrosse captain, one of three residents of 610.
- **Mark Gottlieb**—Sergeant, Durham Police Department. Appointed lead investigator of the lacrosse case.
- **Benjamin Himan**—Detective, Durham Police Department. Sergeant Gottlieb's partner in the lacrosse investigation.
- **Karla FC Holloway**—English and African-American Studies professor at Duke. Group of 88 member, resigned her role as subgroup chair of the Campus Culture Initiative Committee.
- **K. C. Johnson**—Professor of history at Brooklyn College and the CUNY Graduate Center. Author of blog, Durham-in-Wonderland.
- **Chris Kennedy**—Senior associate athletic director at Duke.
- **Nannerl O. Keohane**—Former president of Duke University.
- **Kerstin Kimel**—Head coach for women's lacrosse team at Duke.
- **Mike Krzyzewski**—Head coach for men's basketball at Duke. Known as "Coach K" and described by many as the most powerful man on Duke's campus.
- **Peter Lange**—Provost at Duke.
- **Wahneema H. Lubiano**—Literature and African-American Studies professor at Duke. Group of 88 member and main author of "We're Listening" ad that ran in the *Chronicle.*
- **Crystal Gail Mangum**—Stripper hired to perform at the March 13 party. She later alleged she was beaten, raped, and sodomized by various members of the Duke lacrosse team.
- **Tony McDevitt**—2006 junior Duke lacrosse player.
- **Ryan McFadyen**—2006 sophomore Duke lacrosse player. Suspended for comments made in an email parodying *American Psycho.*
- **Brian Meehan**—Lab director and founder of DNA Security lab.

- **Larry Moneta**—Vice president of student affairs at Duke.
- **Steve Monks**—Chairman of the Durham Republican party. Ran as a write-in candidate against Mike Nifong and Lewis Cheek in the general election.
- **Chauncey Nartey**—2007 senior at Duke. Sent threatening emails to Pressler, was appointed by Brodhead to serve on Campus Culture Initiative Committee.
- **Mike Nifong**—District attorney of Durham County.
- **Mike Pressler**—Former head coach for men's lacrosse at Duke. Now the head coach for the men's lacrosse team at Bryant University.
- **Sue Pressler**—Mike Pressler's wife and mother to their two daughters, Janet Lynn and Maggie.
- **Christiane Regelbrugge**—2007 junior at Duke. She and fellow juniors Brooke Jandl and Emily Wygod founded Duke Students for an Ethical Durham.
- **Kim Roberts**—Stripper hired to perform at the March 13 party. Would also make 911 phone call that night.
- **Debbie Krzyzewski Savarino**—Daughter to legendary Duke basketball coach Mike Krzyzewski. Fifteen-year friend to Sue Pressler and her family.
- **Reade Seligmann**—2006 sophomore Duke lacrosse player. One of first two players to be indicted.
- **Ruth Sheehan**—Columnist, *Raleigh News & Observer.*
- **John Shelton**—Sergeant, Durham Police Department. He and Officer Barfield were the two DPD officers who dealt with the accuser on the night of the alleged rape.
- **Devon Sherwood**—2006 freshman Duke lacrosse player. A walk-on player and the only African-American on the team.
- **Orin Starn**—Cultural anthropology professor at Duke. Suggested Duke should drop out of Division I athletics.
- **Robert K. Steel**—Chairman of the board of trustees at Duke. Largely responsible for bringing Brodhead to Duke; worked closely with him in the handling of the lacrosse case.

- **Bret Thompson**—2006 senior Duke lacrosse captain.
- **Tallman Trask III**—Executive vice president at Duke.
- **Sue Wasiolek**—Assistant vice president for student affairs and dean of students at Duke.
- **William Wolcott**—2006 senior Duke lacrosse player.
- **Peter Wood**—History professor at Duke. Assumed racial slur on an anonymous student survey was from a lacrosse player.
- **Matt Zash**—2006 senior Duke lacrosse captain, one of three residents at 610.